David Kay

Austria-Hungary

David Kay

Austria-Hungary

ISBN/EAN: 9783743320871

Manufactured in Europe, USA, Canada, Australia, Japa

Cover: Foto ©ninafisch / pixelio.de

Manufactured and distributed by brebook publishing software (www.brebook.com)

David Kay

Austria-Hungary

AUSTRIA-HUNGARY.

LOW, MARSTON, SEARLE, & RIVINGTON,
CROWN BUILDINGS, 188, FLEET STREET.
1880.
[*All rights reserved.*]

" Recent events which have had the effect of directing public attention to Austria, have revealed the misconception that prevails, even in educated circles in this country, respecting her character, position, and policy. Little is really known of the nature of her political and social institutions, of the extent of her resources, of the amount of her natural productions, of the condition of her manufactures, or of her influence for good or for evil in the councils of the world. In plain terms, the general public of Great Britain are not in possession of correct information upon these matters. The consequence is, that the acts of Austria have been distorted, her policy has been misrepresented, and her importance under-rated."—*Austria: Her Position and Prospects*, by J. C. Lever.

"It is not only the public in general that knows very little about the Austria of to-day, but very few statesmen indeed are conversant with the present state of affairs in that country. Thus many will consider the Empire greatly weakened by the loss of the Lombardo-Venetian Kingdom and the famous Quadrilateral; but had Austria lost that kingdom before, and kept her soldiers out of the Quadrilateral, the battle of Königgrätz might have taken a different turn. Others think that the defeats she has sustained by the Prussian Zündnadelgewehr (needle-gun) have rendered her powerless for years to come; but at Sadowa and Königgrätz . . . . . . Austria was taught the crucial lesson that she must arm her soldiers better, find younger and fitter generals, and that a sovereign must rely upon the love of his people rather than upon a well-drilled machine-like army. There are still others who think that the finances of Austria are in so deplorable a state that she cannot extricate herself from the unhappy position into which she has drifted; but they forget, or are ignorant of, the fact that the Austrian dominions abound in natural riches, and that no other European State can vie with them in this respect, and that even now the Austrian subject is less taxed than the French. What, however, is least known to the public, and but little understood, even by foreign diplomatists and statesmen, is the complete change which has taken place in the internal government of the country, and, as a necessary corollary, in its politics. Instead of the former despotic and bureaucratic, or so-called paternal government, Austria enjoys now a free, constitutional, and conservative government."—*Austria, a Constitutional State.*

PREFACE.

IT is sometimes said that Englishmen as a rule know comparatively little of foreign countries; and of probably no other foreign country of the same importance—presenting so many points of interest to us, or having so many claims on our attention, do we actually know so little as of Austria of the present day. When we think of it, it is rather of the Austria of the past than of the present—the Austria of before 1848 or 1866—the absolute monarchy; the oppressor of nationalities; the suppressor of free institutions, and of nearly every form of liberty among its people; the upholder of harassing restrictions against trade, commerce, and industry; and in fine so conservative of everything old and established, and so little given to change, as to merit the designation of the "China of Europe."

But these things have passed away, and changes have taken place that one could scarcely have believed to be possible. Austria now enjoys a constitutional representative government, with a responsible ministry; she has free institutions; her citizens, of whatever class or nationality, have equal rights and privileges; and every means are taken to reconcile and unite the different nationalities, and to establish the government upon its only sure basis—the intelligence, good will, and affection of the people. An enlightened system of national education has been introduced; and wise measures are adopted to develop the industrial resources of the country and to encourage trade and commerce, by removing restrictions of various kinds and opening up means of communication. A Power undergoing such radical changes, and seeking thus to establish itself upon a sure foundation, cannot fail to be an object of interest; and it remains to be seen how far Austria-Hungary, out of the heterogeneous elements of which it is composed, will succeed in building up a strong and united monarchy.

Austria-Hungary abounds in natural productions of various kinds, which only require time and means to develop them. To England she can supply many articles of commerce, while at the same time she affords an important market for English manufactures.

The object of the Author, as far as the limits of the work would admit, has been to present the English reader with a sort of "bird's-eye view" of Austria-Hungary as it exists at present; and in this he trusts that he has been in some measure successful.

CONTENTS.

CHAPTER I.
POSITION; EXTENT; BOUNDARIES; PRINCIPAL DIVISIONS. . **PAGE** 1

CHAPTER II.
PHYSICAL FEATURES; MOUNTAINS; PLAINS; GEOLOGY; RIVERS; LAKES; &c. 4

CHAPTER III.
CLIMATE; FLORA; FAUNA 28

CHAPTER IV.
POPULATION; RACES 33

CHAPTER V.
LANGUAGES AND LITERATURES; RELIGION; EDUCATION . . 51

CHAPTER VI.
INDUSTRIES :—AGRICULTURE; MINES; MANUFACTURES . . 70

CHAPTER VII.
MEANS OF COMMUNICATION; TRADE AND COMMERCE . 91

CONTENTS.

CHAPTER VIII.

GOVERNMENT; ARMY AND NAVY; FINANCE 100

CHAPTER IX.

PROVINCES AND PRINCIPAL TOWNS 109

PROVINCES:—Lower Austria (109); Upper Austria (117); Salzburg (120); Styria (122); Carinthia (126); Carniola (128); Maritime District (Görz and Gradisca, Istria and Trieste) (130); Tyrol and Vorarlberg (135); Bohemia (139); Moravia (148); Silesia (152); Galicia (154); Bukowina (160); Dalmatia (162); Hungary (166); Transylvania (177); Croatia-Slavonia (Military Frontier) (181); Bosnia-Herzegovina (187).

PRINCIPAL TOWNS:—Vienna (111); Wiener Neustadt (117); Linz (119); Steyr (120); Salzburg (121); Gratz (125); Marburg (126); Klagenfurt (127); Laibach (130); Trieste (132); Görz (134); Pola (*ib.*); Pirano (*ib.*); Innsbruck (138); Trent (139); Prague (144); Pilsen (147); Reichenberg (*ib.*); Budweis (*ib.*); Eger (*ib.*); Brünn (150); Iglau (151); Prossnitz (152); Olmütz (*ib.*); Troppau (154); Lemberg (158); Cracow (159); Brody (*ib.*); Czernowitz (161); Zara (164); Spalato (165); Sebenico (*ib.*); Ragusa (166); Buda-Pesth (173); Szegedin (176); Pressburg (*ib.*); Debreczin (*ib.*); Temesvar (177); Grosswardein (*ib.*); Kronstadt (180); Klausenburg (*ib.*); Hermannstadt (181); Agram (186); Essek (*ib.*); Fiume (*ib.*); Bosna-Serai (189); Novi-Bazar (190).

CHAPTER X.

HISTORY 191

LIST OF ILLUSTRATIONS.

	PAGE
The River Danube	19
Fishing on the Theiss	23
Magyar costumes	43
A Magyar gentleman on horseback	44
Sloven peasants	47
A Serb peasant woman	48
Young Dalmatian girl	49
Vienna	113
Pirano	135
The Adriatic coast	162
A street in Ragusa	166
Buda-Pesth	173

MAPS.

Physical Map of Austria-Hungary.
Political Map of Austria-Hungary.

AUSTRIA-HUNGARY.[1]

CHAPTER I.

POSITION; EXTENT; BOUNDARIES; PRINCIPAL DIVISIONS.

AUSTRIA-HUNGARY (in German *Oesterreich-Ungarn*, French *Autriche-Hongrie*) is an extensive country situated in the southern portion of Central Europe, and lying between 42° 10′ and 51° 3′ N. latitude, and 9° 31′ and 26° 21′ E. longitude. It thus extends through almost 9 degrees of latitude, and nearly 17 degrees of longitude, and has an area of about 240,000 English square miles,—nearly a sixteenth part of the entire area of Europe.[2] In regard to extent, it ranks third among the countries of Europe, being surpassed only by Russia, and Sweden and Norway. It exceeds in size the German Empire by about 32,000, and France by more than 36,000 square miles. With a population estimated at 38,000,000 in 1878, it is behind Russia and the German Empire, but somewhat in advance

---

[1] An imperial order, of date 14th Nov., 1868, enjoined that the names *Austria-Hungary* and the *Austro-Hungarian Monarchy*, be employed in place of Austria and the Austrian Empire in all official and public documents; and since that time they have come into general use.

[2] We do not include here the territories of Bosnia and Herzegovina, which Austria-Hungary has entered upon the "occupation" and "administration" of, in accordance with the Berlin Treaty of 13th July, 1878. According to a census taken in 1879, these territories have an area of 24,247 square miles, and a population of 1,142,147. See Chapter IX.

B

of France. Politically it is one of the Five Great Powers of Europe,—the others being England, France, Russia, and Germany.

As a country, Austria-Hungary lies very compact, somewhat in the form of a trapezium, with the exception of a long narrow strip of land, extending for several hundred miles in a south easterly direction along the Adriatic and forming Dalmatia, and a pentagonal projection westward, constituting Tyrol and Vorarlberg. Its greatest length from east to west is 810, and its greatest breadth from north to south 667 miles. It is bounded on the north by Saxony, Prussia, and Russian Poland; west by Russia, and the newly formed principality of Roumania; south by Roumania, the principality of Servia, the territories of Bosnia and Herzegovina, Montenegro, the Adriatic Sea, and the kingdom of Italy; and west by Switzerland, the principality of Liechtenstein, and the kingdom of Bavaria. It is thus surrounded on all sides by foreign countries except where it borders on the Adriatic, which forms its boundary for about 1040 miles, or about one-fifth of its entire boundaries. In addition to this the islands belonging to it have sea boundaries amounting in all to about 1380 miles, and the Lake of Constance forms its boundary on the west for fourteen miles. Of the land boundaries amounting in all to 4310 miles, 720 miles are towards Russia, 658 towards Bosnia and Herzegovina, 630 Roumania, 620 Bavaria, 520 Italy, 420 Prussia, 262 Saxony, 238 Servia, and 198 Switzerland. The boundaries are formed in some parts by the courses of rivers as the Unna Save and Danube in the south, the Rhine and Inn in the west, and the Vistula in the north; in other parts by mountain ranges as the Tyrolese Alps in the south-west, the Bohemian Forest, the Erzgebirge, and Riesengebirge in the north-west, and the Carpathians in the south-east; and sometimes they extend through an open country. From the extent of its land boundaries, and the want in many parts of strong natural defences, the country is particularly liable to hostile invasion, and has on several occasions witnessed its capital besieged (as in 1529, and again in 1683 by the Turks), and twice in the hands of the enemy (i. e. the French in 1806 and 1809).

The present Austro-Hungarian Monarchy embraces a number of different countries and territories, which have from time to time been added to the original duchy of Austria, —raised in the middle of the 12th century, from an earlier margraviate of the same name. It comprises the kingdoms of Hungary, Bohemia, Galicia, Dalmatia, and Croatia-Slavonia; the principality of Transylvania; the archduchies of Lower and Upper Austria; the duchies of Salzburg, Styria, Carinthia, Carniola, Bukowina, and Silesia; the margraviates of Moravia and Istria; and the counties of Tyrol and Vorarlberg, and Görz and Gradisca.

Perhaps the clearest idea of the relative position of the different parts of Austria-Hungary may be obtained, by considering Hungary as a centre, and regarding the various divisions as they group themselves round it. Then on the S.E. of Hungary, is Transylvania, N. of this Bukowina, and still farther N., and forming the boundary of Hungary on the N.E., the extensive country of Galicia. On the N. of Hungary is Silesia, N.W. Moravia and Lower Austria, W. Styria, and S.W. Croatia and Slavonia. Forming, as it were, an outer range, westward, of these last, we have Bohemia on the N.W. of Moravia and Lower Austria, Upper Austria W. of Lower Austria, and Salzburg, Carinthia and Carniola W. of Styria. Finally, we have Tyrol and Vorarlberg in the extreme W., bordering on Salzburg and Carinthia; Görz and Gradisca, and Istria in the S.W., adjoining Carniola and Croatia, and also washed by the Adriatic; and lastly, Dalmatia, on the extreme S., extending in a S.E. direction from Croatia, along the Adriatic.

CHAPTER II.

PHYSICAL FEATURES; MOUNTAINS; PLAINS;
GEOLOGY; RIVERS; LAKES, ETC.

AUSTRIA-HUNGARY is, after Switzerland, the most mountainous country in Europe. About three-fourths of its surface is mountainous or hilly, the rest being made up of valleys and plains, and some of the latter are of great extent. The mountains belong to three great systems,—the Alps, the Hercynian mountains, and the Carpathians. The Alps occupy the S.W. portion of the country, and comprise its loftiest summits. They enter from Switzerland, and spread themselves over Tyrol and Vorarlberg, Salzburg, the portions of Upper and Lower Austria lying S. of the Danube, Styria, Carinthia, Carniola, Görz and Istria, and penetrate even into Croatia, Slavonia, and Dalmatia. In the S.W. they have a steep descent to the plains of Venetian Lombardy; in the S.E. they assume the form of terraces, while towards the N.E. they descend in a less regular fashion through a series of hills to the valley of the Danube. Beyond the Danube rise the Hercynian mountains, under which term are comprised the several mountain ranges of Bohemia, Moravia, Silesia, and the northern portions of Upper and Lower Austria. The Carpathians lie eastward of the rivers March and Oder, which separate them from the Hercynian mountains, while the valley of the Danube separates them from the Alps. They rise near Pressburg on the latter river, and describe a great curve, bounding Hungary on the N.W., N., and N.E., and Transylvania on the E. and S., and terminating at Orsova on the Lower Danube, which here separates them from the northern spurs of the Balkan range. Between the offshoots of the Alps on the one side, and the Carpathians on the other, lie the great plains of Hungary.

An idea of the relative height of the different parts of the country will be obtained if we imagine, with a German Geographer, a series of horizontal sections to be made of the surface at the heights of 500, 1000, 2000, 4000, 8000, and 12,000 Paris feet, above the sea.[1] The first section will present to us the country rising gradually from the low-lying lands of the S. stretching along the river valleys and comprehending the great plains of Hungary, and other low-lying tracts. In the N. it is only penetrated by the rivers Elbe and Vistula. The next section at 1000 feet, comprises the lower parts of the Bohemian Basin, the Moravian, Austrian, Hungarian, and Croatian hilly country, the interior valleys of Transylvania, the plain of Galicia, and the upper course of the Danube. In the third section are included the higher terraces of Southern Bohemia and Western Moravia, the elevated plains of Galicia, the lower declivities of the Alps, and the troughs or basins of the Karst. The fourth section at 4000 feet, will present a great number of elevations, forming, as it were, islands on the surface, but the loftier mountain ranges will still appear as compact masses. In the fifth section these show themselves very much broken up with the exception of the central range of the Alps. The next section at 12,000 feet will contain all the loftiest summits of the country with the exception of the Ortler Spitze in Tyrol, which rises to the height of 12,025 Paris or 12,814 English feet.

The *Alps*, the most extensive and loftiest mountain system of Europe, extend in the form of a great curve, open towards the S. from the Gulf of Genoa eastward to the middle Danube and the Adriatic. They lie between 43° and 48° N. latitude

---

[1] A Paris foot exceeds an English foot by .06576, which makes the equivalents of the above sums 533, 1066, 2132, 4265, 8531, and 12,789 English feet respectively. Hence while only one summit is over 12,000 Paris feet in height, there are several over 12,000 English feet.

(midway between the Equator and the North Pole) and extend from about 5° 10′ to 18° 10′ E. longitude. They are bounded on the S. by the Gulf of Genoa, the plains of Lombardy, and the Adriatic; on the N. by the Rhine, the Lake of Constance, the elevated plains of Bavaria, and the Danube; and they stretch from the Rhone in the S.E. of France, eastward to the Danube, in Hungary. They are estimated to cover in all an area of about 77,500 square miles, of which about 33,500 square miles are in Austria, an extent greater than that contained in any other country. Nor are the Austrian Alps deficient in those striking features for which these mountains are so famous. On the contrary there are portions of them that for beauty and grandeur are not surpassed by any other part of the Alps. "Sir Humphry Davy declared that he knew no country to be compared in beauty of scenery with the Austrian Alps. 'The variety of the scenery, the verdure of the meadows and trees, the depths of the valleys, and the altitudes of the mountains, the clearness and grandeur of the rivers and lakes give it, I think, a decided superiority over Switzerland.'" (*Murray's Handbook.*) Like Switzerland, Austria has its lofty peaks with rugged bare and precipitous sides, its snow-crowned summits, its glaciers, its cascades, and its avalanches.

The Alps are naturally divided by deep depressions, and river-courses into three principal groups, known as the Western Middle, and Eastern Alps. Of these the whole of the Eastern and a portion of the Middle Alps are included in Austria. The Brenner Pass is considered as forming part of the line of separation between these two groups. Another natural division is into three parallel ranges, the middle or central range, and the northern and southern ranges. These are not only separated from each other by longitudinal valleys and depressions, but they are also geologically distinct, the central range being composed of crystalline rocks, as granite, gneiss, and mica-schist, while the northern and southern ranges are of limestone, the southern range also containing porphyry.

The limit of perpetual snow varies considerably in different parts of the Alps, being in some about 8000, in others not much less than 9500 feet, above the level of the sea.

The principal Alpine ranges in Austria are the Rhætian, Noric, Carnic, Julian, and Dinaric Alps. The *Rhætian Alps* enter Tyrol from the Swiss Canton of the Grisons, and traverse the country in three principal chains. The northern chain or range extends from the Rhine eastward to the Inn, and is separated from the central range by a deep depression formed by the valleys of the Inn and the Ill. In height, the summits of this range are inferior to those of the other two, only a few of them rising to 9000 feet. The central range extends eastward through Tyrol to the Dreiherrenspitze on the borders of Salzburg and Carinthia. It is bounded by the Inn, the Adige, the Eisack, and the Rienz, and forms the watershed between the affluents of the Danube on the one side, and those of the Adige and the Drave on the other. Its summits are mostly covered with snow and ice, which in many parts form glaciers, some of them, as the Oetzthaler Ferner, being of great size. Several of its peaks rise to the height of 12,000 feet. This range is crossed by the celebrated Brenner Pass, at the height of 4485 feet,—the lowest of all the Alpine passes, and which from a remote period has afforded the easiest way of communication between Germany and Northern Italy. A railway carried over this pass was opened in 1867, and establishes communication between Innsbruck and Botzen. The southern range of the Rhætian Alps occupies the southern portion of Tyrol, and contains the loftiest summits of Austria, the highest being the Ortler Spitze, rising, as we have said, to the height of 12,814 feet above the sea. The deep transverse valley of the Adige divides this range into two groups, the Ortler and the Trientiner Alps. The former occupies the S.W. portion of Tyrol, between the Adda and the Adige, and contains several of the highest peaks in the country. The scenery here is wild and romantic. The fantastic forms, he wild confusion, the rugged peaks, the snow-crowned summits, all combine to render this one of the most striking portions of Alpine scenery. Here is the famous Stelvio Pass (*Stilfser Joch*), the highest carriage road in Europe, being 9176 feet above the sea. It was constructed by the government in 1820-25, amid engineering difficulties of the greatest magnitude, and traverses scenery of the greatest magnificence. It leads from Glurns on the Austrian side, to Bromio on the Italian.

The Trientiner Alps occupy the S.E. portion of Tyrol, from the valley of the Adige, to the sources of the Piave. The mountains here do not attain to the same elevation as those of the Ortler group, none being probably over 11,000 feet, but the same kind of scenery prevails. An experienced Alpine traveller speaking of this region says,—" Nowhere else in the Alps do the peaks rise so abruptly, and with so little apparent connexion, and nowhere are the contrasts depending on differences of geological structure so marked as those which strike the mere passing traveller, when, beside rounded masses of red and black porphyry, he sees white and pink crystalline dolomite limestone rising in towers and pinnacles, of extraordinary height and steepness. Dolomite limestone is found in many other parts of the Alps, but nowhere else is it developed on so grand a scale, and the exquisite beauty of this region has of late years led an increasing number of travellers to spots that before were scarcely known even to the inhabitants of the adjoining valleys." (*J. Ball.*)

The *Noric Alps* are a direct continuation of the central range of the Rhætian Alps, and present the same leading features. They extend from the Dreiherrenspitze eastward through Salzburg, Styria, Northern Carinthia, Upper and Lower Austria, to Hungary, where they gradually sink into the plains. They have the Danube on the N., and the Drave on the S. The principal range is divided into the Greater and Lesser Tauern, which are again subdivided into several smaller groups. Glaciers are found on the highest mountains, some of which, as the Pasterze on the Grossglockner, are of great size. A number of the summits rise to the height of 11,000 and 12,000 feet, as the Grossglockner (12,455), Gross Vendiger (12,053), Wiesbachhorn (11,738), Dreiherrenspitze (11,424). The railway from Vienna to Gratz, crosses this range at the Semmering Pass. It was an engineering work of great difficulty—the line being carried along the face of precipices, through tunnels, and over bridges of great height. In the Pass a tunnel about a mile in length at the height of 2894 feet, saves a farther ascent of 362 feet.

Two offshoots of this range extend northward; the one in Salzburg, and known as the Salzburger Alps, the other in Styria and the duchies of Austria, and distinguished as the Styria-Austrian Alps. Though none of the summits here rise to the height of 10,000 feet, the glaciers are more numerous than might be expected. Among the mountains too are found numerous beautiful and picturesque valleys. The loftiest peaks are the Dachstein (9845) and the Schneeberg (9292).

The *Carnic* or *Carinthian Alps* lie to the S. of the Noric Alps, and are a continuation of the Trientiner group of the Rhætian Alps, running eastward. They extend from the upper courses of the Drave and the Piave to those of the Save and the Isonzo, and together with their branches occupy the S.E. portion of Tyrol, Carinthia, and the N. portion of Carniola. They give off several branches, and two or three of their summits rise to over 9000 feet, the loftiest being the Terglou (9371).

The *Julian* or *Carniolan Alps* are a continuation of the Carnic Alps, and extend from the Terglou in a S.E. direction through Carniola and Croatia. They form the termination of the Alps in this direction, and have but little of an Alpine character, none of their summits with one or two exceptions, rising over 5000 feet in height. Lying S. of this range, in Carniola and Istria is a desert limestone tract of elevated country known as the *Karst*. It contains few elevations over 4000 feet, but many depressions or hollows, and has numerous subterranean Caverns and subterranean water-courses, though the surface is very deficient in water. In it is the celebrated grotto or cavern of Adelsberg (the most noted in Europe) which extends for about 2¾ miles under ground, and comprises a number of very spacious chambers.

The *Dinaric Alps* extend through Croatia and Dalmatia, and are for the most part bare and rugged, and deficient in water. They bear little resemblance to the Alps, and are sometimes regarded as not forming a part of them. They resemble more the region of the Karst, and hence that term is sometimes used in an extended sense to include them. Mount Dinara, from which they take their name, is 5956 feet above the sea.

The *Hercynian Mountains* is a general term used to include the several mountain ranges of Bohemia, Moravia, Silesia, and the northern portion of Upper and Lower Austria. The principal ranges included in it are the Bohemian Forest, Erzgebirge, Riesengebirge and the Sudetes. They have no great elevations, but are of considerable extent, occupying an area of about 32,000 square miles, and are the most densely populated region of the country.

The *Bohemian Forest* (*Böhmerwald*) forms the S.W. boundary of Bohemia towards Bavaria. It extends from the river Eger in a S.E. direction to the Danube, and forms the watershed between the affluents of the latter river and those of the Moldau which falls into the Elbe. This mountain range is abont 140 miles in length, and with its offshoots covers an area of over 4000 square miles. It is composed of gneiss and granite, and presents a variety of ridges, crests, and solitary peaks, but in general the heights are soft and rounded, not rugged and steep. Ridges of less elevation run parallel with the main chain between which stretch wide longitudinal valleys, communicating here and there by means of transverse valleys and mountain gorges. The mountains are lowest in the N.W. and become gradually higher towards the S.E. but the loftiest summit is only 4550 feet above the sea.

The *Erzgebirge* or *Ore Mountain Range*, so called from its richness in ores, extends along the border of Bohemia separating it from Saxony; and from its commencement near the sources of the White Elster to the Elbe, it has a length of about 90 miles. It is composed of gneiss, mica, and clay-slate, with great masses of granite and porphyry and smaller blocks of greenstone and basalt interspersed. Among its ores the principal are those of silver, iron, copper, and tin, and it has also numerous mineral springs among which those of Teplitz, Karlsbad, and Franzensbad are world famous. The soil in general is not fertile, but here and there spots of great fertility occur. None of its summits exceed 4000 feet in height. The range has a gradual descent towards Saxony, but it falls more steeply and rapidly on the Bohemian side.

The *Riesengebirge* or *Giant Mountain Chain* forms the N.E. boundary of Bohemia towards Prussia. It has a gentle declivity towards Bohemia, but a steep descent on the side of Prussia. It contains the loftiest summits of the Hercynian system the principal being the Schneekoppe or Riesenkoppe 5248, and the Great Rad 4920 feet above the sea. The chain consists chiefly of granite and mica-schist, and though its mineral wealth is considerable, it is in this respect inferior to the Erzgebirge. The scenery in many parts is wild and desolate, and has given rise to many sagas. The western extremity forms part of that beautiful and romantic region on the Elbe known as "Saxon Switzerland."

The *Sudetes* is a term sometimes applied in an extended sense to the whole of the mountain system lying between the Oder and the Elbe, and thus including the Riesengebirge. In a more restricted sense, however, it is confined to that range which extends from the Oder to the March, between Moravia and Silesia. It is composed chiefly of granite, gneiss, and mica-schist, and its highest point, the Spieglitzer Schneeberg, is 4774 feet above the level of the sea. A low mountain range forms the boundary between Bohemia and Moravia. The interior of Bohemia thus forms a kind of basin, being shut in on all sides by mountain ranges. The lowest part is the valley through which the Elbe takes its course and which is from 400 to 800 feet above the sea. From this the land rises, on all sides, in the form of terraces.

The *Carpathians*, form the most extensive mountain system in Austria-Hungary, for while much inferior to the Alps in elevation, they cover more than twice the area that the Alps occupy in the country, or about 72,000 square miles. With the exception of their S.E. and S. declivities which are in Roumania, they are entirely within the Monarchy. They rise near Pressburg at the commencement of the Middle Danube, describe a great curve open towards the S.W. and encircling Hungary and Transylvania on the N.W., N., N.E., E., and S.E., and terminate at Orsova on the Lower Danube having thus a length of about 800 miles. They traverse, with their offshoots, Moravia, Silesia, Galicia, Hungary, Bukowina, Transylvania, and the Banat of Hungary. They are divided into three principal groups, the Hungarian Carpathian Highlands in the N.W., the Transylvanian Highlands in the S.E., and the Carpathian Waldgebirge or Forest Mountain range which connects the one with the other. The two former bear a considerable resemblance to each other, being extensive mountain masses, consisting of several groups; the latter is much less elevated, and is composed of ridges of mountains.

The *Hungarian Carpathian Highlands* extend from W. to E. for about 200 miles through Hungary, Moravia, Silesia, and Galicia, and have a breadth from N. to S. of about 120 miles. They are bounded on the W. by the Oder, the Beczwa, and the March, E. by the Dunajec, the Poprad, and the Hernad, N. by the Vistula, and S. by the plains of Hungary. They are composed of several groups of which the principal are, the Little Carpathians extending from the Danube northward to the Beczwa, and having on the W. the March, and on the E. the Waag, the highest point being Javornik, 3489 feet above the sea; the Beskides stretching from the Beczwa, to the Poprad and Dunajec, divided into the Western and Eastern Beskides by the Jablunka Pass 1950 feet high, through which the railway from Oderberg to Sillein now passes, and having as their loftiest peaks the Babia-gora (5620), and the Lissa-hora (4420); and the Tatra group or Central Carpathians, on the N. border of Hungary between the sources of the Arva, Waag, Poprad, and Dunajec. These last are the loftiest of the Carpathians, having a general elevation of more than 6000 feet, while several of their summits are over 8000 feet, as the Gerlsdorfer Spitze (8650), Eisthaler Thurm (8629), and the Lomnitzer Spitze (8400). In character they resemble the Alps more than the Carpathians, and though for a few weeks in the height of summer their summits are free from snow, it lies perpetually in their clefts and chasms. The scenery here is remarkably wild and bleak, characterized by lofty peaks with rugged precipitous sides, deep fissures and gorges, and numerous lakes surrounded by rocky sides. This group has a length of only about 22 miles, with an average breadth of from 5 to 7. The Fatragebirge, or the Hungarian Erzgebirge, so called from its richness in metals, lies between the valleys of the Gran, and the Waag, and has as its highest point the Great Fatra, about 5400 feet in height.

The *Carpathian Waldgebirge* extends in a S.E. direction from the Dunajec, the Poprad, and the Hernad, to the sources of the Viso and the Bistritza, having on the S. and S.W. the great plain of Hungary, and on the N. and N.E. the elevated plains of Galicia with the Vistula, the San, and the Dniester. It has a length of over 200 miles, with an average breadth of about 45, in Hungary, Galicia, and Bukowina. The descent is somewhat steep towards Hungary, but more gradual on the side towards Galicia. It consists chiefly of transverse ridges of moderate elevation and for the most part wooded, without any great connecting chain, and having numerous transverse valleys through which waters flow S. to the Theiss, N. to the Vistula, and N.E. to the Dniester. The general height is from 3000 to 4000 feet, rising in some parts to 6000, while the loftiest summit Mount Pietrosa reaches 7000 feet.

The *Transylvanian Highlands* occupy the whole of Transylvania and a portion of Hungary, and cover an area of about 39,000 square miles. They have the great plain of Hungary on the W. and N., the plains of Moldavia and the Sereth on the E., and the plains of Wallachia on the S. On all the four sides they form lofty ranges of mountains. The Eastern range extends from the sources of the Viso and Bistritza to the Boza, and has an average height of 5000 feet,—Mount Piatra its highest point being about 6600 feet. The Southern range, otherwise called the Transylvanian Alps, extends from the Boza westward to the Danube at Orsova. It rises abruptly from the plains of Wallachia, having an average height of 6000 feet, while several of its summits are over 8000. In the Banat portion of this range are the celebrated hot springs of Mehadia, which were known to the Romans. The Western range or the Transylvanian Erzgebirge extends northward from the Danube to the Szamos, with an average height of 4000 feet, —its highest summit, Bahar, having 5900 feet. It abounds in minerals of various kinds. The Northern range from the Szamos to the sources of the Viso and Bistritza has an average height of 5000 feet, its extreme point being 7500. The interior of Transylvania, which has a general elevation of from 1000 to 1500 feet, is traversed in different directions by river valleys which are generally narrow, but which occasionally open out into plains of some extent,—these valleys being separated from each other by mountain ranges, sometimes of considerable elevation. The principal of these ranges is the Hargitta, which runs parallel to the Eastern range, from which it is separated by a wide and deep valley, through which the Maros flows northward, and the Aluta southward. This range attains the height of 5500 feet.

Plains.—A considerable portion of the surface of the country consists of extensive plains. The largest of these is the Great Plain of Hungary, which comprises a large portion of the area of that country, extending from the Carpathian Mountains on the N. to the Danube on the S., and from the mountain range of the Bakony Forest on the W. to the Transylvanian Highlands on the E. It has an area of about 38,000 square miles, and a general elevation of from 150 to 200 feet above the level of the sea, rising in some parts to 400 or 500 feet. In some places it is of great fertility, and, as in the Banat, produces excellent crops of wheat and other products; in others, it is no better than a barren sandy waste. Extensive marshes also occur in the low-lying districts along the banks of the rivers, particularly of the Theiss, Temes, Körös, and Danube. The Little Hungarian Plain stretches from the Bakony Forest westward into Lower Austria and Styria, embracing the valley of the Danube from Pressburg to Gran. It has an area of 3400 square miles, and an average elevation of about 360 feet above the sea level. In the N. it is generally fertile, but in the S. and W. it is for the most part barren and sandy, or marshy. In the E., in the neighbourhood of the Bakony Forest, occur parts of great natural beauty. The Galician Plain, which comprises the greater part of that country, is rather an undulating plateau than a plain, being traversed in different directions by ranges of hills. It includes the valleys of the Vistula and Dniester, and of their affluents, the San, Bug, and Sereth. Its general elevation is from 750 to 800 feet, rising in some parts to over 1000, and it has an area of 19,000 square miles. It is for the most part fertile, but includes also large barren sandy tracts and marshes. The Croatia-Slavonian Plain extends along the Drave and Save, and has an area of about 3000 square miles. It produces abundant grain crops. The Vienna Plain or Basin extends westward from the Little Carpathians and the Leitha Mountains along both sides of the Danube, and has in its centre the capital Vienna. It has an area of about 1440 square miles, and an average elevation of 500 feet. The Tulner Basin, so called from the town of Tuln, which is situated in it, is the smallest and highest of the plains of the Danube, having an area of about 200 square miles, and an average elevation of 560 feet. In addition to these, considerable plains occur along the courses of certain of the larger rivers, as the Drave, Save, Mur, Elbe, &c.

Geology.—The great central chain of the Alps is composed of crystalline rocks, principally gneiss, with in less measure mica-schist, granite, and syenite,—the gneiss in some parts containing gold and copper. Frequently the gneiss is overlaid by transition rocks, as clay-slate and transition limestone, and in these large deposits of iron ore are found. North of the central chain is a range of transition rocks, which the organic remains contained in them show to belong partly to the Silurian and Devonian systems, partly to the carboniferous and trias formations. In the S. the transition rocks appear as isolated groups, being broken up by masses of syenitic granite and red porphyry, with red sandstone and dolomite. The northern limestone range of the Alps is formed of Jurassic or Oolitic limestone and Muschelkalk, with here and there considerable deposits of chalk. Its northern border is of sandstone with subordinate layers of limestone and clay-slate. In the southern limestone Alps, the limestone rests upon gneiss, which crops out in some places. In the western division, only detached portions of the chalk formation show themselves, but in the eastern, it generally prevails, extending also through the Maritime District and Dalmatia. In several parts of this range, iron, copper, zinc, and lead ores are found, and at Idria, there is a rich deposit of quicksilver.

The Bohemian Forest is composed of crystalline rocks, among which gneiss predominates, and the like holds true in regard to the Erzgebirge. The Elbgebirge is formed of freestone or greensand with the corresponding marl, and limestone. The Sudetes are principally composed of crystalline rocks, with here and there masses of basalt. Rich mines of silver and lead are worked at Pribram and other parts, also mines of iron and tin. Coal is found in many places.

The central chain of the Carpathians is formed chiefly of gneiss and granite, with clay-slate, transition limestone, trachyte, basalt, and diorite. Among these also frequently occur extensive areas covered by tertiary formations. N. and S. of this are ranges of sandstone mountains, on which diluvial and alluvial deposits are also found. The northern sandstone range is rich in salt, while the central chain abounds in iron and copper ore, and the gneiss and granitic rocks in Hungary and Transylvania are rich in ores of gold and silver. Numerous beds of coal are also found in the later formations. At Cracow appears Jurassic limestone, and in the N.E. of Galicia are chalk marl and white chalk, which, entering from the N., traverse the country.

The hilly and flat portions of the country are of tertiary and diluvial formations, which frequently occur also in the valley basins of the three great mountain systems. The low-lying country between the outermost declivities of the three mountain systems belongs throughout to the middle tertiary or miocene period. In Upper Austria it consists principally of marly sandstone, with subordinate layers of marl. In the Vienna and Hungarian basins, marl, clay, and sand form the principal portion, and coarse limestone also occurs. The Transylvanian basin is for the most part made up of sandstone and clay marl. The Bohemian tertiary basin belongs more particularly to the Pliocene period. The Galician plain consists mostly of sand, sandstone, and coarse limestone, resting partly on chalk, chalkmarl, and gypsum, partly on diluvian limestone.

In the great variety of its mineral products, Austria-Hungary is unsurpassed by any other country in Europe. Except platinum, there are none of the useful metals that are not found here, and many of them are in abundance. Besides the precious metals, gold and silver, it abounds in ores, more or less rich, of iron, copper, lead, and tin; while in less abundance are found zinc, antimony, quicksilver, arsenic, cobalt, nickel, manganese, bismuth, chromium, uranium, and tellurium. Coal and salt exist in almost inexhaustible quantities, and there are also sulphur, alum, saltpetre, petroleum, asphalt, graphite, marble, roofing-slate, gypsum, porcelain earth, and potters' clay. Among the precious stones found here may be mentioned the Hungarian opal and the Bohemian garnet, which are famous; in addition to which are the agate, beryl, ruby, sapphire, carnelian, calcedony, topaz, jasper, amethyst, chrysolite, and many others.

Rivers.—As the highlands of Austria-Hungary form part of the great watershed of Europe, which divides the waters flowing northward into the North Sea or Baltic, from those flowing southward or eastward into the Mediterranean or the Black Sea, its rivers flow in three different directions—northward, southward and eastward. With the exception of the small streams belonging to it which fall into the Adriatic, all its rivers have their mouths in other countries, and its principal river, the Danube, has also its source in another country. Of the waters of Austria-Hungary by far the greater portion falls into the Black Sea, the Danube alone draining about 73.5 per cent. of the entire area of the country. The territory so drained, includes the northern portion of Tyrol and a part of Vorarlberg, Salzburg, Upper and Lower Austria, Styria, Carinthia, Carniola, the greater part of Moravia, nearly the whole of Hungary, Croatia and Slavonia, Transylvania, Bukowina, and Eastern Galicia (by the Dniester). The region drained into the Adriatic, includes the southern portion of Tyrol, Görz and Gradisca, Istria, a portion of Croatia, and Dalmatia. The rivers here are all small, with the exception of the Adige. The Rhine drains a portion of Vorarlberg, and the Elbe, Bohemia and a small portion of Lower Austria into the North Sea. The Oder conveys the waters from Silesia and a portion of Moravia, and the Vistula from the western half and a small portion of the eastern half of Galicia, into the Baltic. The Elbe drains 9.3 per cent. of the area of the country, the Vistula, 6.7, the Dniester 5.6, the Adige 1.9, and the other rivers together, 2.6. The country is on the whole, well supplied with streams, and the navigable length of the various rivers within the territory exceeds 4000 miles.

The Danube (*Donau*), which after the Volga is the largest river of Europe, is pre-eminently the river of the country. Of its entire course of 1770 miles, 846 miles are in this territory, and of the 310,000 square miles drained by it 177,000 are in

THE RIVER DANUBE.

Austria-Hungary. It flows from W. to E. through the entire length of the country, and not only affords the means of commercial intercourse between the different places on its banks, but through its numerous tributaries, many of which are of great size and navigable for long distances, it has communication with most parts of the country. In addition to this internal intercourse, a considerable foreign trade is carried on by means of it with Germany on the one side and Servia, Roumania, Turkey, and Russia on the other.

The region drained by the Danube is more enclosed by high mountains than that by any other great river of Europe. On the S. are the Alps and the Balkans, and on the N. the Hercynian mountains and the Carpathians. In some parts these come up quite close to the banks of the river, and in several occasion rapids which impede the navigation by small boats, but present no obstacles to steamers, except the last—the *Iron Gate*, where the river leaves the country and where there is a fall of 42 feet in less than half a mile. The other parts, where the mountains thus approach the river, are at Passau, from Grein to Krems and Greifenstein, at Pressburg, and at Waitzen. In other places the mountains recede to a great distance, and the river flows through wide plains. The principal of these plains or basins are those of Linz, Tuln, Vienna, and the Great and Little Hungarian Plains. Here its course is generally slow and meandering, and it sometimes forms islands of considerable size, as the Lobau and Prater in the neighbourhood of Vienna, the great and little Schütt islands between Pressburg and Komorn, and a number of others.

The Danube rises in the Grand Duchy of Baden, by the union of two small streams, the Brege and Brigach, at Donaueschingen, on the S.E. declivity of the mountain range of the Black Forest, at the height of 2850 feet above the level of the sea. It enters Austria at Passau, when it has fallen to 900 feet and has become navigable for steam vessels. It flows through the duchies of Upper and Lower Austria, first in a S.E. direction as far as Linz, and then generally E., past

Vienna till it enters Hungary, a little above Pressburg. From Pressburg its course is S.E., through the Little Hungarian Plain to its confluence with the Raab, whence it flows eastward to Waitzen. At Waitzen it turns S. and flows with a slow current and numerous windings through the Great Plain of Hungary for nearly $2\frac{1}{2}$ degrees of latitude till its junction with the Drave, when it again has a general S.E. direction to Orsova where it leaves Austrian territory. In the upper part of its course, particularly above Vienna it flows with considerable velocity. Below Waitzen, when it enters upon the great plain of Hungary its course is slow, the banks generally low and marshy, and it forms numerous islets. After passing Moldova it forms a succession of rapids, the last and principal of which is the Iron Gate, where it rushes through a narrow channel with a great velocity. Its height above the sea is at Linz 690, Vienna 480, the mouth of the March 414, Pressburg 380, Pesth 296, the mouth of the Drave 270, the mouth of the Save 202, and at its exit below Orsova only 123 feet. The velocity of its current is at Passau 5, Vienna 3, and Baja 2 feet per second. The width of the river varies greatly in different parts; being at Linz 800, Mauthausen 1250, Tuln 3300, Nutzdorf near Vienna, 1250, Pressburg 900, below which it varies to over 6000 feet.

The principal affluents of the Danube in this country are—following the course of the stream,—on the right the Inn, Traun, Enns, Leitha, Raab, Drave and Save, and on the left, the March, Waag, Gran, Theiss and Temes. The Inn rises in the Swiss Canton of the Grisons, and enters Tyrol at Finstermünz. It flows first N. and then N.E., through the great valley of the Inn, passes Innsbruck, where it becomes navigable, and flows into Bavaria, below Kufstein. After receiving the Salzach, it forms the boundary between Austria and Bavaria, to its mouth at Passau, being there a longer and much broader stream than the Danube itself. Length 320 miles. Its principal affluent is the Salzach, which rises in the Tauern Mountains, passes Salzburg, and for some distance from its mouth forms the boundary between Austria and Bavaria. The Traun rises at the foot of the Styrian Alps, in the N.W. of Styria, flows first westward into Upper Austria, then northward, passing in its course through several lakes, the principal of which is the Traunsee, and falling into the Danube, near Linz, after a course of 110 miles. It is navigable to Hallstadt. The Enns rises in Salzburg, on the northern declivities of the Tauern Mountains, to the S. of Radstadt, flows N.E. into Styria, and afterwards N., forming the boundary between the duchies of Upper and Lower Austria, and falling into the Danube below the town of the same name after a course of 180 miles. The Leitha is formed by the union of two small streams, the Schwartzau and the Pitten, to the S. of Neustadt in Lower Austria. It flows generally in a N.E. direction, forming for some distance the boundary between Lower Austria and Hungary, and after a course of 110 miles, falling into the Danube. The Raab rises in Styria, flows first S.E. then E., enters Hungary, turns to the N.E., and falls into the Danube at the town of the same name, after a course of 150 miles. It is navigable from Körmönd. The Drave (*Drau*), rises in the Pusterthal, in Tyrol, flows E. through Carinthia and Southern Styria, passing Villach, where it becomes navigable, and Marburg, then takes an E.S.E. direction, and forms the boundary between Hungary on the N., and Croatia and Slavonia on the S., to its mouth below Essek. It has a course of 380 miles, in the upper part of which its current is very rapid, but in the lower part it becomes rather sluggish, forming marshes along its low banks. Of its numerous affluents, the principal is the Mur, which rises in Salzburg, and flows first N.E. passing Judenburg, where it becomes navigable. At Bruck, it turns suddenly S., afterwards S.E., forms for a short distance the boundary between Styria and Hungary, enters Hungary, and falls into the Drave at Legrad, after a course of 250 miles. The Save (*Sau*), rises in the Julian Alps, not far from Mount Terglou, flows through Carniola, becoming navigable at Laibach; afterwards for some distance it forms the boundary between

Carniola and Styria, enters Croatia, and after receiving the Unna forms the boundary between Slavonia and Bosnia and Servia to its mouth, between Semlin and Belgrade. It is upwards of 600 miles in length, its general direction is E.S.E., and in the lower part of its course it is sluggish, with in many parts marshy banks. Its principal affluents are the Laibach, the Gurk, the Kulpa, and the Unna, the last forming the boundary between Croatia and Bosnia.

Of the affluents of the Danube here, on the left, the first important one is the March, which rises in the Spieglitzer Schneeberg, in the N. of Moravia, flows S. through that territory, becomes navigable at Göding, afterwards forms the boundary between Lower Austria and Hungary, and falls into the Danube at Theben above Pressburg. It is 220 miles in length, and in the lower part of its course has many windings, and throws out arms which form numerous islands. Its principal affluent is the Thaya (*Thaja*), which rises in the Bohemia-Moravian Mountains, flows first S. then E. on the borders between Moravia and Lower Austria, and finally S.E. to its mouth, having in all a course of 160 miles. The Waag is formed by the union of two streams called the Black and White Waag, in the Carpathians in the N. of Hungary. It flows first W. then S.W. and S., and finally S.E., thus forming in its course a great curve and joining the N. branch of the Danube, near Komorn. It has a course of 180 miles and is navigable to Neustadtl. Its principal affluent is the Neutra which it receives immediately above its mouth, and which has a length of 110 miles. The Gran rises by several sources in the Hungarian Erzgebirge, flows first W. to Neusohl, then turns suddenly S., for some distance flows through an open valley, and falls into the Danube opposite the town of Gran after a course of 160 miles. It is navigable to Helpa, but with many obstacles. The largest affluent of the Danube, and the principal river of Hungary after the Danube is the Theiss. It rises in the eastern part of the kingdom, county of Marmaros, by the union of two streams, the Black

and White Theiss, which descend from the western slopes of the Carpathians near the borders of Galicia. Its course is at first westerly, passing Szigeth where it becomes navigable, but after receiving the Szamos from the S., which brings into it a much larger volume of water than itself, it turns N.W. and afterwards S.W., receiving at Tokay the Bodrog from the N. Farther down it receives the Hernad from the same direction, and tending more and more southward, its course at Szolnok is almost due S.; and it holds this with many windings to its mouth, being almost directly parallel with the course of the Danube in this part of Hungary. Below Szolnok its principal affluents are, the Körös and Maros, both from the left, the latter draining the greater part of Transylvania. It has a length of 800 miles, and drains an area of 56,000 square miles, including the eastern half of Hungary and the greater part of Transylvania. At Titel, near its mouth, it is 750 feet wide. Here it is joined by the small river Bega, by means of which, and the Bega canal in connexion with it, it communicates with the upper part of the Temes. At some distance from its mouth the Bacser or Franzens Canal goes off, by means of which it is connected with the Danube, and the course up that river shortened by many miles. The Theiss is particularly noted for the abundance and excellence of its fish. The Temes rises on the W. declivities of the W. range of the Transylvanian Carpathians, flows first N.W., afterwards S.W., and finally S. to its mouth in the Danube at Pancsova. It is 280 miles in length and is navigable for small vessels to Lugos. In addition to these the Aluta, Sereth, and Pruth affluents of the Danube beyond Austria, drain in their upper courses the eastern portion of the country,—namely the Aluta, Transylvania; the Sereth with its tributaries, the Suczawa, Moldava and Bistritza, Bukowina; and the Pruth, the southern portion of Eastern Galicia.

The Dniester (*Dniestr*), which like the Danube, flows into the Black Sea, rises on the northern declivities of the Carpathians, in Galicia, flows first N. then E., S.E., and finally

E. through that territory, forming for a short distance the boundary between it and Bukowina, also between it and Russia, and afterwards becoming entirely Russian. Of its entire length of 500 miles, 290 are in Galicia, and it drains an area therein of 14,500 square miles. It is navigable in Galicia to Sambor, a length of about 210 miles. It receives numerous affluents here, the principal of which is the Stry. The Podhorce which also falls into it, separates for some distance Galicia from Russia.

The Vistula (*Weichsel*), drains the waters of a large portion of Galicia and a part of Silesia northward into the Baltic. It is formed by the union of three small streams, the White, Black, and Little Vistula, near the small town of Weichsel in Silesia. It flows first N., through Silesia, then turning E., it forms for a short distance the boundary between Austrian and Prussian Silesia. Below Cracow, where its course turns more N., it separates Galicia from Russian Poland, down to below Sandomir, where it receives the San and leaves Austrian territory to pass through Russian Poland, and afterwards Prussia to its mouth. Its entire course is upwards of 600 miles in length, and it drains an area of 75,000 square miles; and of the former, 240 miles, and of the latter 16,000 square miles are in Austria. It is navigable up to Cracow, or for 165 miles in this country. Its principal affluents here are, the Dunajec with its tributary the Poprad, and the San, which rises in the northern slopes of the Carpathians, flows through Galicia in a winding course, and has a length of 170 miles. It is navigable to Przemysl. The Bug, a portion of the upper part of whose course is in Galicia, does not join the Dniester till long after it has left Austrian territory.

The Oder, which also falls into the Baltic, has only a length of 60 miles in this country, for no part of which it is naviable. It rises in the N. of Moravia, and flows first E. forming part of the boundary between Moravia and Silesia, and then N.E., through Silesia, into Prussia. Its tributaries here are unimportant, the principal being the Oppa, which for some distance separates Silesia from Prussia. The Oder drains in Austria, an area of 2400 square miles.

The Elbe, which falls into the North Sea, below Hamburg, has its source, and the upper part of its course, in Bohemia. It is formed by the union of a number of streams in certain of the mountain meadows of the Riesengebirge, not far from the Schneekoppe, and at the height of about 4400 feet above the level of the sea. It flows first S. then W., N.W., and finally N., passing into Saxony, through the district, known as "Saxon Switzerland." Its length in Austria is 230 miles, for 175 of which it is navigable, up to Pardubitz, and it drains an area of 21,000 square miles. At Königgrätz it is 620 feet above the level of the sea, at Melnik 430, and where it leaves the country 350. Its width at Königgrätz is 100, and at Melnik 300 feet. Its principal affluents are, the Moldau and the Eger. The former on account of its greater length and the larger volume of water which it carries down is entitled to be considered the main stream. It rises in the Bohemian Forest, flows first S.E. and afterwards has a N. course to its mouth at Melnik. It has a length of 260 miles, and is navigable to Budweis, steamers coming up to Prague. The Eger rises by several sources on the eastern slopes of the Fichtelgebirge in Bavaria. It flows E. and falls into the Elbe at Theresienstadt, after a course of 160 miles.

The Rhine (*Rhein*), which also flows into the North Sea, can scarcely be claimed as a river of Austria, seeing that it only flows along its western border for about 18 miles, before falling into the Lake of Constance, and the only tributary that it receives from the country is the Ill, which has a course of about 50 miles.

The Adige (*Etsch*), the principal river of Austria, which falls into the Adriatic, rises in the Reschen Lake, in the Oetzthaler district of the Rhætian Alps, flows first S. to Glurns, passing in its course through two other small lakes. It then turns E. to Botzen, where it receives the Eisack, and becomes navigable; adopting then a S. course, it passes Trent, and after a time enters Lombardy; then flowing S.E., and finally E. it falls into the Adriatic, not far from the mouth of the Po. Of its entire length of 230 miles, 140 are in Austria, and of these last, 64 are navigable. Its principal affluents the Eisack, rises on the southern slopes of the Brenner, and has a length of about 50 miles. Of the streams which have their course entirely within the country, and which fall into the Adriatic, the principal is the Isonzo, which rises in the vicinity of the Terglou, flows generally S., and falls into the Gulf of Trieste, after a course of 70 miles; but it is only navigable for a short distance from its mouth.

Lakes.—The lakes are numerous, but are mostly of small size. They occur principally in the region of the Alps, in the valleys, or at the foot of high mountains. In the northern limestone Alps, the principal are, the Hallstädter, Traun, St. Wolfgang, Mond, Atter, and Waller lakes. In the southern limestone Alps are, the Reschen, Millstädter, Ossiacher, and Wörther lakes. In addition to these, many small lakes occur in the high Alps. The Carpathians also in many parts contain numerous mountain lakes, usually of small size, but frequently of great beauty. The largest lake in the country is the Balaton or Platten, in Hungary, which is about 46 miles in length by from 4 to 9 in width, and has an area of about 215 square miles, exclusive of the extensive swamps that occur on its banks. The Neusiedler lake, also in Hungary, had a length of 18 miles, with a width of from 4 to 7, and an area of 127 square miles, but its extent has lately been very much reduced by drainage, and sometimes in summer it is now quite dry. The most eastern portion of Lake Constance, and the northern end of Lago di Garda belong to Austria. In some of the northern parts of the monarchy, ponds, or lesser sheets of water are numerous. They occur particularly in Bohemia, where they are reckoned by hundreds, and cover an area of 150 square miles. In southern Moravia, in Galicia, and in the N. of Bukowina they are also numerous, occupying in Galicia an area of upwards 200 square miles. Swamps and marshes occur in all parts of the country, in the low-lying districts along the banks of rivers and in the vicinity of lakes. They are found particularly in the plains of Hungary along the Danube, Theiss, and other streams, and in connexion with the Platten and Neusiedler lakes. They occupy in all an area of over 4200 square miles, but this is being gradually reduced by embanking and drainage. Turf moors occur in the Bohemian Forest, the Sudetes, and some other parts.

Mineral Springs.—No other country in Europe comes up to Austria-Hungary in the number and value of its mineral springs. These are reckoned at over 2800, and are of almost every variety—hot, cold, saline, chalybeate, sulpureous, gaseous, acidulous, alkaline, containing lime, magnesia, soda, potash, bromine, iodine, and many other minerals. Among the most celebrated of these are—in Bohemia, Karlsbad, Marienbad, Franzensbad, Bilin, Püllna, Teplitz and Sedlitz; in Hungary, Füred, Gran, Ofen, Mehadia, and Piftjan; in Styria, Rohitsch, Gleichenberg, and Aussee; in Upper Austria, Hall and Ischl; in Lower Austria, Baden, and German Altenburg; in Moravia, Lahatschowitz; and in Salzburg, Gastein. These not only serve to attract numerous visitors to them during the season, but at many of them an extensive trade is carried on in bottling and sending the waters to distant parts.

CHAPTER III.

CLIMATE; FLORA; FAUNA.

THE climate of Austria-Hungary, in consequence of the great extent of its surface, its continental position and eastward extension, the great differences in its elevation, and other circumstances, is very various. In general, however, it may be characterized as mild and agreeable—favourable alike to animal and plant life, except in the high mountain regions.

In the extreme E. in Bukowina, the sun rises 1 hour, 2 minutes, 45 seconds earlier than in the extreme W. in Vorarlberg; the longest day to the inhabitants in the farthest N. part of Bohemia is 1 hour, 13 minutes, 41 seconds longer than to those in the most S. part of Dalmatia, being in the former case 16 hours, 18 minutes, 49 seconds, and in the latter 15 hours, 5 minutes, 8 seconds. At Vienna, the length of the longest day is 15 hours, 52 minutes, and of the shortest 8 hours, 8 minutes.

In the little elevated districts near the coast the variations in temperature are much less than in the interior, where hotter summers and colder winters prevail. The greatest variations occur in the plains of Hungary, where the summers are very hot and the winters intensely cold. Those parts which are protected on the N. by mountain ranges enjoy in consequence a comparatively mild climate, and on the other hand those that are shut out from the warm S. breezes by mountains have a colder climate than they otherwise would have. The mean annual temperature varies from about 60° Fahr. in the extreme S., to 48° in the farthest N.; and from 52° in the extreme W., to 49° in the farthest E. These diminish according to the elevation of the place above the level of the sea at the rate of about one degree of mean annual temperature for every 300 feet. The limit of perpetual snow on the Alps, may be taken at about 8500 feet, though it varies considerably in different parts. On the Carpathians it is about 200 feet less.

It is usual in considering the climate to divide it into three zones, one embracing all that portion of the country which lies S. of the 46° of N. Lat., another all lying betwen 46° and 49° of N. Lat., and the third all lying N. of the latter. The S. zone thus includes all Dalmatia, and the country along the coast, together with the S. portions of Tyrol and Carniola, also Croatia, Slavonia, and the most S. portion of Hungary. Here the seasons are mild and equable, the summers last for five months in the year, and the winters are short, with little snow or ice. The vine and maize are everywhere cultivated, as well as olives and other southern products. In the S. of Dalmatia tropical plants flourish in the open air. The central zone includes Lower and Upper Austria, Salzburg, Styria, Carinthia, northern Carniola, central and northern Tyrol, southern Bohemia and Moravia, the main portion of Hungary, Bukowina, and Transylvania. Here the seasons are more marked than in the preceding, the winters are longer and more severe, and the summers are shorter and hotter. The vine and maize are cultivated in favourable situations, and wheat and other kinds of grain are generally grown. The N. zone comprises the N. portion of Bohemia, and of Moravia together with Silesia and Galicia. The winters are here long and cold; the vine and maize are no longer cultivated, the principal crops being wheat, barley, oats, rye, hemp, and flax.

In general the western half of the country receives more rain than the eastern. In some parts in the vicinity of the Alps the rainfall is excessive, sometimes exceeding 60 inches. It is less among the Carpathians, where it usually varies from 30 to 40 inches. In other parts it generally averages from 20 to

24 inches, and in the plains of Hungary it is as low as 16 inches. In the S. the rains prevail chiefly in spring and autumn, and in the N. and central parts during summer. Storms are frequent in the region of the Southern Alps and along the coast.

Flora.—From the varied character of its climate and soil the vegetable productions of the country are very various. It has floras of the plains, the hills, and the mountains; a temperate flora, an Alpine flora, and an Arctic flora; a flora of marshes and a flora of steppes; floras peculiar to the clay, the chalk, the sandstone, and the slate formations. There are reckoned no fewer than 4377 different species of Phanerogamous or flowering plants in the country, and nearly twice that number of species of Cryptogamous, or flowerless plants. The duchy of Lower Austria surpasses any other part of the Monarchy in the number of species which it contains, amounting to about four-ninths of the whole, and more than 1700 species of the flowering plants. The Vienna basin alone comprises 1397 species of the latter. The forests occupy nearly one-third of the productive area of the country, and cover about 66,600 square miles. They exist particularly in the regions of the Alps and Carpathians, and also of the Hercynian mountains. Styria, Carinthia, Carniola, Tyrol, Silesia, and Bukowina, are all richly-wooded districts, as are also Croatia, Slavonia, and Transylvania. On the other hand Dalmatia, Istria, the Great Plain of Hungary, and the E. portion of Galicia, are all more or less deficient in wood. The forests consist chiefly of oak, ash, elm, beech, and the like, which rise on the mountain slopes to the height of about 4000 feet, and are succeeded by pine, fir, larch, &c., to the height of about 2000 feet more. In the S. the chestnut, walnut, and mulberry-trees are common. Among fruit-trees may be mentioned the apple, pear, cherry, plum, peach, apricot, fig, olive, almond, orange, lemon, pomegranate, the last six chiefly in Dalmatia, and the adjoining districts of the S. The vine is extensively cultivated, particularly in Hungary and the southern parts. The chief fruit-growing districts are Lower Austria, Bohemia, Moravia, Upper Austria, Styria, Carinthia, and a part of Tyrol and Vorarlberg. The principal grain crops are wheat, rye, oats, barley, maize, rice, millet and buck-wheat. Among the other vegetable products of the country may be mentioned hemp, flax, tobacco (a state monopoly), potatoes, beans, peas, turnips, carrots, cabbage, beet, hops, rape-seed, &c. Besides these many medicinal plants are found wild or cultivated, and various plants used in dyeing. A large portion of the country is in meadow and pasturage, in moor and marsh, and has the plants peculiar to these parts. The chief pastoral districts are the Alpine lands, Maritime District, Dalmatia, Bukowina, Galicia, Bohemia, Moravia.

Fauna.—The animal kingdom is not less rich and varied than that of the vegetable. Naturalists enumerate no fewer than 90 species of mammals, 250 of birds, 60 of reptiles, 380 of fishes, and more than 13,000 of insects, as belonging to the country. Many animals that were once common have disappeared, and many that were formerly abundant have now become scarce. The buffalo, the giant elk, and the elk which at one time existed here, have now disappeared,—the elk only so recently as 1769 (in Galicia). The wild goat which once had its home on the high Alps, is no longer found there, but the chamois is still common in all the Alpine regions and in Transylvania. The bear, wolf, and lynx have been nearly extirpated in the W., but they are still numerous in the E. The fox is still common all over the country, but especially in the E. part. The otter is to be found near most of the waters where fish are plentiful, and is especially common in Hungary, but the beaver has almost disappeared except where preserved. Of the larger animals of chase are the wild boar and several species of deer, which are still found in the wooded districts of the Alps, the Hercynian mountains, and the Carpathians, but the former is becoming rare and the latter are mostly preserved. The hare is common and to be found in all parts of the country, particularly the N. and the Alpine hare is common in all the Alpine regions. The wild cat, badger, polecat, marten, weasel, stoat, marmot, squirrel, mole, rat, mouse, are all more or less common. The jackal exists only in Dalmatia, and some of the neighbouring islands. The principal domestic animals are the horse, ass, mule, cow, ox, sheep, pig, goat. The number of birds is very great,' including several species of eagle and hawk, the Lämmergeier, bustard, heron, wild goose, wild duck, gull, wood-pigeon, pheasant, red grouse, ptarmigan, blackcock, partridge, snipe, owl, and a great variety of singing birds, besides the ordinary domestic fowls. The rivers and lakes abound in different kinds of fish, which are also plentiful on the sea-coast. Among insects, the bee and the silk-worm are the most useful, and constitute considerable sources of gain. The leech forms an important article of export, and is obtained particularly in Hungary.

CHAPTER IV.

POPULATION; RACES.

The civil population of Austria-Hungary in 1818, amounted to 29,769,263; in 1830, it had increased to 34,082,469; in 1842, to 35,295,957; and in 1857 to 37,339,012. Soon after this it lost its Lombardo-Venetian territories, with more than 5,000,000 inhabitants. Taking the present limits of the Monarchy the civil population in 1857 amounted to 31,993,013; and in 1869 had risen to 35,634,858, being in Austria from 18,224,500 to 20,217,531, and in Hungary from 13,768,513 to 15,417,327. To these have to be added the military in active service, amounting in all to 269,577 men (177,449 in Austria, and 92,128 in Hungary), and raising the population of the Monarchy in 1869 to 35,904,435, of whom 17,737,175 were males and 18,167,260 females. Of the entire population 56·74 per cent. are in Austria, and 43·26 per cent. in Hungary. The civil population of the Monarchy is estimated as, at the end of 1876, amounting to 37,129,968, of which 21,565,435 were in Austria, and 15,564,533 in Hungary. The civil population of Austria at the end of 1878 is estimated at 21,970,649. The following table gives the area and civil population of the several provinces or crown lands of the Monarchy in 1857, and at the 31st of December, 1869. The first 14 provinces constitute the empire of Austria and the remaining four the kingdom of Hungary, or as they are sometimes termed Cis-Leithania and Trans-Leithania, from the small river Leitha, which flows for some distance between the two.

Provinces.	Area in sq. miles.	Population in 1857.	Population in 1869.		
			Males.	Females.	Total.
CIS-LEITHANIA.					
Lower Austria	7,654	1,681,697	967,087	987,164	1,954,251
Upper Austria	4,632	707,450	358,117	373,462	731,579
Salzburg	2,767	146,769	73,468	77,942	151,410
Styria	8,669	1,056,773	555,289	576,020	1,131,309
Carinthia	4,005	332,456	161,519	174,881	336,400
Carniola	3,855	451,941	220,009	243,264	463,273
Görz, Istria, and Trieste	3,082	520,978	288,293	293,786	582,079
Tyrol and Vorarlberg	11,320	851,016	429,241	449,666	878,907
Bohemia	20,119	4,705,525	2,433,629	2,672,440	5,106,069
Moravia	8,582	1,867,094	948,206	1,049,691	1,997,897
Silesia	1,986	443,912	242,574	269,007	511,581
Galicia	30,306	4,597,470	2,660,518	2,757,498	5,418,016
Bukowina	4,034	456,920	255,919	256,045	511,964
Dalmatia	4,938	404,499	220,169	222,627	442,796
Total	115,949	18,224,500	9,814,038	10,403,493	20,217,531
TRANS-LEITHANIA.					
Hungary	87,044	9,900,785	5,499,462	5,618,161	11,117,623
Transylvania	21,214	1,926,797	1,051,145	1,050,582	2,101,727
Croatia and Slavonia	8,864	876,009	1,102,953	1,095,024	2,197,977
Military Frontier	7,308	1,064,922			
Total	124,430	13,768,513	7,653,560	7,763,767	15,417,327
Total of Monarchy	240,379	31,993,013	17,467,598	18,167,260	35,634,858

A comparison of the two divisions shows that as regards extent, Austria is to Hungary as 4 to 4½, while in regard to population the former is to the latter as 4 to 3, denoting that Hungary is considerably more thinly populated than Austria. The density of the population is for the whole Monarchy 149 inhabitants to the square mile—being in Austria 174, and in Hungary 124 per square mile. But these proportions differ greatly in different parts of the country, partly owing to the character of the surface, partly to the presence of active industries. In the mountainous regions the population is generally very sparse, and on the other hand where mining or manufactures are actively carried on, or in the neighbourhood of large towns the population is comparatively dense. In general, the W. portion of the Monarchy is the most densely populated, and it becomes gradually less so as we proceed eastward. The most thinly populated districts are the Alpine lands and Dalmatia. The province of Silesia has a population of 257 inhabitants to the square mile, Lower Austria which contains the capital Vienna 256, Bohemia 254, and Moravia 233, and on the other hand Dalmatia has only 89, Carinthia 84, Tyrol and Vorarlberg 77, and Salzburg 54. This disproportion is still more marked if we take particular districts even in the same province. Thus in the N.E. of Bohemia on the declivities of the Riesengebirge the ratio is as high as 600, 800, and even 900 inhabitants per square mile, while in the S.W. in the neighbourhood of the Bohemian Forest, it is as low as 160 and 150.

It will be observed that in the Monarchy as a whole and in almost every one of the provinces, the number of females exceeds that of males. In the Military Frontier the males considerably exceed the females, and there is a trifling excess also in Transylvania and Bukowina, but in all the other provinces the females are more numerous. This is not different from what is found in other countries. Taking the whole of the Monarchy the proportion is 1041 females to every 1000 males, rising in Austria to 1060, and falling in Hungary to 1014. If we take in the army we have for the whole of Austria 1024 females to every 1000 males. The difference in this respect is considerable when we regard the different provinces. Thus in Silesia the excess of females over males is 109 per 1000, Moravia 107, Carniola 106, and Bohemia 98; on the other hand in Lower Austria it is only 21, in Hungary 17, Dalmatia 11, and Croatia-Slavonia 9. The inequality appears to decrease as we proceed from the north southward, and from the west eastward. It also appears to depend largely upon race—

the greatest differences being found among the Czechs, Slavonians and Germans, differences in a much less degree among the Poles, Ruthenians, and Hungarians, while among the southern Slavs and Roumanians the sexes are about equal.

As regards the condition of the people, 10,299,416 males and 10,006,323 females were single, 6,632,804 males and 6,666,435 females were married, 516,190 males and 1,464,507 females were widowers and widows, and 19,188 males and 29,995 females were separated from their partners. That the number of widows is so much greater than that of widowers is accounted for from the fact that the men marry usually at a considerably later period of life than the women, and their labours are more exhausting. If we consider only those of over 15 years of age we have 35.85 per cent. males and 30.97 per cent. females single, 59.37 per cent. males and 56.40 per cent. females married, 4.62 per cent. males and 12.38 per cent. females widowers and widows, and 0.16 per cent. males and 0.25 per cent. females divorced.

With regard to age, there were 2,453,771 males and 2,480,286 females under five years of age; 1,966,631 males and 2,017,258 females between five and ten; 1,853,204 males and 1,847,824 females between ten and fifteen; 1,602,269 males and 1,956,400 females between fifteen and twenty; 2,706,331 males and 3,077,972 females between twenty and thirty; 3,450,854 males and 2,535,076 females between thirty and forty; 1,940,560 males and 2,008,472 females between forty and fifty; 1,397,800 males and 1,398,499 females between fifty and sixty; 778,117 males and 763,851 females between sixty and seventy; 253,833 males and 237,352 females between seventy and eighty; 40,130 males and 39,710 females between eighty and ninety; 3816 males and 4238 females between ninety and a hundred; and 282 males and 325 females of a hundred and upwards.

Comparing the populations of the two divisions of the Monarchy, we find that of Hungary to comprise a greater proportion of young persons than that of Austria. In Hungary the proportion of persons not exceeding 30 years of age was, of males 62, and of females 64 per cent. of the entire population, while in Austria the numbers were respectively 59.68 and 59.52. The individual average of life, however, is greater in Austria than in Hungary, and of persons over 60 years of age there were 1.5 per cent. more men and 1.8 per cent. more women in the former than in the latter. Of the productive ages, taken at between 16 and 60, Austria contains a larger proportion than Hungary, being in the former 58.15 per cent. of males and 60.22 of females, and in the latter 57.37 per cent. of males and 58.13 of females. It may also be mentioned that in Hungary, while the number of females exceeds that of males up to 30 years of age, from 30 up to 90 the number of males is in excess of that of females, which is not the case in Austria, where only between the ages of 80 and 90 do we find the males slightly more numerous than the females.

The number of blind was 29,509, or one in every 1208 of the population; of deaf mutes 39,205, or one in every 909; of insane 32,957, or one in every 1081; and of Cretins 28,802, or one in every 1220.

In Austria the native population amounted to 15,925,924, or 78.77 per cent. of the whole; in Hungary to 14,776,383, or 95.84 per cent., and in the Monarchy to 30,702,307, or 86.16 per cent. The greatest number of foreigners are found in Lower Austria, and especially in Vienna, where no less than 55 per cent. of the inhabitants are not natives of the city. Of the foreigners in Austria, 66,400 were Germans, 29,400 Italians, 4500 Swiss, 4100 Russians, 3000 Turks, 2300 French, 1700 Roumanians, and 1500 British. In Hungary there were 5700 Germans, 4100 Italians, 1100 Turks, 600 Swiss, and 400 British. Of the natives of Austria who were abroad, 41,500 were in Germany, 17,300 in Italy, 11,400 in Russia, 10,600 in Turkey, and 9900 in America: of Hungarians there were in Roumania 17,100, in Servia 3300, in Germany 2000, and in Turkey 1700.

In 1869 there were in Austria 738 cities and large towns, 1270 market towns, 52,919 villages, and 2,766,314 inhabited and 121,045 uninhabited houses. In Hungary there were 189 cities and large towns, 769 market towns, 16,373 villages, and 2,450,213 houses inhabited and uninhabited. The cities containing more than 100,000 inhabitants were Vienna (607,514), Pesth (200,476), and Prague (157,713). Seven cities contained between 50,000 and 100,000 inhabitants, 42 between 20,000 and 50,000, and 90 between 10,000 and 20,000.

Of the entire population, 31,389 in Austria and 10,858 in Hungary were ecclesiastics; 72,147 in Austria and 35,540 in Hungary officials; 40,503 in Austria and 28,221 in Hungary teachers; 75,642 in Austria and 63,437 in Hungary students; 15,888 in Austria and 12,018 in Hungary literary persons and artists; 7230 in Austria and 4884 in Hungary lawyers and notaries; 28,142 in Austria and 14,283 in Hungary medical practitioners; 7,497,500 in Austria and 5,015,899 in Hungary engaged in agricultural pursuits; 104,342 in Austria and 48,854 in Hungary employed in mining; 2,706,960 in Austria and 833,885 in Hungary engaged in various branches of industry, manufacture, and trade; 817,835 in Austria and 1,143,075 in Hungary employed as domestic servants; and 8,404,663 in Austria and 8,117,693 in Hungary of no fixed occupation.

Taking the number of births in Austria from 1868 to 1876, and in Hungary from 1868 to 1874, we find the annual average to be in the former 814,152, or 40.2 per thousand of the population, and in the latter 648,428, or 42.1 per thousand, making together 1,462,580, or 41.0 per thousand. Of these 752,429 were males and 710,151 females, being at the rate of 105.9 males to every hundred females. The illegitimate births were 12.6 per cent. in Austria, and 6.3 in Hungary; but they varied greatly in the different provinces, being in Carniola as high as 46, and in the Military Frontier and Dalmatia as low as 2 and 2.2 per cent. The still-born averaged about 20,000 annually, or 1.6 of the entire number of births.

The annual average number of marriages was 359,579, being for Austria 190,904, or 9.4 per thousand of the population, and for Hungary 169,675, or 10.9 per thousand. The number of marriages varies greatly in different parts of the Monarchy, being in some as high 11 per thousand of the population, in others little more than half of that number. In general they are more frequent in the eastern than in the western half. Of the bridegrooms 19.8 per cent in Austria and 37.4 per cent. in Hungary did not exceed 24 years of age; and 35.9 per cent. in Austria and 34.5 per cent. in Hungary were between 24 and 30. Of the brides 19.8 per cent. in Austria, and 37.4 in Hungary were not over 20 years of age; and 35.9 per cent. in Austria and 34.6 per cent. in Hungary were between the ages of 20 and 24. Thus in Austria the greatest number of marriages take place in males beween the ages of 24 and 30, and in females between 20 and 24; while in Hungary most marriages take place in males not exceeding 24, and in females not over 20 years of age. In districts wholly German the majority of males do not marry till between 30 and 40 years of age, and of females till between 24 and 30. Among the Slav population marriages take place much earlier:—in Bohemia, Moravia, and Silesia more than one-third of the males are married between 24 and 30, and in Galicia and Bukowina more than a third before they are over 24. Of the entire number of marriages, 74.9 per cent. were between persons neither of whom had been previously married; 7.4 between persons both of whom had been previously married; 12.3 where the male only had been previously married; and 5.4 where the female only had been previously in that state.

The annual average number of deaths for the period above stated amounted to 643,379 (334,320 males and 309,059 females) in Austria, and 642,248 (333,900 males and 308,348 females) in Hungary, making together 1,285,627 (668,220 males and 617,407 females) as the total number. This was at the rate of 31.8 per thousand of the population for Austria, and not less than 41.6 per thousand for Hungary. These are high death-rates, particularly that of Hungary, and are to be partly accounted for by the prevalence of the cholera epidemic, especially in Hungary, during several of the years from which the average has been taken. In Hungary, in 1872 the number of deaths exceeded that of births by 17,800, and in 1873 by more than 300,000. The number of deaths among young children is very great, and is greater in Hungary than in Austria. Altogether 34.8 per cent. of the males and 30.3 per cent of the females were children who had not completed their first year, and 17.6 per cent. of the males and 17.9 per cent. of the females were between the ages of 1 and 5 years. Thus nearly a third of the deaths are of children of one year and under, and about a half are not exceeding 5 years of age. Taking the two divisions of the Monarchy, we find that in Austria 50.1 per cent. of the males and 45.9 of the females, and in Hungary 52.3 per cent. of the males and 48.9 of the females had not completed their fifth year. Under five years of age 112.2 males die for every 100 females, and taking all ages, 108.2 males for every 100 females.

Races.—The population of Austria-Hungary is made up of a number of distinct races, differing from each other in manners, customs, language, and religion; and united together only by living under the same government. No other state in Europe, except Russia, embraces within it so many distinct nationalities, and nowhere else at the present time do quessions affecting the relations of different nationalities present so many interesting features.[1] To these questions the present emperor has addressed himself with intelligence and zeal, and, by means of wise

[1] Austria "is charged with a task unique and exceptional among the powers and nations of modern Europe. German and Slav, Czech and Magyar, Christian and Mussulman, Jew and Gentile, all have to be reconciled to a common rule, and to be welded, if possible, into a single nationality. Nowhere perhaps in Europe are the rivalries of race and religion, of political and social aims stronger and more conflicting, and yet it is the singular fortune of Austria to control and to harmonize them all. The task is not accomplished of course without continual friction and difficulty, but somehow or other it never entirely fails, and year by year it seems to approach towards fuller and more permanent success. We have only to think of the condition of Austria before 1848, and again after 1866, to realize the substantial progress that has been made. . . . Matters are very different now,—Austria has long been reconciled to Hungary; and Bohemia is at last preparing to accept its allotted place in the National Constitution."—(*The Times*, October 9th, 1879.)

legislation, of liberal concessions, and the substitution of direct for indirect representation, has sought to promote the best interests of all classes of his subjects. It remains to be seen how far it may be possible by these means to reconcile and fuse together the different nationalities.² The Germans are the dominant race in Austria, and the Magyars in Hungary, but in neither do they form a majority of the population. The various divisions of Slavs constitute the most numerous race in the country, making about 45.5 per cent. of the whole population. No official census has been taken of the different nationalities since 1850, but the following table, based on the census of 1869, and taken from the best German authorities, is believed to be a pretty close approximation to the truth.

Nationalities.	Austria.	Hungary.	Total.
Germans	7,108,800	1,894,800	9,003,700
Czechs	4,718,800	1,840,800	6,559,600
Poles	2,443,500	. . . .	2,443,500
Ruthenians	2,584,600	448,000	3,032,600
Slovens	1,196,200	58,000	1,254,200
Croats and Serbs	522,400	2,405,700	2,928,100
Magyars	17,700	5,688,100	5,705,800
Italians	587,500	600	588,100
Roumanians	207,900	2,477,700	2,685,600
Jews	820,200	552,100	1,372,300
Various	9,800	51,200	61,000
Total	20,217,400	15,417,000	35,634,400

² Many persons seem to think that there exists some mysterious quality in race that tends to keep nationalities distinct under all circumstances. As against this view Mr. Arthur J. Patterson says, " In Hungary we find many instances of loss or rather change of nationality. The Germans have in many, perhaps in the majority, of their settlements lost their German character and become here Magyars, there Slovacks, in the third place Wallachs. There are besides undoubted cases where Magyars have become Slovacks, Ruznieks, or Wallachs. Again several Slovack communes have become Magyars. It must be borne in mind that I am at present not taking into account individual cases, butt only those in which whole villages, parishes, and communes have gone over from one nationality to another." (*The Magyars.*)

The Germans constitute 25.27 per cent. of the entire population, being 35.16 per cent. of the population of Austria, and 12.30 per cent. of that of Hungary. They form almost the entire population of the provinces of Upper Austria and Salzburg, and 90 per cent. of that of Lower Austria, 63 of Styria, 69 of Carinthia, 60 of Tyrol, and 51 of Silesia. They also form 38 per cent. of the population of Bohemia, and 26 per cent. of that of Moravia.

The German of Austria is in general well built, of middle size, bony and muscular, but rather spare than corpulent. He is possessed of the general characteristics of the German race, has good natural abilities, and displays a considerable degree of aptitude, skill, and inventive genius. What particularly distinguishes him among Germans is his light-hearted, joyous, and happy disposition, together with great good humour and equanimity of mind, so that he is not easily put out of temper, and manifests great forbearance under sometimes trying circumstances. He is fond of pleasure and of society, open and trustful, but still not without some degree of seriousness, and a certain amount of reserve. He is also brave, true-hearted, kind, hospitable, industrious, a lover of order, and in a high degree a law-abiding man. He manifests a strong attachment to old customs and usages, and a great disinclination to change; and he is also characterized by an intense love of "Fatherland," for which he will submit to any hardships, dare any dangers.

The Magyars constitute in Hungary and Transylvania 42 per cent. of the entire population of these parts, and though not forming an absolute majority, none of the other races nearly come up to them in point of numbers. They form 16.01 per cent. of the entire population of the monarchy. Unlike the Germans, Slavs, and Roumanians, who are European races, the Magyars are of Asiatic descent, and have only been established in the country since the end of the ninth century. They are believed to be of Tartar origin, and to be allied to the Fins; but they have become very much mixed with the Huns, Slavs, Germans, and others among whom they have lived, so that they are by no means a pure race, though they have maintained their individuality and still present many traces of their Oriental extraction. They have the free gait, the dignified bearing and open glance of the warrior. They are proud, high-minded,

MAGYAR COSTUMES.

brave, honourable, hospitable, fond of convivialities and fine clothes, and but little inclined to steady, patient labour. There are only two classes among them, the nobles and peasants, and even the latter have the bearing and manners of gentlemen— respectful to those above them without being servile. They have an intense love of liberty, and their warlike spirit and courage have gained renown for the Hungarian regiments wherever they have been engaged. The Magyar is a born soldier; to carry arms is his greatest pride, and he remains true to the flag to which he has sworn. It is as a hussar that he is most distinguished, and indeed he has given name to this species of light cavalry, which was first introduced by the Hungarians. From his earliest years the Magyar and his horse are inseparable companions; they are constantly together, and in accordance with this custom he prefers to fight on horseback. The Magyar is of average height, well-formed, and muscular, with regular, well-cut features, aquiline nose, finely formed mouth, strong moustache, and oval chin. The hair is usually black, or at least dark; and the women, particularly of the higher ranks, are distinguished for their beauty. Even among the upper classes, the ladies of the family perform almost all those services for which in England we have special servants. "The young ladies of a large family will all be employed together on the arrival of an expected visitor—one assisting to cook, another bringing the dishes to table, a third seeing that all the guests are provided for, and a fourth clearing away." (Prof. Ansted).

The Slavs form the most numerous race of people in the monarchy, but unfortunately they are broken up into several branches, speaking different languages, and having little in common. Farther they are almost exclusively confined to the northern or southern regions of the country, and are thus separated from each other by a wide middle tract inhabited by Germans, Magyars, and Roumanians. The northern Slavs belong to three distinct nations, speaking different languages, namely the Czechs (including the Moravians and Slovaks), the Poles, and the Ruthenians. The southern Slavs include the Slovens or Wends, the Croats, and Serbs. Of late years, attempts have been made to bring about a closer union between the different tribes of Slavs, Panslavic congresses have been held and the movement has been gaining strength and importance. One difficulty they have to contend with is the

A MAGYAR GENTLEMAN ON HORSEBACK.

want of a common language, so that they are obliged, however unwillingly, to make use of the hated German at their congresses, and in their communications with each other. The Slavs are in general a strong, patient, laborious, undemonstrative race of people. They number altogether 16,218,000 persons (45.5 per cent. of the entire population), of whom 11,035,700 are northern, and 4,182,300 southern Slavs.

The Czechs (including the Czechs Proper who inhabit Bohemia, the Moravians who dwell in Moravia, and the Slovaks who live in the N.W. of Hungary) are the most numerous branch of the Slav population, and are on the whole the most advanced. They possess an ancient history, rich in the great deeds of their ancestors, an early and polished literature, and are distinguished by many mental endowments. The Czech is laborious and painstaking; has a good natural understanding, comprehension, and imagination; an excellent memory so that he readily acquires foreign languages; and he also distinguishes himself in the study of various of the higher branches of knowledge, particularly mathematics and astronomy. For art, and especially for music, he displays great talent, and Bohemian musicians are known throughout Austria, and Germany, and even much more widely. In body he is strong and muscular, capable of enduring a great amount of fatigue; so that he makes a good soldier, and is also to be found in most of the provinces employed in the hardest kinds of work. The Czechs form 18.41 per cent. of the entire population of the monarchy. They occur chiefly in Bohemia where they form 60 per cent. of the population, and in Moravia where they form 72 per cent. They also form 10 per cent. of the population of Silesia. With their neighbours, the Germans, whom they look upon in the light of foreign intruders into their country, they live on anything but friendly terms, and a great deal of mutual enmity and mistrust exists between the two races. The Czech still obstinately holds to his own manners and customs, and will by no means assimilate himself to the German. Hence mistrust, reserve, and stubbornness in opinion, have come to be marked features of the Czech character.

The Ruthenians are a branch of the great stock of Little Russians, and inhabit chiefly Eastern Galicia, Bukowina, and the N.E. of Hungary. They form 44 per cent. of the population of Galicia, and 40 per cent. of that of Bukowina. They are a strong and hardy race of men, and are mostly employed in agriculture or cattle-rearing, in wood-cutting or charcoal-burning. There is no burger or citizen class among them, and the middle and upper classes in the country are almost all Poles. The soil is but rudely cultivated, and is besides so subdivided into small lots as to afford but a very precarious and insufficient subsistence. Hence they are mostly all poor, living in wretched wooden or mud huts under the same roof with their cattle. They have, however, a strong love of freedom, and manifest an intense dislike to foreigners, including the Poles. They are very superstitious, and still retain many of the heathenish customs that prevailed among them before the introduction of Christianity.

The Poles form 6.86 per cent. of the entire population. They occur chiefly in Galicia where they constitute 42 per cent. of the population, and in Silesia where they form 29 per cent. They are mostly confined to the W. half of Galicia as the Ruthenians are most numerous in the E. half. The Poles in the upper ranks of life are a handsome, well developed, active, and intelligent class of men; but unfortunately the majority of the people have, as the result of many generations of penury and hardship, very much degenerated, as is seen in their wasted forms, their indolent and spiritless movements, and their gross ignorance. The former are brave, frank, and generous, but at the same time proud and haughty, while the latter are cringing and servile, their whole behaviour evincing a state of the most abject servility.

The Southern Slavs consist of the Slovens or Wends, who exist chiefly in the S. of Styria, Carinthia, Carniola, and the Maritime District, and the Croats and Serbs who inhabit chiefly

Croatia and Slavonia, Dalmatia, the S. of Hungary, and Transylvania. They are generally characterized as cheerful, contented, happy, good-natured, upright, honest, frank, open, kind, and hospitable. For this last quality, they are particularly distinguished. They are at the same time, however, very ignorant and superstitious, and strongly attached to traditional usages. They are very primitive in their habits, content with the produce yielded by their fields and cattle, and having no wish to travel beyond

SLOVEN PEASANTS.

the limits of their native districts. They usually live together in large families of from 6 to 10, and often many more members. The oldest member of the family, or his representative is the "House father," who directs the labours of each individual, both in the house and in the field, and to whom the most implicit obedience is rendered. Hence, love to his family and to his paternal home is one of the strongest features in the character of the Southern Slav. The Croats and Serbs, in particular, are brave and warlike, but are at the same time said to be treacherous and cruel. The former have long manifested a feeling of hostility against the Magyars, which showed itself in

A SERB PEASANT WOMAN.

1848-49 in their taking up arms on behalf of the empire against Hungary.

The Roumanians, or East Romans, called also Wallachians and Moldavians, constitute 7.54 per cent. of the population of

YOUNG DALMATIAN GIRL.

Page 49.

the Monarchy. They live chiefly in the E. provinces, and form in Transylvania 52 per cent. of the population, in Bukowina 39 per cent., and in Hungary 10 per cent. Next to the Magyars they form the most numerous race in Trans-Leithania. In appearance they bear a strong resemblance to the Italians, clearly showing, as does also their language, that they are both connected with the same root. The head and face are long, the complexion dark, the eyes large, black, and deep, flashing up suddenly under excitement, the nose of a pure Roman form, the mouth well shaped, with beautiful white teeth, the hair long, dark, thick, hanging wild and disorderly round the head, a long thick moustache—the priests only wearing beards. They are well formed, of middle size, but slow and heavy in their movements and extremely lazy, their great delight being to spend their time in doing nothing. They are ignorant, superstitious, bigoted, and improvident; but their mental faculties are good, and they display a considerable amount of mechanical genius, and are skilful in the use of their hands. On the other hand they are said to be cowardly, deceitful, crafty, malicious, and cruel. The Roumanian looks to his wife to labour for him, and besides her domestic duties she works for him in the garden, field, vineyard, and forest. The females of the family also spin, weave, and make all the garments of the household, male as well as female. They are rarely to be seen abroad without the spindle and distaff. When young they are reckoned very beautiful. Their movements are easy and graceful, the figure faultless, hands and feet small, head and face beautifully oval, the eyes dark, generally quite black, and full of life and animation, with long eyelashes, thick eyebrows, and a well-formed nose and mouth.

The Italians, with the Ladins and the Friulians are known as West Romans, and inhabit certain of the W. provinces. In the Maritime District they form 31 per cent. of the population, and in Tyrol 39 per cent. There are a considerable number also in Dalmatia. The Italians are most numerous in the district around Trent in Southern Tyrol where they form a compact body. They are active, pushing and industrous, and are rapidly extending. The love of their native country and the desire to promote its best interests are ever strong in the breast of the Italian. The Ladins, a corruption of Latins, inhabit certain valleys of Tyrol. They were formerly much more numerous than at present, but they have been gradually Germanized, and now number in all probably not more than 10,000 persons. The Friulians inhabit a district in the south-west of Görz-Gradisca.

The Jews form about 3.86 per cent. of the population. They are most numerous in Galicia, Bukowina, Transylvania, Hungary, Bohemia, Moravia, and Lower Austria. In the Alpine provinces they are rarely met with. Their character and pursuits here are not different from what they are in other countries and are sufficiently well known.

Among other races are Bulgarians of whom there are 26,000 in Hungary; Albanians, in Dalmatia and Croatia-Slavonia; Greeks in Lower Austria (1000), and Transylvania; Armenians in Hungary, Transylvania, Galicia, and Bukowina. The Gipsies are numerous in Hungary where according to some authorities they exceed 150,000; but by the author we have followed they are included in the Magyars.

CHAPTER V.

LANGUAGES AND LITERATURES; RELIGION; EDUCATION.

AUSTRIA-HUNGARY being composed of different nationalities, has also different languages and different literatures. It has not, as is the case in most other states, one national language, and one national literature. The number of distinct languages or dialects spoken in the country, exceeds twenty. German is indeed the language of the court, and of the upper classes generally, and is the language in which the great mass of the literature of the country is written. It is besides the common language of a large portion of the country, is used to some extent in almost all the large towns, and is generally understood by the educated classes in all parts of the country. To the great majority of the people, however, and in most parts of the country it is an unknown tongue. German is the spoken language of Lower and Upper Austria, Salzburg, Middle and N. Styria, N., Middle, and W. Carinthia, N. and Middle Tyrol, also of the N.W. of Bohemia, the N. of Moravia, and Upper Silesia. There are likewise in all the provinces, isolated districts, inhabited by Germans, where the language is spoken. Altogether it is estimated to extend over 55,000 square miles. Except in some districts of Hungary and Transylvania where Low German is spoken, the language in use is the modern High German, but in different dialects. That which is most extensively and indeed generally spoken, is known as the Bavaria-Austrian dialect. In Vorarlberg the Swabian dialect is spoken, in the N.W. of Bohemia the Franconian, in the E. of Bohemia the Upper Saxon, and in the N. of Moravia and Upper Silesia, the

Silesian. The German literature of Austria is the German literature generally. The history and present condition of the one is likewise that of the other. In general, however, in Austria speculative subjects do not receive so much attention as they do farther north. The people here incline more to the useful and practical, and their books treat more of the arts and manufactures, of trade and commerce, natural history and geography, natural philosophy, medicine, surgery, and the like.

The Magyar language is a branch of the Ugric group of the Finnish family. In the course of time, it has come to acquire a number of words from other languages, as the Slavonic, German, French, Latin, Greek, Armenian, Hebrew, Persian, Arabic, but it has digested them all in its own way, and according to its own nature. Though till recently almost entirely neglected, it is a polished language, rich in expression, and remarkable, particularly for its system of suffixes. It is very terse, a decidedly soldierly language, and well adapted for purposes of oratory. It is not so vocalic as the Italian, nor so consonantal as the German or Slavonic tongues. The Latin language was introduced into the country with Christianity and western civilization, and for more than eight centuries it was the language of the educated classes generally, used in the state assemblies and courts of law, in all state and public documents, and in the schools. The oldest literary remains of Hungary are therefore in the Latin language; and though in the latter half of the fifteenth and earlier part of the sixteenth century, a number of distinguished writers appeared, particularly in history, medicine, natural science, philosophy, mathematics, and poetry, their works were mostly in the Latin tongue. It was only towards the close of the eighteenth century that partial efforts began to be made for the cultivation and general adoption of the mother tongue, and only within the last fifty years that these efforts have become general, and have been followed by the most marked success. The Magyar is now the language in which all state affairs are conducted, the language of the law courts, and of society generally, and is taught in all the schools. Many works too of the highest class are annually issuing in it from the press; so that altogether, Hungary possesses to-day a literature which, both as regards its quantity and quality, will bear comparison with that of most other nations.

The Czech or Bohemian language is the richest and most developed, but at the same time the harshest and strongest (owing to its abounding in consonants) of the Slavonic tongues. Its forms are less developed than the Polish and its consonants less softened. It is distinguished among its sister dialects by its copiousness of root-words, great flexibility in combination, precision of expression, and accurate grammatical construction. Its grammar is complicated, and more difficult to master than that of most other languages. It differs from most European languages in the use of quantity instead of accent in its poetry, as in Greek and Latin, and hence it can accurately copy the different metres of these tongues; and, indeed, in no other modern language can the ancient classics be so faithfully and forcibly translated. It is spoken in three dialects, the Bohemian Proper, the Moravian, and the Slovak. The oldest forms exist in the Moravian dialect. The Bohemian literature is older than that of the other Slavonic tongues, and dates from the tenth century. The improved language dates from the time of John Huss, who, like Martin Luther, was a reformer of language as well as of religion. He revised and improved the Bohemian translation of the Bible, and wrote about twenty other works, great and small. The period from 1526 to 1620 is called, by the Bohemians, the golden age of their literature. During this period the arts and sciences were cultivated with diligence, knowledge was sought after, and generally diffused, and the language attained a high degree of excellence. There were two universities at Prague, and numerous other educational institutions there and elsewhere over the country. The most disastrous period for Bohemian literature, was during and subsequent to the Thirty Years' War (1618—1648), when the best of her people were either slain or obliged to leave the country, and their places were supplied by Italian, Spanish, Dutch, German, and other adventurers, who came in troops and possessed themselves of all dignities and offices. Jesuit missionaries went from place to place and from house to house, accompanied by soldiers, searching for and destroying all books that were suspected of heresy. This destruction of books continued to far into the eighteenth century. It is impossible to form an estimate of the vast amount of valuable literature that thus perished. One Jesuit who died in 1760, boasted that he had destroyed 60,000 Bohemian books. In 1774, an imperial decree ordained the establishment of German schools throughout the country, and in 1784 it was decreed that instruction in the higher schools should be given only in German. These measures caused great dissatisfaction, and met with much opposition, and, at length, in 1818 a decree was issued recommending the use of the Bohemian language in the gymnasia. Since that time the progress of the language has been very rapid. Many books now appear in it, and a strong attachment to it is manifested by all classes of society.

The Polish language is, after the Bohemian, the principal dialect of the Northern Slavs. It is a remarkably rich, flexible, harmonious, and expressive language. Its grammatical structure is fully developed and firmly established, and its orthography precise and perfect. The verb is exceedingly rich in forms which serve to express frequency, intensity, inception, duration, and other modes of action or being. There are three principal dialects, the Mazurish, which is spoken in the plains, the Cracovian, and the Silesian. After the introduction of Christianity, Latin became the common language of the educated classes of the country, and continued to be so for centuries. It is only in the beginning of the sixteenth century that Polish can be said to have become a literary language, and that books began to appear in it. It soon made rapid progress and supplanted the Latin, becoming the language of the state and of the higher classes generally. Many books now came out in it, particularly in poetry, history, and theology, and this is commonly reckoned its golden age. In the seventeenth century it declined, the influence of the Jesuits prevailed, and Latin again came into common use. In the eighteenth century, during the reign of Stanislaus Augustus, it revived, and in spite of the great political changes that have since taken place, it has continued to advance. Now its literature is extensive and flourishing. It possesses a number of distinguished writers, as poets, dramatists, historians, novelists, and the like, but few or no distinguished names have yet appeared in philosophy, theology, or natural science.

The Ruthenian language is a branch of the Russian, but it has been greatly modified and changed by the Polish, so that it may be said to be a sort of intermediate language between the two. It is very flexible and rich in expression, being remarkable for the richness of its forms, and the softness of its sounds. Its popular poetry is particularly rich and beautiful, but beyond this its literature is poor, and of little value, though it goes back for a considerable time. Since 1845, instruction in the Polish language has been generally introduced into the schools, and now such of the Ruthenians as may be said to be educated, are able to speak and write the Polish language. Thus the Ruthenian is rapidly passing out of use, though of late, interest in it has been reviving.

The Southern Slavonic dialects are the Serbian, the Croatian, and the Slovenian or Wendic, which are sometimes collectively termed the Illyrian language. These dialects are nearly related to each other. The Serbian most nearly resembles the Russian, and is one of the most harmonious and vocally richest of the Slavonic tongues. The Croatian and Slovenian more nearly resemble each other than either does the Serbian. The Serbians use in writing a modification of the Cyrillic characters, of which the Russian characters are also a modification, while the Croatians and the Slovenians employ the Latin alphabet. Cyrillus based his characters upon the Greek alphabet. It was he and Methodius who translated the Bible into the ancient Slavonian or ancient Bulgarian in the middle of the ninth century, and this is still the authorized version of the

Scriptures for the whole of the Slavonic race. The language in which it is written is called the ecclesiastical Slavonic, and is to the student of the Slavonic languages very much what the Gothic is to the student of German. The Serbians belong to the Greek Church, while the Croatians and Slovenians are Roman Catholics. There is little in the literatures of these peoples calling for special notice, though some fragments of Slovenian literature go back as far as the tenth century. Several small colonies of Bulgarians exist in the Banat of Hungary and Transylvania who speak the modern Bulgarian. This, so far as grammatical forms are concerned, is the most reduced among the Slavonic dialects.

The Romance languages or those derived from the ancient Latin are in this country the Italian, the Rhæto-Romanic, and the Roumanic. The Italian of all the Romance languages is that which stands most nearly related to the ancient tongue. About the end of the seventh century Latin began to acquire the character of the modern Italian. Its formation may be said to have been completed by Dante in the beginning of the fourteenth century, and it was still farther polished by the classical writers who immediately succeeded him. As it at present stands it is essentially a dialect of the Latin, although its grammatical construction is considerably changed by the infusion of the modern spirit into the antique as the character of the people underwent the same change. It contains many German words derived from the different nations who occupied in succession the northern parts of Italy, and some Arabic, Norman, and Spanish, left by occasional visitors in the S. The Italian is the most beautiful and harmonious of European tongues, and is rightly considered to be the best medium for the interpretation of real poetic feeling. The Friulian or Friaulian is a dialect of the Italian spoken in a small district in the S.W. of Görz-Gradisca. It has been considerably modified by the introduction of foreign elements.

The Rhæto-Romanic or Romanic is spoken in the Swiss canton of the Grisons and in the adjoining districts of Tyrol, forming a portion of the Ancient Rhætia. It is nearly related to the Italian, but characterized by the presence of Rhætian elements. Nearly allied to it is the Ladin, which is still spoken in some of the remote valleys of Tyrol, but both these dialects are gradually dying out and German taking their place.

The Roumanic or Wallachian is the least genuine or marked of the languages derived from the Latin. It is descended from the language spoken in the Roman province of Dacia, but so little does it contain of the Latin element that it is only recently that scholars have agreed upon classing it among the Romance languages. Its grammatical construction and material composition however testify to its Latin extraction. About one half of it is borrowed from the German, Slavonian, Turkish, and other sources. The Latin part of the language has much of the Italian form, and had assumed it as early as the fifteenth century. There are two dialects, the Dacian or Daco-Roumanic, which is spoken N. of the Danube, and the Thracian or Macedo-Roumanic S. of that river. The former has received a certain amount of literary polish, the latter is more mixed with Greek and Albanian words.

Among the other languages spoken less extensively in the country may be mentioned the Albanian, which is a strange admixture of Greek, Latin, German, Slavonic, and Turkish terms, and shows in many of its grammatical forms a closer affinity to the Sanscrit than the ancient Greek. The Modern Greek and the Armenian are also spoken in some few parts. The Jews, though a pretty numerous race, have no special language, but make use of that of the people among whom they are; and the same may be said of the gipsies, who while using their own language among themselves adopt one or other of the languages of the country for intercourse with others.

The number of newspapers published in the monarchy in 1875 was 1201, of which 876 appeared in Austria and 325 in Hungary. The languages in which they were severally printed were: German 663, Magyar 194, Czech 116, Italian 62, Polish 53, Slovenian 35, Servian and Croatian 13, Ruthenian 9, Slovak 14, Roumanic 12, Greek 2, Hebrew 15, French 2, several languages 11. Of these 293 in Austria and 151 in Hungary were political papers. The entire number of sheets issued amounted to 83,100,000 in Austria and 19,000,000 in Hungary. In 1876, 1902 books were printed in German, 692 in Slavonic, 19 in Italian, and 727 in Magyar.

Religion.—The religion of the people corresponds very much with their nationality, a circumstance which no doubt tends greatly to keep up their differences. The Germans, as a rule, are Roman Catholics where they form the great mass of the population, but where they have come into the country as colonists, they are generally Protestants. The Czechs and Moravians are almost entirely Catholics, while the Slovaks, though when near the Moravians and Poles Catholics, are when among the Magyars in a large degree Protestant, and when near the Ruthenians many of them belong to the Greek Catholic Church. The Poles, Slovenians, and Croatians are Roman Catholics, while the Ruthenians belong to the Greek Catholic Church, and only a small portion of them in Bukowina and the neighbouring part of Hungary are attached to the Oriental Greek Church. The Latin races in the W. are throughout Roman Catholics, while the Roumanians in Hungary and Bukowina belong for the most part to the Oriental Greek Church, and in Transylvania the majority are connected with the Greek Catholic Church. The Serbians belong almost entirely to the Oriental Greek Church. The following table gives the numbers belonging to the principal religious sects according to the Census of 1869.

	Austria.	Hungary.	Monarchy.
Roman Catholics	16,248,776	7,502,000	23,750,776
Greek Catholics	2,330,421	1,587,585	3,918,006
Oriental Greek Church	458,128	2,579,048	3,037,176
Lutherans	247,157	1,109,154	1,356,311
Calvinists	104,017	2,024,332	2,128,349
Unitarians	161	54,438	54,599
Jews	820,200	522,133	1,372,333
Other Christian sects	8,306	8,423	16,729
Sects not Christian	365	214	579

RELIGION.

The Roman Catholics form 66.65 per cent. of the entire population, and are in a majority in almost all the provinces. They are much more numerous however in Austria, where they form 80.37 per cent. of the population, than in Hungary where they do not exceed 48.67 per cent. In Salzburg, Carniola, and Tyrol, they comprise almost without exception the entire population. In Styria, the Protestants form only 1 per cent. of the population, in Upper Austria 2, and in Carinthia 5, the rest being Roman Catholics. In Lower Austria, there are 96 per cent. Catholics, 2 per cent. Protestants, and 2 per cent. Jews; in the Maritime District, 99 per cent. Catholics, and 1 per cent. Jews; in Bohemia, 96 per cent. Catholics, 2 per cent. Protestants, and 2 per cent. Jews; in Moravia, 95 per cent. Catholics, 3 per cent. Protestants, and 2 per cent. Jews; in Silesia, 85 per cent. Catholics, 14 per cent. Protestants, and 1 per cent. Jews. In Galicia, there are only 46 per cent. Roman Catholics to 43 per cent. Greek Catholics, and 11 per cent. Jews; in Bukowina, 11 per cent. Roman Catholics and 4 per cent. Greek Catholics to 73 per cent. belonging to the Oriental Greek Church, 2 per cent. Protestants and 10 per cent. Jews. In Dalmatia, there are 82 per cent. Roman Catholics and 18 per cent. belonging to the Oriental Greek Church. In Hungary and Transylvania, there are 45 per cent. Roman Catholics, 12 per cent. Greek Catholics, 23 per cent. Protestants (8 Lutherans and 15 Calvinists), 13 per cent. Oriental Greek Church, 5 per cent. Jews, the rest Unitarians and other smaller sects. In Croatia and Slavonia, the Roman Catholics amount to 84 per cent., and there are 14 per cent. of the Oriental Greek Church, 1 per cent. Protestants, and 1 per cent. Jews. Finally in the Military Frontier, there are 43 per cent. Roman Catholics, 1 per cent. Greek Catholics, 55 per cent. of the Oriental Greek Church, and 1 per cent. Jews.

The Roman Catholic is the established religion of the country, and Austria has always remained strongly attached to that faith; but her sovereigns have in general resisted the pretensions of the popes to temporal power, so that their authority is not so unlimited here as in some other Catholic countries. Papal bulls and decretals are valid only after they have received the sanction of the monarch, who also has the nomination of the bishops and archbishops, and the power of imposing taxes on Church property. There are 11 archbishops, 7 in Austria (at Vienna, Salzburg, Görz, Prague, Olmütz, Lemberg, and Zara), and 4 in Hungary (at Gran, Erlau, Kalocsa, and Agram). There are also 45 bishops, 22,305 secular clergy, 9820 monks, and 7754 nuns.

The Greek Catholic Church or the United Greek Church is composed of those Greek Christians who have been induced to acknowledge the supremacy of the Pope, while on the other hand they are permitted to hold to all the peculiar usages of the Greek Church which do not affect fundamental doctrines, as the use of the Greek language in divine service, the giving of the cup to the laity in the communion, the marriage of the priests, &c. It has 2 archbishops, 1 at Lemberg and 1 at Blasendorf in Transylvania, and 4785 secular clergy. There is also a small body of Armenian Catholics similarly connected with the Roman Catholic Church, and having an archbishop at Lemberg, but altogether it numbers only about 8000 adherents.

The Protestants rank, in point of numbers, next to the Roman Catholic and the Greek Catholic churches, and comprise 10.1 per cent. of the population, being 1.8 per cent. in Austria, and 8.3 per cent. in Hungary. Of these 3.9 per cent. are Lutherans, and 6.2 per cent. Calvinists, the former being the more numerous in Austria, the latter in Hungary. In Austria and Hungary ecclesiastical affairs are conducted separately. In the former they are managed by an Upper Ecclesiastical Council in Vienna, and a General Synod. The former is the highest governing body in spiritual and administrative matters. It is composed of representatives of each division, and in all that concerns the Protestant Church generally, the members act together, but in what more particularly concerns only one of the divisions of it, they act separately. The General Synod is composed of representatives of the inferior courts of each division, namely, the superintendents, the superintendential curators, the seniors, a lay representative from each seniority, and a representative of the Protestant Theological Faculty at Vienna. They, as a rule, meet every six years, usually in Vienna, and consider matters more particularly relating to ecclesiastical law and government. They sit separately, but may come together for the consideration of matters of common interest. There are 9 Superintendencies (5 Lutheran), having each a superintendent as its head, with a managing committee, and a superintendential assembly. Under these are the Seniorities, of which there are 21 (15 Lutheran), with similarly a senior, a managing committee, and a seniorial assembly. Following these are the Presbyteries and local assemblies, for the management of parochial matters. In Hungary the Synod passes the laws for the government of both sections of the church, while the General Convention directs and controls matters connected with the churches and schools. Under these are 8 Superintendencies (4 Lutheran), and superintendential Conventions; 74 Seniorities (36 Lutheran) and seniorial Conventions; Presbyteries and local Conventions.

The Eastern or Oriental Greek Church embraces 8.52 per cent. of the entire population, being 16.73 of that of Hungary, and 2.27 of that of Austria. Its affairs are conducted by an Episcopal Synod, and it has in Austria 3 bishops, at Czernowitz, Zara, and Cattaro; and in Hungary, 2 archbishops, at Karlowitz and Hermannstadt, the former having the title of Patriarch, and having under him 6 bishops, the latter having under him 2 bishops. There are also 3 Church Congresses for the management of internal affairs—one for Bukowina, and one each for the Serbian and Wallachian races. The dioceses or eparchs are divided into Proto-presbyteries, and these into parishes. There are altogether about 4000 secular clergy, and about 300 monks in 40 cloisters.

The Unitarian Church (in Transylvania) has an Upper Consistory and a Synod for the direction of its affairs.

Under these are 8 Dioceses, in which Diocesan Assemblies are held.

The Jewish religion is conducted by rabbis, preachers, and religious teachers, of which there are in Austria about 390, and in Hungary, about 350.

Education.—Previous to 1848, the monarchy was very far behind in the matter of education; but since that time great improvements have been effected, and an entire change has taken place. The greatest attention is now given to the subject of education, schools of all kinds have been established throughout the country, improved systems of teaching have been introduced, and instruction is open to all, without regard to class or creed, at a very small cost, or even gratuitously to such as are unable to pay for it.[1] It still, however, continues to be very much under the control of the priests, and many of the teachers are ecclesiastics. The Roman Catholic religion forms an essential part of the instruction in all public schools, except those established for special subjects. The Protestant and Oriental Greek Churches have, as a rule, their own common schools, and where this is not the case, they have to send their children to the public schools. The Jews, also, in places where they have no schools of their own, are obliged to send their children to Christian schools.

Matters connected with education are now managed in Austria under a law passed in 1869; in Hungary, under one passed in 1868; and in Croatia and Slavonia, under one of 1874. The school age in Austria extends from the end of the 6th to the completion of the 14th year, and in Hungary, Istria, Dalmatia, Galicia and Bukowina, to the end of the 12th year; but in the latter case the children are expected to attend a repetition school (*Wiederholungschule*) at least once a week

---

[1] The Right Hon. W. E. Forster, speaking at Bradford on 9th October, 1879, said that "he had just come from Austria, and in going through the towns and villages of the Tyrol, he found good schools, compulsory by-laws, and technical schools meeting him everywhere; and that it was quite evident that as far as education goes, Austria will obtain an advantage for its workpeople.

for three years more. The necessity for the erection of a school exists in all places where, within a circle of three miles, there are 40 children who are more than two miles from a school. The number of teachers depends on the number of scholars, so that when these amount to more than 80, a second teacher is deemed necessary, and when over 160, a third. According to the census of 1869, the number of persons in Hungary over six years of age, who were able to read and write was 3,990,519 or 31.3 per cent.; who could merely read, 1,344,292, or 10.5 per cent.; and who neither read nor write, 7,416,503, or 58.2 per cent. The proportions varied in different parts of the kingdom: thus, in Hungary and Transylvania 32.7 per cent. could read and write, in the Military Frontier 20.7 per cent., and in Croatia and Slavonia, only 15 per cent. We do not possess the same means for determining the state of education in Austria, but taking the number of recruits joining the army during the years 1872-74, we find that for the entire Monarchy only 52.5 per cent. of them are able to write, being for the western half 54.7, and for the eastern 51.4. In many of the provinces of Austria, however, the percentage is much higher. Thus, in Lower Austria, it amounts to 94.2; in Silesia to 91.2; in Salzburg to 88.5; in Bohemia to 84.7; and in Styria to 73.7; while on the other hand it is as low as 15.3 in Galicia; 7.3 in Carniola; 6.2 in Bukowina; and 1.6 in Dalmatia.

The educational institutions may be divided into four classes: the lower, middle, and high schools, and the schools devoted to special subjects. The lower schools include the common elementary schools, and the burgh or higher elementary schools. In 1875 there were altogether in the Monarchy 31,418 of the former, and 322 of the latter; with 43,494 male and female teachers, and 3,723,600 scholars out of 5,463,900 within the school age. This gives 67 per cent. attending school out of those that ought to be there—66.2 for Austria, and 68.1 for Hungary. In some of the provinces of Austria, however, the proportion is as high as 94 and 96; in others, as low as 17 and 2?. In the common elementary schools, the subjects taught are reading, writing, arithmetic, religion, singing, the elements of natural science and history, with gymnastics. In addition to these, there are taught in the burgh schools, literary composition, advanced natural science, geometry, book-keeping and drawing. Besides these, there are a number of Kindergartens, and establishments for the care of children under the school age during the day, so as to enable the mothers to go out and work. In 1875 there were 142 establishments for the care of young children and 75 Kindergartens in connexion with the common schools, and 235 independent establishments of both kinds in Austria; and 211 similar establishments in Hungary. Some are maintained by societies, others by private individuals; at some a small charge is made, at others the benefits are afforded gratuitously. In 1876, there were in Austria 26 orphan asylums, having 556 boys, and 833 girls. There are also numerous industrial schools for girls, and trade and agricultural schools for boys. The schools are under the management of local, district, and provincial school boards; and there are district and provincial school inspectors, for visiting and reporting upon the different schools.

The middle schools comprise the gymnasia, the real schools, and the real gymnasia. The gymnasia are preparatory institutions to the universities. A complete gymnasium provides for a course of eight years' study, and is divided into two parts of four years each. The lower course not only prepares for the higher, but is also complete in itself, for those that do not wish to go any farther. The branches of study include Latin, Greek, and modern languages, geography, history, religion, mathematics, natural history, physics, writing, drawing, singing, and gymnastics. In passing from one class to another, the scholars undergo a very searching examination. The under gymnasia, of which there are a considerable number, only provide for a four years' course. The real schools are designed to afford a course of instruction, preparatory to the technical high schools, and also suitable for those intending to enter upon industrial pursuits. The course extends over seven years, of which four are spent in the under, and three in the upper school. The former not only serves a preparation for the latter, but is also complete in itself,—fitting for the lower kinds of industrial occupations. The branches taught include history, geography, arithmetic, mathematics, writing, drawing, book-keeping, exchanges, natural history, technology, &c. The real gymnasia combine the leading features of the two others, the under course of four years being a common one, and the upper course also of four years, being divided into a humanity side and a real side. In Austria in 1876 there were 91 gymnasia with 24,030 scholars; 61 real gymnasia with 11,898 scholars; and 78 real schools, with 10,237 scholars. In Hungary in 1875, there were 155 gymnasia, with 29,189 scholars, and 410 real schools, with 9,186 scholars. With the exception of the gymnasium at Teschen, which is Lutheran, and the gymnasium at Suczawa and the real school at Czernowitz, which belong to the Oriental Greek Church, the middle schools in Austria are all Roman Catholic, but they are open to scholars of every creed. Of the gymnasia in Hungary:—88 are Roman Catholic; 3 Greek Catholic; 3 Oriental Greek; 57 Protestant; and 4 Unitarian: of the real schools, 38 are established by the state or the town, and are therefore unsectarian; 2 are Jewish; 1 Roman Catholic; and 1 Greek Catholic. In Austria, 72 gymnasia, 35 real gymnasia, and 4 real schools, are either wholly or partly supported by the state. Of the rest, 9 real gymnasia, and 12 real schools, are supported by the provinces; 13 gymnasia and 2 real schools by religious bodies; 6 gymnasia, 17 real gymnasia, and 17 real schools, by communities, and 3 real schools by private individuals.

The high schools are the universities and the technical institutions. Of the former, there are 7 in Austria, namely, at Vienna, Gratz, Innsbruck, Prague, Lemberg, Cracow and Czernowitz; and 3 in Hungary—at Buda-Pesth, Klausenburg and Agram, having in all 990 professors and teachers, and 11,850 students. The university of Vienna is the largest—not only in Austria, but in Germany—having (in 1876) no fewer than 283 professors and teachers, and 3810 students. It is particularly distinguished in the departments of medicine, law, natural science, and Oriental languages. The medical school in Vienna is reckoned the first in Germany. The university of Buda-Pesth had 149 professors and teachers, and 2566 students, and that at Prague 172 of the former, and 1885 of the latter. Each university—except those after mentioned—has four complete faculties, for theology (Roman Catholic), law and political economy, medicine and surgery, and philosophy. The universities at Lemberg and Czernowitz have no medical faculty, and the theological faculty in the latter is of the Oriental Greek Church. In Hungary, the university of Buda-Pesth is the only one having four faculties, that at Klausenburg having only a medical and a philosophical faculty, and that at Agram, theological, law, and philosophical faculties. The theological and law courses occupy 4 years each, the medical 5, and the philosophical 3.

The technical high schools have for their object, the imparting of a high scientific education to their pupils. These generally enter from the upper real schools, and the complete technical course extends over five years. There are 8 of these institutions in the Monarchy, namely:—at Vienna, Gratz, Prague (a German and a Czech), Brünn, Lemberg, Cracow, and Buda-Pesth—having in all 346 teachers, and 4273 pupils. Those of Vienna, Prague and Lemburg, have each four departments—for engineering, architecture, machinery, and technical chemistry; those of Gratz, Brünn and Buda-Pesth have no architectural department, and that of Cracow has only a technical and a commercial course.

The special high schools or educational institutions include a number of theological seminaries connected with the different religious sects of the country, and academies and schools for law, commerce, navigation, mining, manufactures, agriculture, forest-management, the fine arts, military training, and the training of teachers. Besides the theological faculties in the universities, the Roman Catholics have theological faculties at

Salzburg and Olmütz, 17 episcopal seminaries, and 46 other seminaries, having in all 1775 students. The Greek Catholics have 4 theological seminaries with 217 students; the Oriental Greek Church 5 seminaries with 246 students; the Protestants, a theological faculty at Vienna, and 13 seminaries with 473 students; the Unitarians, a college at Klausenburg with 23 students; and the Jews, a rabbinical school at Pressburg, with 8 students. The Oriental Academy at Vienna, for the training of officials for diplomatic and consular service in the east, has 11 teachers and 38 students; besides which there are 14 law academies in Hungary (6 royal, 2 episcopal, and 6 Protestant), having together 103 teachers, and 1580 students. The trade and manufacture schools are numerous and of different kinds—some for special, others for more general objects—but all having more or less in view, the improvement of apprentices and journeymen, in their special callings. They are established usually by corporations, companies, or private firms, and are mostly devoted to affording instruction in such arts as building, weaving, turning, cabinet-making, wood-cutting, glass-making, printing, drawing, modelling, lace-making, straw-plaiting, sewing, knitting and the like. The principal of these are at Vienna, Gratz, Prague, and Buda-Pesth. The art school in Vienna has 13 teachers, and 240 scholars. Altogether there were in the Monarchy in 1876, 197 of these schools, having 782 teachers, and 18,500 scholars. There is a commercial and nautical school at Trieste, having 20 teachers and 106 scholars, and nautical schools at Zara, Spalato, Ragusa, Cattaro, &c. There are mining academies at Leoben and Pribram, and a mining and forest academy at Schemnitz, with various schools for miners, in the different mining districts. In 1873 an agricultural school was established in Vienna, which in 1876 had 41 professors and 170 pupils. In addition to these there were in Austria 36 agricultural schools, 22 for vine and fruit culture, 6 for forest management, and 5 for farriery, having in all 389 teachers and 1880 pupils. In Hungary there are 3 agricultural academies—at Altenburg, Reszthely, and

Kreutz, having 54 teachers and 270 scholars; and 14 agricultural and the like schools with 600 scholars. For the fine arts there are the Academy of the Fine Arts at Vienna, having 22 teachers, and, in the 12 special schools, 215 pupils; the Academy of Painting at Gratz with 40 pupils; the Art Academy at Prague with 70 pupils; and the school for the fine arts at Cracow. For instruction in music there are the Conservatoire of Music in Vienna (650 pupils), that in Prague (120), the Academy of Music in Buda-Pesth, the school of the Society of the Friends of Church Music in Vienna (150), that of the Music Society of Linz (210), of the Cathedral Music Society at Salzburg, and numerous other music-schools, amounting in all to about 150, with about 450 teachers and 8000 pupils.

Of late years special attention has been given to the training and properly qualifying of teachers for the common schools; and normal schools for both sexes have been established, where a course of instruction, extending over four years, is imparted. In Austria, in 1876, there were 42 of these schools for males, and 23 for females, with 6900 male, and 3362 female pupils; and in Hungary, in 1875, 61 schools, with 2800 pupils of both sexes.

The military special schools for the training of officers, are the Military Academy in Wiener Neustadt for the infantry and cavalry, with 48 teachers and 300 pupils; the Technical Military Academy in Vienna for the artillery and engineers, with 43 teachers and 250 pupils; the veterinary school in Vienna with 12 teachers and 118 pupils, and the marine academy in Fiume with 37 teachers and 110 pupils. There are also special courses of instruction given in Vienna for staff-officers; advanced instruction for officers in the infantry, cavalry, artillery, and engineer branches of the service; and instruction in the art of war. In addition to these a number of cadet schools have recently been established in Vienna, Prague, Buda-Pesth and other places.

There are 14 deaf and dumb institutions in Austria, having in all 850 pupils, and 1 in Hungary (at Waitzen); and 6 institutions for the blind with about 500 pupils. In addition to these there are a number of private schools for special objects in all the large towns.

In connexion with the universities and many of the higher educational institutions are libraries, museums of natural history and antiquities, botanic gardens, observatories, chemical laboratories, &c. There are also valuable libraries belonging to various ecclesiastical bodies, to societies of different kinds, and to many of the large towns.

CHAPTER VI.

INDUSTRIES :—AGRICULTURE ; MINES ; MANUFACTURES.

THE great majority of the people of Austria-Hungary are engaged in agricultural pursuits, or in connexion with the forests, which are extensive and valuable. According to the last census, 7,497,500 males or 37.13 per cent. of the population of Austria, and 5,015,899 males or 32.54 per cent. of that of Hungary were thus employed. These sums are exclusive of women and children, which, if we include will raise them to more than double, so that it is estimated that probably nearly three-fourths of the entire population are so employed.

The land in general is very fertile, although great differences exist in different parts owing to special circumstances. It is estimated that 93.56 per cent. of the entire area of Austria, and 83.11 per cent. of that of Hungary are productive. The proportion is highest in Bohemia, Silesia, Dalmatia, and Galicia, where it exceeds 96 per cent., and Moravia, and Lower Austria, where it exceeds 95 ; and lowest in Salzburg, Tyrol, and the Military Frontier, where it is between 80 and 82 per cent. Of the productive land, 36.5 per cent. is arable ; 1.1 in vineyards, 13.4 gardens and meadows, 16.1 pasturage, 32.6 forests, and 0.3 reeds and rushes. The following table gives the area occupied by each in English acres :—

	Austria.	Hungary.	Monarchy.
Arable	25,107,538	26,960,351	52,067,889
Vineyards	506,708	999,884	1,506,592
Meadows and gardens	8,820,648	10,226,406	19,047,054
Pasturage	11,381,525	11,601,595	22,983,120
Forests	23,514,803	23,045,072	46,559,875
Reeds and rushes . .	79,998	390,161	470,159
Total.	69,411,220	73,223,469	142,634,689

The provinces having the largest proportion of arable land are Moravia, Bohemia, Silesia, Galicia, Lower and Upper Austria, Hungary, Croatia, and Slavonia. Austria is still behind many other countries in agricultural matters, although in this respect great improvements have recently taken place. The most extensively wine-producing districts are Hungary and the adjoining lands, with Dalmatia, Lower Austria, the Maritime District, and Southern Tyrol. The Alpine lands proper, the Maritime District, Bukowina, Dalmatia, and the Military Frontier, are on account of their great extent of pasture-land, great cattle-rearing districts. Particularly rich in forests are the Alpine lands, Upper Austria, Bukowina, Transylvania, Croatia, and Slavonia.

The acreage under the principal crops was, according to the latest returns, as follows:—

	Austria.	Hungary.	Monarchy.
Wheat	674,402	5,549,455	6,223,857
Rye	4,812,478	287,631	5,100,109
Barley	2,694,223	2,307,263	5,001,486
Oats	4,351,197	2,589,835	6,941,032
Maize	733,007	3,960,096	4,693,103
Potatoes	2,350,734	890,353	3,241,087
Total	15,616,041	15,584,633	31,200,674

These six principal crops occupied 69 per cent. of the arable land in Austria, and 67.3 per cent. in Hungary. The rest was taken up with less extensive crops, or was lying fallow. The principal of the less extensive crops, were olives, 52,174 acres (38,301 being in Dalmatia, and 10,625 in Istria); chestnuts, 3130 acres (2322 being in Southern Tyrol); fruits of different kinds, 655,208 acres in Hungary, and 49,287 in Austria; flax, 259,849 acres in Austria, and 21,162 in Hungary; and hemp, 91,822 acres in Austria, and 116,533 in Hungary.

The estimated average annual produce of the six principal crops in English bushels, is as follows :—

	Austria.	Hungary.	Monarchy.
Wheat .	34,114,000	64,486,000	98,600,000
Rye . .	68,862,000	43,385,000	112,250,000
Barley .	47,430,000	30,152,000	77,582,000
Oats .	63,718,000	40,551,000	104,269,000
Maize .	16,214,000	69,962,000	86,170,000
Potatoes	257,978,000	30,098,000	281,076,000

The value of an average crop of the different kinds of grain is estimated at 95,000,000*l*. being 48,400,000*l*. for Austria, and 46,600,000*l*. for Hungary. The grain produced is not only sufficient for home consumption, but usually affords a considerable amount for export, which varies greatly in different years, but may be taken to average in value, from 2,000,000*l*. to 3,000,000*l*. The principal grain producing districts are Hungary, Bohemia, Galicia, Moravia, Lower and Upper Austria. The potato is extensively cultivated only in the north, chiefly in Bohemia, Moravia, Silesia, Galicia, Bukowina, and the north of Hungary. In the south it is much less cultivated, and only to a small extent in the Alpine districts. Flax and hemp are grown in all parts of the country, flax prevailing in the north-west, and hemp in the east and south. The annual produce is estimated at 293,000,000 lbs. of which about ⅖ are flax, and ⅗ hemp. Tobacco is a state monopoly, and confined to Hungary, Galicia, Bukowina, and Tyrol. The annual produce is about 101,250,000 lbs., of which Hungary yields about 93,000,000 lbs. Hops are grown to a great extent in Bohemia, and of late years also in Upper Austria. The average crop is reckoned at about 44,000,000 lbs., of which Bohemia produces about half. The valley of the Eger is considered to yield the best hops. The cabbage is very extensively cultivated, being much used by the inhabitants, especially in the form of Sour Krout, and is also largely given to cattle. Turnips are extensively grown, especially in the S., and beet-root more particularly in the N. The growth of rape-seed has of late become much more extensive than formerly, especially in Bohemia, Moravia, Galicia, Upper and Lower Austria, Hungary, and Transylvania. The average annual produce is about 4,320,000 bushels.

Austria-Hungary ranks third among the wine-producing countries of Europe—after France and Italy, and some of the wines of Hungary, as Tokay, are justly celebrated. The amount annually produced in the country is estimated at 332,200,000 gallons, of which Hungary produces more than two-thirds. The principal of the other wine-producing provinces are Dalmatia, Lower Austria, Styria, and Moravia. After corn and timber, this forms the most valuable product of the soil. Fruits are largely grown, particularly in Lower Austria, Bohemia, Moravia, Upper Austria, Styria, Carinthia, and parts of Tyrol and Vorarlberg. Much of the fruit produced is used in the manufacture of cider and other drinks. In the S. of Hungary, and adjoining lands, the plum ranks first among fruits, and from it a kind of plum brandy is very largely made. The W. and S. of Hungary, Transylvania, Croatia, Slavonia, and the Military Frontier are great fruit-producing districts. A considerable quantity of the fruit grown is annually exported. The forests occupy nearly one-third of the whole of the productive area of the country, and are estimated to yield annually about 7,416,482,000 cubic feet of timber. The annual value of the various productions of the soil, exclusive of grain, is reckoned at 91,600,000*l*. for Austria, and 78,000,000*l*. for Hungary, being together 169,600,000*l*., or including the grain crops no less a sum than 264,600,000*l*.

The Monarchy is particularly distinguished for the number and the superiority of its horses, for the improvement of which numerous studs exist all over the country. The breeding of horses is more or less extensively carried on in all the provinces, but more especially in Hungary, Transylvania, Bukowina, Galicia, Styria, Bohemia, Moravia, Lower and

Upper Austria. The total number of horses in the country in 1869 was, 3,525,842 of which, 2,158,819 were in Hungary. Comparing the number of horses with the population, we find that for every 1000 of the latter there were 140 of the former in Hungary, and 70 in Austria. Galicia is the only province of Austria which has over 100 horses to every 1000 of its inhabitants, having 128. In Hungary, the Military Frontier stands first, having 147 horses to every 1000 of its population. Since the date of the last census, the number of horses has been increased, and more attention has been given to their improvement owing to the stimulus imparted by prizes, exhibitions, races, &c. All kinds of horses are found here from the heaviest to the lightest, from the largest to the smallest. The most beautiful horses are those of Transylvania and Bukowina, the lightest and fleetest those of Hungary, and the largest and strongest those of Salzburg. The smallest horses are found in Croatia, and the neighbouring lands. The horses of Styria, Carinthia, Northern Tyrol, and Upper Austria, are also famous. In Dalmatia, the Maritime District, and Southern Tyrol, horses are less numerous, and mules, and asses, in a great measure take their place. Of the 13,981 mules in Austria, 45 per cent. were in Dalmatia, and 30 per cent. in the Maritime District and Southern Tyrol; and of the 61,831 asses 28 per cent. were in the former, and 21 per cent. in the latter. In Hungary there were 2266 mules, and 30,482 asses.

Austria-Hungary is not remarkable as a cattle-rearing country. Indeed except in certain districts, particularly among the Alps, it must be considered to be much behind in this branch of industry. The finest cattle are to be found in the Alpine regions, —in other parts the breeds are generally very inferior. In 1869 the Monarchy possessed 12,704,405 head of cattle, of which 5,279,193 were in Hungary, 2,070,572 in Galicia, and 1,602,015 in Bohemia. The cattle of Hungary are generally of very inferior quality. In proportion to their extent, Upper Austria, Silesia, Bohemia, Styria, and Galicia, contain the greatest number of cattle, and on the other hand Hungary, Tyrol, the

Military Frontier, the Maritime District, and Dalmatia, contain the smallest number,—attention in these latter provinces being more given to sheep. In proportion to the population, Austria had 367 cattle for each 1000 of its inhabitants, Hungary 341, and the Monarchy 357. In Salzburg the proportion was as high as 1105 per 1000, Carinthia 692, Upper Austria 650, Styria 527, and Tyrol 525. The rearing of sheep receives a large share of attention. It is carried on to a considerable extent in all the provinces, and in some, very extensively. Much has been done of late years in the way of improving the breeds, particularly in Moravia, Silesia, Bohemia, Lower and Upper Austria, and Hungary. In no part of the Monarchy has sheep-rearing reached so high a point as in Moravia, and Silesia. The main object has been the improvement of the wool, and with this view the merino and the other fine-woolled breeds have been introduced. Some attention, however, is also given to the fattening qualities. For mutton, the best sheep are those of Lower Austria, Carinthia, the Maritime District, Dalmatia, and the Military Frontier. The sheep are frequently driven for the sake of pasture, from one part of the country to another, and even into other countries, as Italy, Roumania, &c. The total number of sheep, in the country in 1869, was 20,102,393, of which over 15,000,000 were in Hungary. Dalmatia, Hungary, and the Military Frontier, are most largely stocked with sheep. Dalmatia had 1520 sheep to every 1000 of its population, Hungary 1053, and the Military Frontier 574. Sheep are least plentiful in Styria, and Carniola. The goat, which has been called the poor man's cow, is also to be found in all parts of the country, but is most common in the mountainous districts, and is owned chiefly by the poorer classes of the rural population. The total number of goats in the country, in 1869, was 1,552,055, of which 572,951 were in Hungary. Dalmatia, however, is the great country of the goat, where there are no fewer than 280,656, after which follow Bohemia with 194,273, Tyrol with 137,698, and Moravia with 8,383. The number of swine in the Monarchy was 6,994,752, of which 4,443,279 were in Hungary. They are most numerous in those provinces that contain extensive oak and beech forests, or where there are many distilleries or breweries. Hence they are most plentiful in Croatia and Slavonia, the Military Frontier, Hungary, Transylvania, Galicia, Styria, Upper and Lower Austria, and Bohemia.

Since the date of the last census the numbers of these animals in the Monarchy have generally diminished, except that in Hungary the sheep and the goats have largely increased. It is estimated that nearly 12,000,000 cwt. of flesh, 1,960,000 cwt. of butter, and 1,658,000 cwt. of cheese are annually produced. The annual produce of wool is about 400,000 cwt., but mostly of common or inferior kinds. The finer wools are chiefly produced in Moravia, Silesia, Bohemia, Lower Austria, and certain parts of Hungary and Galicia. Poultry are common in all parts of the Monarchy, particularly in the neighbourhood of large towns where they are in demand. The common fowl is the most abundant, and after it the goose. In Bohemia alone there are about 15,000,000 common fowls and 4,000,000 geese. In Moravia, Silesia, Lower Austria, Hungary, Transylvania, and the Military Frontier, they are also common. Ducks, capons, and turkeys are more common in the South than in the North. The capons of Styria are especially noted. Pigeons are everywhere common. The value of the poultry of all kinds in the Monarchy is estimated at not less than 10,000,000*l.*

Bees are extensively kept, particularly in the provinces of Hungary, Transylvania, Galicia, Bohemia, Styria, and Carinthia. In Carinthia and Lower Austria they are kept most skilfully, although not so extensively as in some of the other provinces. In 1869, there were 1,531,150 hives in the Monarchy, of which 517,710 were in Hungary and Transylvania, 257,493 in Galicia, and 140,892 in Bohemia. The annual average produce is estimated at 25,000,000 lbs. of honey, and 1,980,000 lbs. of wax. The silkworm is cultivated in certain parts of the Southern districts, particularly in Southern Tyrol.

The annual yield of cocoons is about 3,520,000 lbs., of which nearly one-half is obtained in Southern Tyrol. Game of various kinds are common, particularly in Bohemia, Moravia, Silesia, Lower and Upper Austria, Hungary, Galicia, and Bukowina. The hare is common everywhere; red deer are found in Hungary, Upper Austria, Salzburg, Styria, Carinthia, and Tyrol; and wild boars in Bohemia, Moravia, Silesia, Galicia, and Hungary. Partridges are common in most parts of the country; pheasants are most numerous in Bohemia, but are found also in Hungary, Styria, Moravia, and Lower Austria. Bears are met with in the Carpathian and Alpine regions, and also in Dalmatia and the Maritime District; and the wolf is common in Hungary, Transylvania, Croatia, Slavonia, Galicia, and Bukowina. The rivers and lakes in general abound in fish, which are also plentiful along the coast. In Dalmatia in particular, fishing constitutes an important branch of industry, affording employment to many of the population. In the season of 1875-6, the fishing along the coast, and on the islands, was estimated to yield 174,000*l*. The tunny and sardines are largely caught.

Mining[1] with the industries depending upon it forms one of the most important pursuits of the people after agriculture. In 1869, 104,342 men were employed in the mining and smelting works in Austria, and 50,143 in Hungary, making together

[1] Mining and every form of manufacturing industry suffered greatly from the monetary crisis of 1873. This was occasioned by over-speculation, induced by previous years of unusual prosperity. One form in which it manifested itself was in the construction of new lines of railway. In the five years from 1863 to 1868 scarcely 140 miles of new railway were opened annually, while in the six following years the annual average reached 930 miles. Iron, coal, and almost every other branch of industry enjoyed for a time the like success. The crisis came with the sudden failure of one of the largest financial houses of Vienna, in consequence of which a large amount of stock of various kinds was at once thrown upon the market; great depression of prices followed, the Bourse became profoundly agitated, and hundreds of failures followed. The result was years of depression in almost every branch of industry, so that in 1877 many of them were not much in advance of what they were in 1869. Coal is almost the only object of mining industry that has shown a large increase. The great want of the country is the want of capital to develope its great and varied resources.

154,485 exclusive of women and children, of whom a great many are thus employed. In 1875 there were directly employed in the mines, including the salt works, but excluding the smelting works, 76,100 men, 5700 women, and 1800 children in Austria, and 36,400 men, 1400 women, and 4600 children in Hungary, making in all 124,400 persons. The provinces in which mining operations are chiefly carried on are Styria (iron and coal), Carinthia (lead and iron), Carniola (quicksilver), Hungary (gold, silver, copper, iron, and coal), Transylvania (gold and silver), Salzburg (iron), Bohemia (silver, lead, iron, and coal), Moravia (iron and coal), Galicia (salt).

Gold has been obtained in the Monarchy from very early times, and was formerly found in greater abundance than at present. Yet even now Hungary and Transylvania rank among the first gold-producing districts of Europe. More than half the gold produced, is obtained in Transylvania, principally at Zalathna on the southern range of the Behar Mountains, where affluents of the Körös and Maros take their rise, in which, as well as in the Theiss and Danube, gold is also found. In Hungary, gold is obtained chiefly at Schemnitz and Kremnitz. It is also found in small quantities in Salzburg, Tyrol, Styria, and the Military Frontier. In 1875, Hungary produced 12,145 lbs. of gold ore, and Austria 242 lbs., making together 12,387 lbs. and yielding 51,166 ozs. of metal of the value of 221,500*l*. Silver has also been obtained from an early date and formerly in larger quantity than at present. Even now, however, this country ranks next to Russia, which produces the largest quantity of silver of any country in Europe. Bohemia and Transylvania yield the largest quantities of silver ore. Pribram and Joachimsthal are the parts in Bohemia where it is chiefly found, also Zalathna in Transylvania and Schemnitz and Kremnitz in Hungary. It is also found in small quantities in Bukowina, Tyrol, Salzburg, and Styria. In 1875, Austria produced 27,751 lbs. of silver ore, and Hungary 229,891 lbs., making together 247,642 lbs.; from which 1,610,168 ozs. of metal were extracted, of the value of 419,300*l*.

Iron is found in all the provinces, with the exception of the Maritime District and Dalmatia. It is found in the Alps (in Styria, Carinthia, Lower Austria, Salzburg, and in a less degree in Carniola), in the southern declivities of the Carpathians (Hungary and Transylvania), the northern declivities of the Carpathians (Galicia, Bukowina and Silesia), and the mountains of Bohemia, Moravia, and Silesia. Styria and Carinthia form a compact iron-producing region which yields more than a third part of all the ore obtained in the Monarchy. The principal mines are at Eisenerz and Mariazell in Styria, and Hüttenberg in Carinthia. After these come Hungary (at Schmölnitz and Dios-Györ, in the neighbourhood of Miskolez), Bohemia (Platten), Moravia (Blansko), Galicia (Sambor, Stry, and Sandec), and Transylvania. In 1875, Austria produced 14,099,680 cwt. of iron ore, and Hungary 7,964,860 cwt., making together 22,064,540 cwt., and yielding 8,267,800 cwt. of wrought and 995,460 cwt. of cast iron, of the value of 2,545,000*l.*

Copper is principally obtained in Hungary, particularly in the neighbourhood of Schmölnitz; then in Tyrol, Transylvania, Bukowina, Styria, Salzburg, and Bohemia. In 1875 442,760 cwt. of copper ore were produced, from which 28,800 cwt. of copper were extracted, of the value of 132,700*l.* Lead is found principally in Carinthia, which yields about as much as all the rest of the country put together. The other provinces in which lead is found are Bohemia, Tyrol, Styria, Hungary, and Transylvania. The amount of lead ore produced was 22,064,540 cwt., yielding 117,320 cwt. of lead, and 63,560 cwt. of Litharge, the value being 145,600*l.* Quicksilver is obtained at Idria in Carniola, where is the richest quicksilver-mine in Europe, after Almaden in Spain. In 1875 it produced 655,940 cwt. of ore which yielded 7760 cwt. of pure metal valued at 131,000*l.*

Tin is only found in Bohemia, which produced 40,430 cwt. of ore, from which 3180 cwt. of metal were obtained. Zinc is found chiefly in Western Galicia in the neighbourhood of Cracow, and in smaller quantities in Carinthia, Tyrol, and

Croatia. The amount of ore produced was 514,580 cwt., and of metal 69,060 cwt. The principal of other metals found in the country are antimony, manganese, nickel, arsenic, uranium, chromium, and wolfram. Antimony is obtained in Hungary, Bohemia, and Transylvania; manganese in Hungary, Bohemia, and Carniola; nickel in Hungary, Salzburg, Bohemia, and Styria; arsenic in Salzburg, Bohemia, and Silesia; chromium in the Military Frontier and Styria, uranium and wolfram in Bohemia.

The country possesses almost inexhaustible beds of coal of which a great part has not yet been touched upon. It exists in all the provinces, but the richest seams are in the mountain systems of Bohemia and Moravia. Bohemia yields more than half of the entire amount of coals raised in the country, Hungary (12 per cent.), Silesia (10), Styria (11), Moravia (6.5); then follow Galicia, Upper Austria, Carniola, Carinthia and Lower Austria. An immense advance has been made in coal-mining of late years. In 1831, the output of coals only amounted to about 4,000,000 cwt., in 1865, it had risen to 101,386,103 cwt., and in 1875, to 257,040,960 cwt. Of this last sum 228,017,800 cwt. were raised in Austria and 29,023,160 in Hungary; 153,336,260 cwt. were brown coal and 103,704,700 cwt. black coal. Brown coal is obtained in Bohemia (Teplitz), Styria (Köflach), Upper Austria (Wolfsegg), Carniola (Zagor), Moravia, Carinthia, Lower Austria, and Hungary (Losonez and Orawitza); black coal in Bohemia (Pilsen and Schlan), Moravia (Rossitz and Moravian Ostrau), Silesia (Polish Ostrau), Galicia (Javorzna, near Cracow), Lower Austria, Styria, Upper Austria, and Hungary (Fünfkirchen). Peat is also common, and is found to a greater or less extent in all the provinces. It is, however, found in greatest abundance in Upper Austria, Salzburg, Styria, Carinthia, Carniola, Tyrol, Bohemia, and Galicia.

Austria-Hungary is particularly rich in salt. Immense beds of rock salt exist on both sides of the Carpathians, particularly at Wieliczka in Western Galicia, where are the far-famed salt-works, Solotwina and Delatyn in Eastern Galicia, Marmaros in

Hungary, and the neighbourhood of Thorda in Transylvania. Salt is also largely obtained in the district of Salzkammergut in Upper Austria and Styria (at Hallstadt, Ischl, Ebensee and Aussee), in Salzburg (Hallein), and in Tyrol (Hall). It is also obtained from salt springs in Galicia, Hungary, and Transylvania. In addition to this it is manufactured from sea water at various places along the coast, at Pirano in Istria, and Pagno and Stagno, in Dalmatia. In 1875, 1,494,800 cwt. of rock salt were obtained in Austria, 2,797,520 cwt. of salt from brine, and 741,580 cwt. of sea salt, besides 211,420 cwt. of salt for industrial purposes, making in all 5,245,320 cwt.; while Hungary yielded of all sorts 2,210,780 cwt., the total being 7,456,100 cwt., and the total value 3,080,000*l.* Sulphur is found in Galicia, Bohemia, Moravia, and Salzburg; alum, in Bohemia, Hungary, Moravia, and Salzburg; sulphates of of iron and copper, in Bohemia and Carniola; petroleum, especially in Galicia; asphalt in Dalmatia and Tyrol; and graphite, in Lower Austria, Carinthia, Bohemia, and Moravia. Clay is found in most of the low-lying parts of the country; and at Inzensdorf in Lower Austria is said to be the largest brick and tile work in the world. Porcelain clay exists in Bohemia and Moravia; white, red, black, and variously coloured marble in Tyrol, Salzburg, Silesia, and Galicia; alabaster in Galicia; and gypsum in Silesia.

Manufactures.—The manufactures of Austria-Hungary have made great progress during the last five-and-twenty years, and notwithstanding the check they received a few years ago, many of them are now extensively and actively carried on. They include cotton, flax, hemp, woollen and silk stuffs; gold, silver, iron, lead, copper, tin, and zinc articles; leather, paper, tobacco, beer, brandy, and sugar; glass, porcelain, and earthenware; chemical stuffs; scientific and musical instruments, &c. The manufactures are principally carried on in the W. provinces, and more particularly in Bohemia, Moravia, Silesia, and Lower Austria. In the Hungarian provinces, in Galicia, Bukowina, and Dalmatia they are comparatively neglected. The principal seats of the woollen, linen, and cotton manufactures are in Bohemia, Moravia, and Silesia, and of the last also in Lower Austria and Vorarlberg; of iron in Styria, Carinthia, Bohemia, Hungary and Moravia; iron and steel wares chiefly in Vienna, Waidhofen on the Ybbs in Lower Austria, and the town of Steyer in Upper Austria; leather in Moravia, Lower Austria, and Bohemia; leathern articles in Vienna and Prague; glass, porcelain, and earthenware in Bohemia; beetroot sugar in Bohemia, Moravia, Hungary, Silesia, Galicia; silk in Vienna; beer in Vienna and Bohemia; brandy in Galicia, Moravia, and Bohemia; cabinet wares and musical instruments in Vienna and Prague; and scientific and surgical instruments in Vienna. The annual value of the manufactures is estimated at 180,000,000*l*., of which about one fourth is produced in Bohemia and Silesia, and after them come Styria, and the other Alpine provinces. The manufactures in Hungary are extensively carried on only in the larger towns and particularly in the capital, Buda-Pesth. According to the census of 1869, 2,920,280 persons were employed in the manufactures, of whom 2,273,316 were in Austria, and 646,964 in Hungary. Of these, 890,951 were engaged in industries connected with weaving; 677,740 in producing articles in metal, stone, and wood; 298,113 in the building arts; 330,285 in the production of articles of food, chemicals, and tobacco; 478,704 in leather, paper, and other productive industries; and 244,487 in non-productive industries. These figures, however, by no means represent the total number of persons employed in the manufactures. They only include those that are directly so employed without taking account of the members of their family who may also be engaged therein, or of the great numbers that practise some manufacture as secondary to husbandry. The number altogether of those who are employed in some kind of manufacture is estimated at not less than 7,000,000.

The cotton manufacture is one of the most extensive and flourishing in the country, and it has also risen up very rapidly.

In 1831, the import of cotton was 101,000 cwt., and the export 175 cwt., ; in 1850, the former had risen to 522,000, and the latter to 1270; and in 1875, the former was 1,186,552, and the latter 37,949 cwt. In 1870, there were in the country 134 spinning factories, with 1,405,000 spindles, and employing 20,500 work-people. Of the factories 67 were in Bohemia, 29 in Lower Austria, and 24 in Tyrol and Vorarlberg. The weaving of cotton is still mostly done by hand, and as a domestic branch of industry, being frequently carried on as a secondary occupation by persons engaged in agricultural pursuits. There are in all about 200,000 hand looms. Power-loom weaving has, however, lately been introduced, and in 1875, there were about 20,000 of these in operation, 8000 being in Bohemia, 4000 in Vorarlberg, and the rest in Lower and Upper Austria, Moravia, and Silesia. Weaving is most extensively carried on in Northern Bohemia, Moravia, and Silesia. The annual value of the cotton goods produced in the Monarchy is estimated at about 6,000,000*l*. In connexion with this manufacture there are printing works, of which there are several large establishments in Bohemia, Lower Austria, and Vorarlberg.

The flax and hemp manufacture is one of the oldest in the country, and was long the most important; but in consequence of the rapid advance of the cotton manufacture, it is no longer of the same importance as formerly. It still, however, affords employment to a great number of persons, and is very generally extended over the country. It is principally carried on as a domestic industry, the yarn being mostly spun by hand, and the weaving generally carried on in the cottages as a secondary occupation, the linen produced being chiefly of the commoner kinds and intended for domestic use. As a domestic industry it is most extensively carried on in Upper Hungary, Galicia, and Bukowina, but the production though large comes little into the market. There are also, however, a number of spinning factories, chiefly in Bohemia, Silesia, Moravia, and Lower and Upper Austria. In 1870, the number of spindles was 403,000, of which 260,400 were in Bohemia, 71,600 in Silesia, and 57,000 in Moravia. For the weaving of fine linen the most noted places are Rumburg, Schönhaide, and Reichenberg, in Bohemia ; Schönberg, in Moravia ; and Freudenthal, in Silesia. The number of looms for weaving linen in the Monarchy is 560,000.

The woollen manufacture is also an old-established branch of industry, and is still actively carried on. It is estimated that about 600,000 cwt. of wool are spun annually, the principal seats of it being in Bohemia, Moravia, Silesia, and Upper Austria, where it has been brought to a high state of perfection. The number of spindles in 1870 was 580,000. The weaving of woollen stuffs of a middling or inferior quality which are largely exported to America, Northern Europe, Italy, and the East, is extensively carried on in Moravia (especially at Brünn), Silesia (Bielitz), and Bohemia (Reichenberg). Fine cloths are manufactured at Namiest, Brünn, and Iglau in Moravia, and Klagenfurt in Carinthia. Shawls are manufactured only in Vienna ; carpets there, and in Linz and Reichenberg. About half the entire quantity of woollen goods produced in the country are manufactured in Bohemia and Moravia. The prosperous state of the woollen manufacture is owing to its being mostly in the hands of large manufacturers who employ the most improved kinds of machinery. In E. Hungary, Galicia, and Bukowina, as well as in Tyrol, Carniola, and Styria, the manufacture of coarse woollens is carried on to a considerable extent, but chiefly in the cottages and for home use. Little of this comes into the market.

If we except a few establishments in Bohemia and Moravia, the manufacture of silk stuffs is confined to Lower Austria, and principally to Vienna. In 1870, there were 165 silk and velvet factories, aud 119 ribbon factories in Vienna and the neighbourhood. Silk is produced in any considerable quantity only in Southern Tyrol, but to some extent also in the Maritime District and the S. of Hungary. The amount produced, however, is not equal to what is required, and about 1,700,000 lbs. are annually brought from other countries. The spinning of silk is principally carried on in Southern Tyrol. The annual value of the silk stuffs manufactured is about 900,000*l*.

The iron and steel manufactures form one of the most important branches of industry in the Monarchy, and afford employment to a great number of persons. They are more or less extensively carried on in all the provinces except the southern ones of Dalmatia, Croatia, Slavonia, and the Maritime District; but their principal seats are in Lower and Upper Austria, Bohemia, Moravia, Styria, and Carinthia. One of the most important of these seats is Steyer, and its neighbourhood in Upper Austria, where there are about 700 establishments producing goods to the value of 400,000*l*. annually, chiefly cutlery, scythes, sickles, arms, &c. There are also numerous ironworks in Vienna, and Waidhofen on the Ybbs, in Lower Austria. Bessimer steel is now largely manufactured in Styria, Lower Austria, and Carinthia. The principal casting works are in Bohemia, Moravia, and Lower Austria. The making of steam-engines and other kinds of machinery has made great progress of late years, its chief seats being Vienna, Wiener-Neustadt, Prague, Brünn, Buda-Pesth, and Trieste. The Austrian Lloyd's Company has large workshops at Trieste. Agricultural implements and machinery are largely made in Vienna, Wiener-Neustadt, Prague, and Brünn. Vienna is particularly noted for its manufacture of fire-proof safes, also for its lamps, and of late years it has done a large business in the making of sewing-machines. Among the other iron and steel manufactures may be mentioned tools of various kinds, files, wire, nails, jews' harps (which find a ready market in the East and in other parts), steel pens, needles, &c. Still English and American goods meet with a good sale in the Monarchy.

The principal copper works are at Brixlegg and other places in Tyrol, in Galicia, Bukowina, and Hungary. The annual value of the articles produced is about 293,000*l*. Leaden wares are manufactured to the annual value of about 155,000*l*., and zinc and tin goods to about 45,300*l*. These manufactures are mostly in the hands of small manufacturers. Gold and silver articles are worked chiefly in Vienna, and to some extent also in Prague,—the annual value being about 1,141,600*l.* The mixed metals are also made and manufactured to a considerable extent, as brass, bronze, bell-metal, gun-metal, pinchbeck, &c Vienna is particularly noted for its production of beautiful articles in bronze—ornaments, lustres, candelabra, church furnishings, and utensils of various kinds.

The manufacture of scientific instruments—mathematical, physical, surgical, optical, has of late years risen rapidly into importance, particularly in Vienna and Prague, and now these are to be found among the exports to other countries. Austria is also distinguished for the manufacture of musical instruments, both wind and stringed, particularly the former, the chief seats being Vienna, Prague, and Königgrätz. Pianofortes are largely made in Vienna, and form a considerable article of export. Clock or watchmaking is not extensively carried on, and is declining.

The glass manufacture has its principal seat in Bohemia, where there are not only the greatest number of works, but where the articles produced are of very superior quality. The crystal glass of Bohemia surpasses both English and Belgian for hardness and polish, and the articles are noted for the beauty of their forms and the skill of their workmanship. Artificial pearls and precious stones in glass are largely manufactured in the neighbourhood of Gablonz, and looking-glasses in W. Bohemia. Besides Bohemia there are glassworks in Moravia, Styria, Lower Austria, and Hungary, but they produce chiefly the commoner kinds of glass for home use. The annual value of the glass produced in the glassworks of Austria is estimated at 2,530,000*l.*, besides which there are about 30 glassworks in Hungary.

The manufacture of leather constitutes an important branch of industry, and is chiefly carried on in Lower Austria, Bohemia, and Moravia. There are in all about 8000 establishments great and small in the Monarchy, yet the amount produced falls considerably short of the demand. Boots and shoes are made to a considerable extent in all the large towns, but principally in Vienna, Prague, and Münchengrätz in Bohemia; and they form a considerable article of export. Gloves are also largely manufactured in Vienna and Prague, and find a ready market abroad, being considered little inferior to those of France. Vienna is also noted for its manufacture of fancy articles in leather, and trunks. Saddlery is principally carried on in Vienna, Prague and Buda-Pesth.

Paper-making has of late made considerable progress in Austria. The most important works are in Lower Austria, Bohemia, Styria, and Fiume. Vienna is noted for its variegated and wall papers, also for its pasteboard and cardboard. The manufacture of papier-maché goods employs many persons in the districts of Gablonz and Teplitz, in Bohemia.

The manufacture of sugar from beet-root is actively carried on, and is year by year increasing in importance. In 1876, there were 231 factories in operation in the Monarchy, of which 150 were in Bohemia, 48 in Moravia, 18 in Hungary, and 8 in Silesia. They consumed in all over 30,000,000 cwt. of beet-root and produced about 1,072,000 cwt. of sugar. This not only supplies the home demand, but furnishes a considerable surplus for exportation. The manufacture as well as the growth of tobacco is a government monopoly. There are 27 tobacco factories in Austria, and 10 in Hungary, employing in all 39,380 persons, and producing annually 1,756,000,000 cigars, 98,000,000 cigarettes, 78,288,000 lbs. of common tobacco, 4,920,000 lbs. of roll tobacco, and 5,535,000 lbs. of snuff. The largest factories are those of Hainburg in Lower Austria, Fürstenfeld in Styria, and Sedler in Bohemia.

Austria is noted for its beer, of which that of Vienna and Bohemia are particularly celebrated. In 1876 there were no fewer than 2504 beer breweries in operation in the Monarchy, of which 2272 were in Austria, and 232 in Hungary. Of the former there were 928 in Bohemia, 271 in Upper Austria, 230 in Galicia, 228 in Moravia, 142 in Tyrol, 128 in Carinthia, and 110 in Lower Austria. The quantity of beer annually produced exceeds 248,500,000 gallons. Fifteen of the breweries each produced over 2,200,000 gallons—ten being in the neighbourhood of Vienna, and 4 of these producing each from 4,500,000 to 8,500,000 gallons annually. Beer forms an important article of export, particularly bottled beer made in the breweries around Vienna. Brandy is largely made in the N.E. and E. districts, in Hungary, Galicia, and Bukowina, and to a less extent in Bohemia, Moravia, and Lower Austria. Liqueurs of superior quality are made in Dalmatia (Maraschino), Moravia, Bohemia, and Lower Austria.

The manufacture of porcelain articles is actively carried on in the N.W. of Bohemia, where there exist rich beds of porcelain clay. The number of porcelain works in the Monarchy is 36—of which 25 are in Bohemia, 10 in Hungary, and 1 at Linz in Upper Austria. The articles produced meet the home demand and also afford a considerable surplus for exportation. Earthenware goods are made mostly in Moravia, but also in Bohemia, Galicia, and Lower Austria. Terra Cotta wares —which have lately come much into use for the ornamenting of buildings, &c.—are made in the neighbourhood of Vienna. The porcelain works in 1870 employed 3850 men, and produced 168,000*l*. worth of goods; while the earthenware and other works employed 2830 men, and yielded 138,000*l*. The making of bricks and tiles is actively carried on, there being in Austria 80 large works, and over 4000 lesser ones, employing 22,000 workmen, and producing annually to the value of 1,500,000*l*. In Hungary there are 184 larger and many smaller brickworks.

The manufacture of chemicals has of late years been greatly extended, and now forms an important branch of industry—not a few of the products being to be found among the exports of the country. Sulphuric and muriatic acids are largely made in Bohemia, Lower Austria, and Silesia; pharmaceutical preparations and perfumes are made chiefly in Vienna; and dyestuffs in Lower Austria and Bohemia. Tartar and potash are produced chiefly in Hungary; petroleum is obtained in

Galicia, where is also obtained ozokerit or earth-wax, now largely employed in the manufacture of candles. The manufacture of candles and soap is largely carried on in Vienna and some other parts. The value of the soap, oil, perfumes, &c , produced in Austria in 1870, was estimated at 1,398,200*l.* ; of chemical products 220,200*l.*; petroleum, 126,700*l.* ; colours and dyes, 117,200*l.*

The manufacture of wooden articles is extensively carried on over the country, and affords employment to a great number of persons. Articles of furniture are largely made in Vienna, and Buda-Pesth, particularly of bent wood, which owing to their cheapness and durability are in demand both at home and abroad. Artistic cabinet work is also largely done in these towns, and of late has been greatly improved through the influence of the art schools and museums. The making of wooden toys is chiefly a domestic industry carried on by the peasantry in the mountainous and rural districts—particularly in the Bohemian Erzgebirge, the Salzkammergut district, and the Grodnerthal in Tyrol. It has lately been much improved through the establishment of special schools. Shipbuilding is carried on particularly at Trieste, Pola, and Fiume. Railway and other carriages are largely made at Vienna, Prague, and some other places. Vienna is also noted for its manufacture of meerschaum and amber articles.

The total number of mills for the grinding of corn, in the Monarchy in 1874, was 56,504, of which 31,548 were in Austria, and 24,956 in Hungary ; 47,829 were water-mills ; 1469 windmills; 707 steam mills ; 128 steam and water mills ; and 6361 mills worked by animal power. In that year there were in Austria 12,268 baking establishments, employing 10,910 workmen, and producing to the value of 3,652,000*l.* ; 1165 confectionary establishments, employing 2780 workmen, and yielding 260,000*l.* ; and 76 chocolate factories employing 820 men, and yielding 210,000*l.* There are over 500 printing and lithographic establishments in the country, of which 44 of the former, and 78 of the latter, are in Vienna alone.

A rough estimate of the annual value of the industrial products of the Monarchy, published in 1872, gives the total amount as not less than 130,000,000*l.*, of which 33 per cent. belonged to the E., and 67 to the W. half of the country. Taking the provinces, no less than 18 per cent. belonged to Bohemia alone, 15 to Lower Austria (including Vienna), 15 to Hungary, 6 to Transylvania and the other Hungarian provinces, 11 to Galicia and Bukowina, 10 to Moravia, 6 to Tyrol, 4 to Styria, and 4 to Upper Austria. Since the time when this estimate was made, the value of the industrial products of the Monarchy must have largely increased.

CHAPTER VII.

MEANS OF COMMUNICATION; TRADE AND COMMERCE.

THE great means of communication are roads and railways, navigable rivers and canals, and seaports with shipping. Except as regards her navigable rivers, Austria-Hungary has not been greatly favoured by nature in this respect. The mountainous character of much of the country presents obstacles to easy communication between its different parts, while the small extent of its seaboard does not afford great facilities to commercial intercourse with other countries. Much, however, has been done—particularly of late years—in the way of making and improving roads, opening up mountain passes, and especially in constructing railways throughout the country, and in establishing lines of steamers.

The roads are generally in good condition; and at the end of 1874 there were 33,250 miles of state, provincial, and district roads in Austria, and at the end of 1871, 19,200 miles of state and county roads in Hungary, making together 52,450 miles. They are more numerous and in better condition in the W. than in the E. portion of the Monarchy. Bohemia in particular is distinguished for the number and excellence of its roads.

In 1837 the Monarchy possessed only 160 miles of railway; in 1849 it had 1214 miles; in 1857, 2260 miles; and in 1867, 4170 miles. Within the next eight years this last sum was more than doubled, for at the end of 1875 there were no less than 10,345 miles of railway in operation. Of these 4754 miles were in Austria, 2441 in Hungary, and

3150 common to both. Of this last there were 1650 miles in Austria, and 1500 in Hungary. In the course of the year 1876 there were 580 miles of new railway opened in Austria, and 295 in Hungary, making in all 11,220 miles in operation at the end of that year—besides 414 miles in course of construction, and 408 miles conceded. During 1875, 41,348,200 passengers were carried by rail, and 1,221,000,000 cwt. of goods. Of the former, 532,900 were first class; 5,449,100 second class; 26,086,600 third class; 8,253,700 fourth class; and 1,025,900 military. The receipts from passenger traffic amounted to 4,346,000*l.*; from goods, to 13,455,200*l.*; and from sundries, to 514,600*l.*—making a total of 18,315,800*l.* The total working expenses were 10,850,500*l.*, leaving a balance of 7,465,300*l.*, of which 3,666,600*l.* was on the Austrian lines, 605,300*l.* on the Hungarian lines, and 3,193,400*l.* on the common lines. This surplus had to meet the interest on capital and other charges. The capital of the Austrian lines amounted in all to 119,223,100*l.*, of the Hungarian lines to 43,943,400*l.*, and of the common lines to 104,775,600*l.*—making a gross total of 267,942,100*l.* The surplus would thus yield 3.08 per cent. on the capital of the Austrian lines, 3.04 per cent. on the common, and 1.31 on the Hungarian, or 2.80 per cent. on the whole. Individual lines, however, differ considerably from these averages—some being much higher, others considerably lower.

The River Danube, which traverses the country from W. to S.E., is navigable for steamers for its entire length within the territory, from Passau to Orsova. Many of its affluents are also navigable for a considerable length, particularly the Theiss, Drave, and Save. It affords means of communication, not only between the different parts of the country, but also with Germany, Turkey, Servia, Roumania and Russia; and notwithstanding the railway competition the traffic is yearly increasing. In 1865, it amounted to 60,000,000 cwt., in 1870 to 90,000,000 cwt., and in 1875 to 120,000,000 cwt. Nearly one half of this is timber brought down in rafts, about one fourth is grain, and the rest coal, charcoal, salt, stone, lime, flour, wine, wool, skins, &c. Nearly one-fourth of the entire traffic is carried on by the Austrian Steam-Ship Company, which in 1876 possessed 196 steamers and 696 towed boats, and carried 26,921,000 cwt. of goods, besides 2,554,700 passengers. The Elbe, so far as it is navigable serves principally for the export of Austrian raw and manufactured articles to Saxony and Prussia, and also to some extent to Hamburg. These consist chiefly of brown coal, timber, and corn, and amount in all to about 10,000,000 cwt. annually. The Vistula enables western Galicia to communicate with the Baltic, and the principal traffic consists in sending down timber, corn, salt, and other products, to the amount of about 4,500,000 cwt. annually. There are steamers and other vessels on a number of the larger lakes, but the traffic is not considerable. The navigable canals in Austria are not numerous. The principal are the Wiener-Neustädter Canal, which connects Vienna with the Leitha; the Bacser or Francis Canal, between the Theiss and Danube; and the Bega Canal, between the Bega and the Temes. The Monarchy possesses in all about 4240 miles of navigable river and canal communication, of which the greater part (60 per cent.) is in Hungary.

The Monarchy includes in all 112 seaports at which trade is carried on, of which 44 are in the Maritime District, 57 in Dalmatia, and 11 in Croatia. The principal of these are Trieste, Fiume, Pola, Spalato, Rovigno, and Zara. At the end of 1876 the number of vessels belonging to these ports was 7538, having in all 330,300 tons, and 27,650 men. Of these 98 were steamers with 56,900 tons; 573 with 282,100 tons were large vessels sailing to distant parts; 73 with 6700 tons were large coasting vessels; and 1885 with 27,800 tons were small coasting vessels; the rest being fishing and other barks and lighters.

Formerly the trade of Austria-Hungary was very much hampered by high duties and restrictions of various kinds, but of late these have all been removed or very much modified, and the trade in consequence, has greatly increased. The whole country has, with certain exceptions, been formed into one customs territory, within which trade is perfectly free and the goods are subject to no duties. The duties on imports into this territory are in general moderate, and have in view chiefly the protection of native industries. There are no duties levied on exports—except on a very few articles, as raw skins and hides, bones, rags and other substances used in the manufacture of paper. There are no duties levied on goods in transit. The parts not included within this customs territory are Dalmatia (which forms a customs district by itself), Istria and the islands in the gulf of Quarnero, the six free ports of Trieste, Fiume, Buccari, Zengg, Portore and Carlopago, the town of Brody in Galicia, and the small village of Jungholz in Tyrol.[1]

According to the census of 1869, there were 567,225 persons engaged in trade, of whom 400,644 were in Austria, and 133,582 in Hungary. The internal trade of the country consists chiefly of the exchange of the products of one part of the country with another—more particularly of the agricultural products of the E. with the industrial products of the W. Important markets are held at fixed times in the principal towns, for the different kinds of produce. Vienna, as being the capital and the seat of so many different branches of industry, and having also ready means of communication with all parts of the country, is the principal seat both of the home and foreign trade, and the great resort of merchants and capitalists.

The external trade of the country is principally carried on overland. Of the imports, in 1876, 82.8 per cent. in value were brought overland, and 17.2 per cent. by sea; and of the exports, 84.8 per cent, were sent landwards, and 15.2 by sea. The following are the principal countries with which trade was carried on, and the percentage falling to each. Imports:—Saxony, 30.1; South Germany, 19.7; Prussia, 14.1;

---

[1] Since the above was written the imperial assent has been given to a bill by which Istria, Dalmatia, and Brody, together with Bosnia and Herzegovina, are to be included within the Austro-Hungarian Customs limit.

Trieste, 13.7; Roumania, 6.2; Turkey, 5.1; Italy, 4.1; Seaports, 3.5; Russia, 2.9; Switzerland, 0.6. Exports:—South Germany, 25.6; Saxony, 23.9; Trieste, 12.9; Prussia, 15.6; Italy, 7.0; Russia, 5.2; Roumania, 4.9; Seaports, 2.2; Turkey, 2.1; Switzerland, 0.6. The total value of the imports was 54,805,000*l.*; and of the exports 60,338,800*l.* The principal imports with their values in round numbers were cotton (from North America, the East Indies, Turkey), 3,380,000*l.*; grain (Roumania, Russia, Italy), 2,550,000*l.*; silk goods (France, Switzerland, Prussia, Italy), 1,480,000*l.*; cattle for slaughter and draught (oxen from Russia and Roumania, swine from Servia), 4,220,000*l.*; coffee (Brazil, Java), 3,590,000*l.*; wool (Australia and Cape, England, and the Zollverein), 2,740,000*l.*; woollen goods (England and Germany), 2,200,000*l.*; skins and hides (America, Russia, Turkey), 1,660,000*l.*; leather (Germany), 1,810,000*l.*; ironwares (England, Belgium, Germany), 580,000*l.*; woollen yarn (France, Belgium, England), 990,000*l.*; cotton yarn (England, Switzerland, Germany), 1,820,000*l.* The exports, in like manner, were small wares (to the Levant, Germany, England, the United States, Italy), 3,470,000*l.*; grain (Switzerland, France, Belgium), 6,890,000*l.* wool (France and Germany), 2,670,000*l.*; flour (the Levant, Germany, Switzerland, Holland, Brazil), 2,480,000*l.*; wood (Germany, France, Italy), 3,640,000*l.*; glass, 1,540,000*l.*; woollen goods (the Levant, North America), 2,130,000*l.*; linen goods (Germany, the Levant), 1,390,000*l.*; cattle for slaughter and draught (oxen, England and Germany; swine, Germany; sheep, France), 3,740,000*l.* The total value of the imports into the United Kingdom from Austrian territories in 1877 was 1,540,980*l.*; and of the exports, 1,397,322*l.* The chief articles of import were wheat and flour (1,335,921 cwt.), and of export cotton manufactures and iron.

The number of trading vessels that entered the various seaports with cargoes in 1871 was 25,999 having in all 2,684,900 tons, and in ballast 14,621 vessels, with 892,000 tons. In like manner in 1875, 30,604 vessels having 3,384,800 tons entered laden and 16,169 vessels with 1,041,200 tons in ballast. In 1871 the number of trading vessels that left the different ports with cargoes was 25,790, numbering in all 2,512,700 tons, and in ballast 14,368, with 1,159,500 tons. In 1875, the numbers that left laden were, 28,905 vessels, tonnage 3,126,100, in ballast 17,593 vessels, tonnage 1,301,600. Of those in 1875, 10,377 vessels having 1,314,000 tons entered from foreign countries, and 9658 vessels having 1,327,300 tons left for foreign countries. Taking the tonnage of these, 29 per cent. of the foreign trade was with Italy, 25.6 with Turkey, 12.6 Great Britain, 11.9 Greece, 8.4 France, 5.6 Egypt, and 6.9 other countries.

The principal seaport of the country is Trieste, at which nearly one-third of the whole sea trade of the Monarchy is carried on. In 1875 8,152 trading vessels, having in all 1,003,900 tons entered this port. The principal of the other ports with the amount of tonnage that entered them in 1875 were Pola 372,600, Lussin-piccolo 224,800, Zara 198,300, Spalato 197,800, Gravosa 183,700, Pirano 172,300, Fiume 167,300, Rovigno 155,300, Parenzo 154,600, Sebenico, 151,400.

The total value of the imports at the different ports in 1875 was 18,700,000*l.*, and of the exports 13,700,000*l.* The principal articles of import were coffee 321,000 cwt., leaf tobacco 142,000 cwt., manufactured tobacco 21,000 cwt., wheat 3,620,000 bushels, flour 738,000 cwt., olive oil 471,000 cwt., pitch, turpentine, and rock oil 338,000 cwt., raw cotton 712,000 cwt., cotton goods 84,000 cwt. The chief articles of export were refined sugar 224,000 cwt., manufactured tobacco 19,000 cwt., maize 2,606,000 bushels, flour 1,505,000 cwt., olive oil 335,000 cwt., staves 68,079,000, raw cotton 133,000 cwt., cotton goods 114,000 cwt.

In addition to these there is a considerable transit trade through the country, chiefly from the seaports and the eastern borders towards the N. and N.W. It is estimated at about 25,000,000*l.* annually.

In 1868 there were 20 banks in Austria, of which 10 were in Vienna, and 10 in the provinces, and which had altogether a capital of 18,216,600*l*. Then followed a period of over-speculation, so that in May, 1873 the number of banks had risen to 137, of which 69 were in Vienna, and the share capital had increased to 61,889,000*l*. The monetary crisis followed, and in the end of 1873 the number of banks had fallen to 92, and the share capital to 48,063,600*l*. In 1874, –75, and –76 the numbers were still farther reduced, so that at the end of the last-named year there were only 51 banks with a share capital of 26,948,600*l*., of which 18 banks having a capital of 22,850,000*l*. were in Vienna. In Hungary in like manner, the number of banks in 1867 was only 5. From that time to 1873, 126 new banks were founded, and of these in 1874 and 1875 31 were in liquidation. At the end of 1875 the number of banks in Hungary was 97 with a total share capital of 5,690,000*l*. The principal Austrian Banks are the National Bank, founded in 1816, and having a capital of 9,000,000*l*.; Trade and Manufactures Credit Institute, founded 1855, capital 4,000,000*l*.; Anglo-Austrian Bank, founded 1863, capital 2,400,000*l*.; Franco-Austrian Bank, founded 1869, capital 1,000,000*l*.; Vienna Banking Union, founded 1869, capital 1,200,000*l*.; Union Bank, founded 1870, capital 2,170,000*l*.; Austrian Banking Company, founded 1873, capital 1,000,000*l*. The principal Hungarian Banks are, the Pesth Hungarian Commercial Bank, founded 1842, capital 250,000*l*.; General Hungarian Credit Bank, founded 1867, capital 1,200,000*l*.; Anglo-Hungarian Bank, founded 1868, capital 384,300*l*.; Franco-Hungarian Bank, founded 1869, capital 1,000,000*l*.; Hungarian General Municipal Credit Institute, founded 1872, capital 400,000*l*.

The country also contains a number of savings-banks. The first institution of this kind was founded at Vienna in 1819, and in 1850 there were 19 in Austria. In 1860 there were 60 having deposits to the amount of 10,500,000*l*.; in 1870 192, with 28,570,000*l*. of deposits; and in 1875 289, with 58,930,000*l*.

of deposits. The number of depositors was 1,340,700, being one in every 15 of the population, and each depositor had on an average 44*l*. In Hungary in 1875, there were 328 savings banks, having in all 18,346,500*l*. In addition to these there are a number of provident institutions for receiving small sums on deposit, and making advances, in cases of necessity, of small sums at a moderate rate of interest, repayable by instalments. There are also numerous societies established for the furthering in various ways of industry and commerce.

The number of joint-stock companies in Austria, at the end of 1875 was 557, having altogether a paid-up share capital of 161,600,000*l*. The Banks and Credit Institutes are included here, which if we deduct will leave 497 joint-stock companies of various kinds, with a paid-up capital of 129,500,000*l*. Of these the railway companies rank first, and among the rest are numerous industrial, mining, and other companies. There are no statistics of a similar kind for Hungary.

In 1850, 32,300,000 private letters passed through the post office; in 1860, 79,300,000; in 1871, 162,982,677; and in 1876, 300,749,000 (including post cards). Of these last, 230,293,000 were in Austria, and 70,456,000 in Hungary. Besides the letters there were 88,630,000 newspapers carried, and 34,936,000 samples, &c. These gave on an average 10.9 letters and 2.9 newspapers to each inhabitant in Austria, and 4.5 letters and 2.0 newspapers to each inhabitant in Hungary during the year 1876. There were in all 6074 post offices in the Monarchy. Telegraph lines were first laid in the country in 1847, and in 1850 there were 1880 miles of them with 37 stations; and 14,400 despatches were forwarded during the year. In 1860 there were 516 stations, with 7964 miles of wires, and 727,300 despatches were forwarded. In 1876 the number of stations had increased to 3240, of which 2329 were in Austria, and 911 in Hungary; the lines over which the wires extended measured 22,220 miles; and the number of despatches transmitted was 7,531,900. The principal places from which despatches were sent were Vienna

3,180,000, Buda-Pesth 2,540,000, Prague 1,080,000, Trieste 782,000, Cracow 680,000, and Lemberg 576,000.

There are Exchanges at Vienna, Trieste, Prague, and Buda-Pesth—that of Vienna generally regulating the rates that prevail in the others, and being itself mainly regulated by the state of the foreign exchanges, particularly those of Frankfort, Paris, and London.

Chambers of trade and manufacture are established in all the principal towns, each having as its district a province or part of a province. They were first established in 1850, and in 1868 the acts were passed under which they are now regulated. There are 29 of these chambers in Austria, and 14 in Hungary. The members are elected by the chambers, each for five years. Besides these ordinary members there are corresponding members. It is the duty of the chambers to take account of all that concerns trade or manufacture, and to bring their observations and opinions before the proper authorities. They also act as judges in disputes connected with trade or industry, and they keep registers of various kinds and draw up periodical reports on the actual condition of the people within their districts.

CHAPTER VIII.

GOVERNMENT; ARMY AND NAVY; FINANCE.

THE head of the Austro-Hungarian Monarchy is the emperor and king in whom the executive power is vested. He bears the three titles of Emperor of Austria, King of Bohemia, &c., and Apostolic King of Hungary. The basis of the present constitution is the Pragmatic Sanction of Charles VI., of date 6th December, 1724. It declares the different parts and provinces of the Monarchy to be inseparable and indivisible, and fixes the succession to the throne in the male line of the House of Hapsburg-Lothringen or Hapsburg-Lorraine, in the order of primogeniture, or failing males then in the female line.

The monarch comes of age on the completion of his eighteenth year, and must belong to the Roman Catholic faith. On assuming the reins of government he must take an oath to the constitution (in Austria, in presence of both Houses of the Reichsrath, and in Hungary on his coronation). He is in exclusive possession of the executive power, but shares the legislative power with the representative bodies of the two states. He is Commander-in-Chief of the army, and Grand Master of the seven Orders of Knighthood, which are conferred by him. These are the Order of the Golden Fleece (for sovereigns, and persons of the highest rank), the Military Order of Maria Theresa (3 classes), the Royal Hungarian Order of St. Stephen (3 classes), the Order of Leopold (3 classes), the Order of the Iron Crown (3 classes), the Order of Francis Joseph (3 classes), and the Military Order of the Cross of Elizabeth Theresa.

The form of government in Austria down to 1848 was an

absolute monarchy, the provincial diets having no voice in the management of affairs; while in Hungary the monarchical power was limited by the National Diet. The disturbances of 1848-49 led to the abolition of the old form of government in Austria, and a constitution with popular representation was introduced, which, however, did not long continue, and absolutism was again established. The disastrous war with Italy in 1859, led to the adoption in the following year of a constitutional form of government, the power being vested chiefly in the provincial diets in Austria, and in the National Diet in Hungary. Difficulties being found in the way of carrying out this system, a central Reichsrath was established, composed of a House of Lords, and a House of Deputies, representing all the provinces of the empire. This scheme did not meet with the approval of the Hungarians, who claimed the right to have a constitution of their own, and a system of government independent of Austria. They therefore declined to send representatives to the Reichsrath, and this continued for some years, till at length in 1867 the laws were passed (during the Ministry of Baron Beust), which regulate the present constitution. The claims of Hungary to a form of government and to certain rights independent of Austria were recognized; and the monarchy declared to consist of two states, each having its own constitution and laws, but united under one ruler, and for certain common purposes. Thus they act together in all matters affecting their interests with foreign countries, in what concerns the army and navy, and other things in which they have a common interest, particularly as affecting industry or commerce,—as commercial treaties with foreign countries, the levying of duties on commodities, the arrangement of railways, the coinage, &c.

These are under the direction of a controlling body called the Delegations consisting of 60 members for each state chosen annually by the assemblies, one-third being elected by the House of Lords and the House of Magnates, and two-thirds by the House of Deputies, and of Representatives. They sit alternately at Vienna and Buda-Pesth, and elect their own presidents. They conduct their business in distinct chambers, communicating their decisions to each other in writing. Should three written messages on any subject be exchanged without bringing the two bodies into accord, they meet together, and without discussion proceed at once to vote by ballot, the majority of votes deciding the question. Their resolutions require neither the approval nor the confirmation of the representative assemblies by which they are chosen, but only imperial assent. The executive is vested in three departments: (1) a ministry of the imperial house and of foreign affairs; (2) a ministry of war; and (3) a ministry of finance. These are responsible to the Delegations.

The Reichsrath, imperial council, or parliament of Austria consists of a House of Lords and a House of Deputies. The former is composed of (1) princes of the imperial house who are of age (at present 13); (2) hereditary members, heads of noble houses of high rank (54); (3) archbishops (10); bishops with the rank of princes (7); and (4) life members nominated by the emperor on account of distinguished services (105). The House of Deputies is composed of 353 members elected to represent different classes of the inhabitants of the several provinces. Of these 85 are chosen by the large landed proprietors; 21 by the chambers of trade and manufacture; 116 by electors in the cities, towns, and places of industry, directly; and 131 by electors in country districts, not directly but through representatives chosen for that purpose every six years. The number of deputies for the different provinces are, Lower Austria 37, Upper Austria 17, Salzburg 5, Styria 23, Carinthia 9, Carniola 10, Trieste (city and district) 4, Görz-Gradisca 4, Istria 4, Tyrol 18, Vorarlberg 3, Bohemia 92, Moravia 36, Silesia 10, Galicia 63, Bukowina 9, and Dalmatia 9. The elections are for six years, and the emperor nominates the presidents and vice-presidents of both houses.

The Reichsrath has the right of legislation in all matters affecting the rights, duties, or interests of the several provinces in so far as these, from equally affecting Hungary, do not come within the province of the delegations. It deals with matters connected with industry, commerce, and finance, the the post office, railways, telegraphs, customs, the mint, raising of new loans, imposing of new taxes, the budgets, matters relating to military service and defence, &c. The members of either house have the right to propose new laws on matters within their province; but the consent of both houses as well as the sanction of the emperor is required to render them valid. The excutive is vested in the president of council and ministries for the interior, religion and education, commerce, agriculture, national defence, justice, and finance. The ministers form also a ministerial council, which is presided over by the emperor or a minister president. The ministers are responsible to the Reichsrath.

Each province or electoral district, has its provincial diet, which deals with such matters affecting it as do not come before the Reichsrath, such as local taxation, religion, education, public works, charitable institutions, industry, trade, &c. There are 17 of such diets in the country, and the number of members in each, varies according to the size and importance of the district, from 20 or 30, up to 100 for Moravia, 151 for Galicia, and 241 for Bohemia. Each diet is composed of the archbishops and bishops of the Roman Catholic and Greek Catholic churches, the rectors of the universities, representatives chosen by the great landed proprietors, representatives of the chambers of trade and manufacture, and representatives of the rural districts. In all these cases except the last, the members are chosen directly by the electors. In the last case, the electors choose a certain number of persons to rerepresent them, and by them the election is made. The members are elected for six years, and sit under a president, who together with his deputy, is nominated by the emperor for the same period of six years.

The Hungarian Reichstag, national diet, or parliament consists of an Upper and Lower House, the former known as the

House of Magnates, the latter as the House of Representatives. The Upper House is composed of 3 royal archdukes, having estates in the kingdom; 48 Roman and Greek Catholic archbishops, bishops, and archabbots; 10 royal barons; 71 supreme counts; the Governor of Fiume; 18 princes; 380 counts; 208 barons; 11 deputies from the Croatia-Slavonian diet, and 6 regalists of Transylvania. The Lower House is composed of 445 members of whom 88 represent the towns, 289 the counties and districts, 34 the sees, and 34 Croatia and Slavonia. They are chosen directly by the electors, for a term of three years, and are summoned annually by the king to meet in Buda-Pesth. The president and vice-president of the House of Magnates are nominated by the king from among the members, and the president and two vice-presidents of the House of Representatives, are chosen by themselves. The executive is vested in a president of council and ministries for the interior, religion and education, agriculture, industry and commerce, public works and communications, national defence, justice, finance, Croatia and Slavonia, all in Buda-Pesth, and a ministry for the Court, at Vienna.

Croatia and Slavonia also have a diet for the management of their affairs, consisting of 134 members, of whom 9 are archbishops and bishops, 8 supreme counts, 40 magnates, 26 representatives of towns, and 51 representatives of country districts.

Army.—Since the war with Prussia in 1866, Austria-Hungary has been making every effort to raise the strength and efficiency of her army. The military system has been entirely remodelled; and her educational establishments and system of training, both elementary and professional, for officers and men are of a very high order. The present organization of the army is based on the law of 1868. Every male citizen capable of bearing arms becomes liable for military service on the completion of his twentieth year, and must serve personally, substitutes not being allowed. Temporary exemptions are granted in certain cases, as where an only son is the sole support of his parents, or a grandson of his grandparents, or the like. Those who from physical incapacity, are unfit for service, are required to contribute a sum of money in proportion to their means to the military pension fund.

The military strength of the country consists in the standing army, marines, landwehr, ersatz-reserve, and landsturm. The standing army is maintained for the defence of the country against a foreign foe, and for the preservation of peace and order at home. The period of service in the standing army and in the marines, extends over twelve years, three of which are in the line, 7 in the reserve, and two in the landwehr. The men in the reserve are only called out periodically for exercise. The landwehr is intended to support the standing army in time of war, and for home defence. Those in the landwehr are liable to serve for twelve years. They are usually called up for eight weeks training on first joining, and for fourteen days annually afterwards. The ersatz-reserve is a body of reserve, designed to furnish recruits to the standing army and marines in time of war, and to replace the casualties of the field. They are not trained at all, but for ten years remain liable to be called up in the event of war. The number may not exceed that of one year's contingent to the active army, and the annual addition to it is one-tenth of this number. The landsturm is made up of volunteers who are not included in any of the above classes. Its business is to support the standing-army and the landwehr in the time of war, and to engage the enemy if he should invade the country. At present it exists only in Hungary, and Tyrol and Vorarlberg, where all males from 18 to 45 (in Vorarlberg to 50) not included in the other classes are enrolled in the landsturm. Besides these, there has lately been introduced a system of military training for youths on leaving school, who volunteer for that purpose. They equip and maintain themselves, and if in the cavalry, provide and maintain a horse; but for youths of promise who are without means these expenses are provided for by the state. They spend a year in active service, and then pass into the reserve.

The number of young men coming of age, and fit for military service amounts to from 140,000 to 150,000 annually. Of these about 95,500 are passed into the army, about 9500 into the ersatz-reserve, and the balance, averaging about 40,000, into the landwehr. The landwehr thus comprises two years contingents of old soldiers, which may be estimated at about 150,000, and 12 years contingents of 40,000, making a total of about 500,000. The actual organization, however, only provides for incorporating about 200,000 of this number.

The total strength of the Austria-Hungarian army, in active service, at the end of 1876 was, on the peace footing 267,005 men, to be raised during war to 800,000. The annual contingent for the standing army and marines, amounts to 95,474, of which Austria furnishes 54,541, and Hungary 40,933. The army on the peace footing, consists of 80 regiments of infantry numbering 148,320 men; 1 regiment of Tyrolese rifles, and 6 battalions of rifles with 21,451 men; 41 regiments of cavalry (41 dragoon, 16 Hussar, and 11 lancers) with 43,993 men; 13 regiments of field artillery and 12 garrison battalions with 30,795 men; 2 regiments of engineers and 1 regiment of pioneers with 9462 men; and others. According to the army registers there were in active service or on leave at the end of 1876 15,702 officers and 828,320 men, to which if we add the landwehr amounting to 213,375, we have a total force of 1,057,997 men. In addition to this the landsturm of Hungary, Tyrol, and Vorarlberg is available in the case of the country being invaded by an enemy.

The Austrian Navy at the end of 1876, consisted of 69 vessels of all sizes, having in all 17,796 horse power, carrying 443 guns, and manned by 8459 men. Of these 8 were iron-clad ships, 3 iron-clad frigates, 2 frigates, 10 corvettes, 9 gun-boats, and 2 river monitors.

Finance.—The revenue and expenditure are presented in three distinct budgets: (1) that of the Delegations for the whole Monarchy, (2) that of the Austrian Reichsrath for Austria, and (3) that of the Hungarian Reichstag for Hungary.

By an arrangement of 1868, Austria pays 70 per cent., and Hungary 30 per cent. towards the common expenditure of the monarchy. Subsequently when the Military Frontier was included in Hungary, it became liable for 2 per cent. more. In the budget for 1879, the total expenditure of the Monarchy is given at 13,853,738*l.*, of which 10,356,584*l.* is ordinary and 3,497,153*l.* extraordinary, the latter being chiefly made up of a sum of 3,357,786*l.* required for the army of occupation in Bosnia and Herzegovina. Of the ordinary expenditure 402,513*l.* was for foreign affairs, 9,007,519*l.* for the army, 745,152*l.* for navy, 188,850*l.* for finance, and 12,550*l.* for Board of Control. The receipts were, from the different branches of the administration 326,358*l.*, from the customs 1,184,100*l.*, leaving 12,343,279*l.*, of which 2 per cent. to be raised by Hungary on account of the Military Frontier, and the remainder by Austria and Hungary respectively, in the proportions of 70 per cent. and 30 per cent.

The budget of Austria for 1879, gives the total expenditure at 47,116,365*l.*, and the revenue at 39,256,514*l.*, showing a deficit of 7,859,851*l.* The principal branches of the revenue are direct taxes 9,108,000*l.*; custom duties 2,396,900*l.*; duties on articles of consumption 6,608,300*l.* (of which beer 2,200,000*l.*, brandy 900,000*l.*, and sugar 1,800,000*l.*); salt monopoly 1,938,800*l.*; tobacco monopoly 5,900,000*l.*; stamps 1,724,000*l.*; judicial fees 3,196,000*l.*; state lottery 2,011,770*l.*; post office and telegraphs 1,826,300*l.*; mines 559,760*l.*; domains and forests 377,505*l.*; octroi 254,300*l.*; state property and mint 174,400*l.* The ordinary expenditure amounted to 43,501,446*l.*, and the extraordinary to 3,614,918*l.* Of the former there were for the imperial household 465,000*l.*; Reichsrath 66,530*l.*; Council of Ministers 85,297*l.*; ministries—of interior 1,562,154*l.*, national defence 787,721*l.*, religion and education 1,452,965*l.*, finance 7,592,630*l.*, commerce 2,165,710*l.*, agriculture 945,247*l.*, justice 1,964,190*l.*; pensions, grants, and subsidies 1,493,900*l.*; share of interest on public debt 11,538,499*l.*; proportion of general expenditure 13,280,204*l.*

The extraordinary expenditure consisted chiefly of pensions, grants, and subsidies 2,344,493*l.*; share of interest on public debt 277,835*l.*; ministries—of interior 151,453*l.*, national defence 49,400*l.*, religion and education 196,976*l.*, finance 48,620*l.*, commerce 214,210*l.*, agriculture 106,575*l.*, justice 138,290*l.*; Reichsrath 80,000*l.* The budget for 1880 estimates the entire income for that year at 39,999,500*l.*, and the expenditure at 41,271,200*l.*, showing a deficit of 1,271,700*l.*

The Hungarian budget for 1879, estimates the expenditure at 25,643,638*l.*, and the income at 22,220,860*l.*, leaving a deficit of 3,422,778*l.* The receipts include direct taxes 8,263,550*l.*; indirect taxes 8,467,785*l.*; state domains, mines, mint, &c. 2,515,519*l.*; post office 1,986,844*l.* The chief branches of expenditure are the royal household 465,000*l.*; Reichstag 130,996*l.*; ministries—of interior 749,246*l.*, war 639,801*l.*, religion and education 422,841*l.*, justice 991,436*l.*, agriculture and commerce 1,057,237*l.*; roads, &c. 1,247,088*l.*; finance 3,948,735*l.*; Croatia and Slavonia 532,220*l.*; general debt of Hungary 4,335,280*l.*; share of common expenses 3,875,789*l.*; share of interest on public debt 3,047,343*l.*

The national debt of Austria in 1815, amounted to 82,500,000*l.*; in 1830 to 108,000,000*l.*; in 1848 to 125,000,000*l.*; in 1866 to 291,000,000*l.*; and in 1878 to 318,587,455*l.* The debt of Hungary at the end of 1877 amounted to 66,017,696*l.*; in addition to which there is her share of the common debt of Austria as at 1868, and also her share (30 per cent.) of the common floating debt, which amounted in 1878 to 41,199,998*l.*

CHAPTER IX.

PROVINCES, AND PRINCIPAL TOWNS.

LOWER AUSTRIA, *Vienna, Wiener Neustadt;* UPPER AUSTRIA, *Linz, Steyr;* SALZBURG, *Salzburg;* STYRIA, *Gratz, Marburg;* CARINTHIA, *Klagenfurt;* CARNIOLA, *Laibach;* MARITIME DISTRICT, *Trieste, Görz, Pola, Pirano;* TYROL and VORARLBERG, *Innsbruck, Trent;* BOHEMIA, *Prague, Pilsen, Reichenberg, Budweis, Eger;* MORAVIA, *Brünn, Iglau, Possnitz, Olmütz;* SILESIA, *Troppau;* GALICIA, *Lemberg, Cracow, Brody;* BUKOWINA, *Czernowitz;* DALMATIA, *Zara, Spalato, Sebenice, Ragusa;* HUNGARY, *Buda-Pesth, Szegedin, Pressburg, Debreczin, Temesvar, Grosswardein;* TRANSYLVANIA, *Kronstadt, Klausenburg, Hermannstadt;* CROATIA-SLAVONIA (including *Military Frontier*), *Agram, Essek, Fiume;* BOSNIA-HERZGOVINA, *Bosna-Serai, Novi-Bazar.*

LOWER AUSTRIA (Ger. *Niederösterreich* or *Oesterreich unter der Enns*) forms the E. part of the Archduchy of Austria, and is that part of the country in which the present powerful Monarchy took its rise, containing also the capital, Vienna. It lies between 47° 26′ and 49° N. latitude, and 14° 26′ and 17° 1′ E. longitude; and is bounded on the N. by Moravia and Bohemia, W. by Bohemia and Upper Austria, S. by Styria, and E. by Hungary. Area 7654 square miles, and civil population (in 1869) 1,954,251, of whom 967,087 were males and 987,164 females. The military numbered 36,457, making a total of 1,990,708.

The Danube flows from W. to E. through the province, dividing it into two nearly equal parts. The river here has a length of about 156 miles and drains the whole territory, with the exception of a small portion in the N.W. Its affluents here are, except the March, all of small size, the principal being, on the right, the Enns, Ybbs or Ips, Erlaf, Traisen, Wien, Schwechat, Fischa, and Leitha; and on the left, the Isper, Krems, Kamp, Schmieda, Göller, and March with its affluents the Thaya and the Zaya. In the N.W. rises the Lainsitz, which falls into the Moldau. The Enns and the March only are navigable, but the others are useful for floating down timber, and for various industrial purposes. The numerous streams from the Alps afford abundant water-power for the many mills and other works on their banks.

About three-fourths of the surface is hilly or mountainous. In the S. portions of the northern limestone range of the Alps enter the country from Upper Austria and Styria, and in the S.E. occur some of the last ridges of the Central Alps. The principal summits of the former are the Dürnstein 6040 feet, Oetscher 6189, Göller 5776, and the Schneeberg 6810, this last being the highest point in Lower Austria. The principal summit of the Central Alps here is the Wechsel 5700 feet high. The Wienerwald or Forest of Vienna is an offshoot of the limestone range, and extends in a N.N.E. direction to the Danube. Its highest point, the Schöpfel, is 2928 feet above the sea. The Kahlengebirge is a branch of the Wienerwald, and the Leithagebirge in the extreme E. of the province is an offshoot of the Central Alps. North of the Danube the southern declivities of the Bohemian and Moravian Mountains form ridges and elevated plains, the boundary of which towards the E. is the Mannhartsberg. East of this the surface presents no great elevations, but descends gradually to the plain of the March. The southern valleys are noted for their natural beauties, and are much frequented as summer resorts. Of those in the N. the valleys of the Isper and Kamp are regarded as the most beautiful. The plains lie principally along the banks of the principal stream. The chief are the Vienna Basin, the Kremser Basin, the Tulner Basin, the Marchfeld, and the Ipsfeld.

The climate is in general mild and salubrious, particularly to the N. of the Danube and in the hilly parts. In the neighbourhood of Vienna and in the Eastern portion of the country the temperature is more variable. The most fertile portion of the province is in the centre, along the Danube. The valley of the March and the N.E. portion generally are also fertile. The S. and N.W. portions are not so productive to the husbandman, though fertile valleys and tracts occur here and there. About 40 per cent. of the entire area of the province is arable, 34 per cent. in woods and forests, and 14 per cent. in meadows and gardens. Oats and rye are the principal grain crops, but wheat, barley, and buckwheat are also largely grown. Potatoes, various kinds of kitchen vegetables, flax, hemp, and other products of the country, are grown here. In the W. the rearing of cattle is extensively carried on, and in the E. the vine is largely cultivated, particularly in the valley of the Danube. The wine produced averages from 18,000,000 to 20,000,000 gallons annually. Mining and quarrying are actively carried on in some parts, principally in coal, iron, antimony, alum, graphite, limestone, gypsum, building-stones, and millstones. Extensive beds of clay also occur, from which bricks and earthenware goods are largely made.

Lower Austria occupies the first rank among the provinces of the empire as a seat of manufacturing industry, the great centre of which is Vienna and the neighbourhood. The annual value of its products is estimated at over 21,000,000*l.*, of which about two-thirds are yielded by the capital. They include cotton, woollen, linen, and silk goods; paper, leather, sugar, iron, and earthenwares; glass, beer, brandy, chemicals, machinery, &c. In 1877 there were 370 miles of railway, 3260 miles of roads, and 250 miles of navigable water, in the province.

The people are mostly Germans, but the capital contains a very mixed population, and on the borders towards Hungary, Moravia, and Bohemia, dwell about 200,000 Slavs. About 96 per cent. of the population are Roman Catholics, 2 per cent. Protestants, and 2 per cent. Jews.

Vienna (Ger. *Wien*), the chief town of Lower Austria, and the Capital of the Monarchy, stands on the right bank of the river Danube, and partly on an island formed by a branch of that river known as the Wiener Donau or the Donaukana (Danube canal), which separates the city proper from its suburb Leopoldstadt, and into which flows the small stream Wien, from which the city takes its name. It is pleasantly situated in the fertile plain of the Vienna Basin, and covers an area of about 22 square miles, or including the suburbs about 36 square miles. In 1872 it contained 10,896 houses, 60 churches, (53 Catholic, 1 old Catholic, 4 Protestant and 2 Greek Churches), 27 cloisters, and 2 synagogues. The population in 1875 amounted to 673,865, or with the suburbs 1,020,770. Latitude 48° 12′ N., longitude 16° 22′ E.

Vienna is the fourth, if not the third largest city of Europe, being surpassed only by London and Paris, and perhaps Berlin, "It yields to few cities in architectural splendour, and in the charms of its environs," and "is one of the most gay, but at the same time, most agreeable places of residence on the Continent, whether the sojourner devote himself to pleasure, science, literature, or art." (*Murray's Handbook.*) It consists of the old city or inner town (*Innere Stadt*) and 9 other districts which form a circle round it. The names of these districts are (1) Leopoldstadt, (2) Landstrasse, (3) Wieden, (4) Margarethen. (5) Mariahilf, (6) Neubau, (7) Josefstadt, (8) Alsergrund, and (9) Favoriten. The old city was formerly surrounded by fortifications, but these have been demolished since 1858, and the space which they occupied laid out in streets. The principal of these is the Ringstrasse, which forms a belt round this part of Vienna $2\frac{2}{3}$ miles long and averaging 186 feet wide. It is planted with trees and lined with palatial buildings. Almost equally fine streets cross it at different points, and this now constitutes the favourite quarter of the wealthy classes. In the inner town the streets are generally narrow and irregular, but it contains the palace of the emperor, and the palaces of some of the principal nobility, the public offices, most of the museums and public collections, the finest churches, and the best shops.

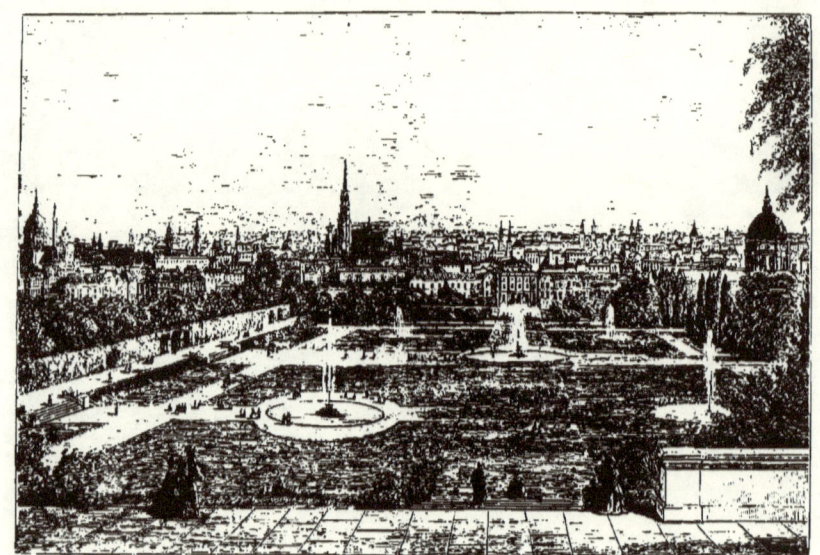

VIENNA.

Since, however, the laying out of the site of the old fortifications, many of the aristocracy have gone to live there, and there too the new public buildings are being generally erected. The Danube Canal is crossed by 8 bridges, and the Wien by 15, the finest being the Elizabethbrücke over the latter, constructed in 1854, and adorned in 1867 with 8 marble statues. Many of the principal squares are adorned with monuments and fountains. The most important square is the Stephansplatz, with the cathedral and episcopal palace, constituting the centre of Vienna. The Graben, with its attractive shops, is one of the most frequented and leading business streets of the city. In the centre stands the Trinity column, 66 feet high, representing a confused group of figures among clouds, erected by the Emperor Leopold I., on account of the cessation of the plague of 1679.

The most imposing edifice in Vienna is St. Stephen's Cathedral, erected between 1359 and 1500, on the site of an earlier building which dated from the beginning of the twelfth century. It is built in the form of a Latin cross, is 354 feet long, 230 broad, and 89 high, and has a beautiful tower 453 feet in height, erected in 1860-64 in place of an earlier one which was removed owing to its unsafe condition. The Cathedral has also lately undergone thorough restoration. The Augustine Church is an elegant structure erected in 1327-39 and restored 1783. It contains a monument of the Archduchess Christina of Saxe-Teschen by Canova, which is considered one of his finest works, and in an adjoining chapel are preserved in silver urns the hearts of the departed members of the imperial house. The church of the Capuchins is only remarkable as containing the sepulchral vault of the imperial family. The church of St. Carlo Borromeo was erected by the Emperor Charles VI. between 1716 and 1737 in grateful acknowledgment of the plague having been stayed. It is a large imposing structure surmounted by a dome, and having on each side of the portal a colossal column 145 feet in height and 13 feet in diameter with a spiral band of reliefs running round each, representing the life and actions of the saint. The Votive Church erected by the Emperor Francis Joseph in commemoration of his escape from assassination in 1853 was begun in 1856 and finished in 1879. It is a beautiful Gothic structure with a handsome façade in front and two slender towers and spires, richly embellished with delicate and beautiful tracery and carvings.

The imperial palace (*Hofburg* or *Burg*) is a large irregular pile of buildings, erected at different times and in different styles of architecture. It encloses several courts, the principal of which are the Franzensplatz, with a colossal bronze statue of the Emperor Francis I., and Josephsplatz, with a fine equestrian statue of Joseph II. Within the precincts of the palace are the imperial library, containing 410,000 volumes of books, and 20,000 MSS.—many of them of great value; the treasury; cabinets of natural history, minerals, coins and antiquities; the winter and summer riding-schools; the court theatre; and chapel. In front of the palace is a large open space termed the Outer Burgplatz, separated from the Ringstrasse by a railing, and having as an entrance the Outer Burg Thor—a massive structure erected in 1822, with five passages, and adorned with twelve Doric columns. Adjoining the Outer Burgplatz is the Volksgarten, laid out by the Emperor Francis in 1824. It contains pleasure-grounds and a café, and is much frequented in summer. In the centre is the temple of Theseus, built on the model of that in Athens, and containing a fine marble group of figures by Canova, representing the victory of Theseus over the Minotaur. The Belvedere, once the residence of Prince Eugene of Savoy, by whom it was erected in 1724, consists of two buildings—the Upper and the Lower Belvedere, separated by a large garden laid out in the French style. The Upper Belvedere contains the imperial picture-gallery—one of the best collections in Europe, and particularly rich in works of the Flemish and German schools. The Lower Belvedere contains the Ambras collection of ancient armour and curiosities—so called from the castle of Ambras in

Tyrol, where it was first formed—and the collection of antiquities, including the Egyptian collection. The imperial arsenal, erected 1849-55, covers a large space of ground outside the city, and contains an interesting collection of weapons of war.

Vienna is possessed of many excellent educational institutions, at the head of which is the university, founded in 1365, and reorganized under Maria Theresa by the celebrated physician Van Swieten. It has a library of over 220,000 volumes, an astronomical observatory, a botanic garden, and various museums and laboratories connected with it. In 1875, it had 283 professors and teachers, and 3810 students. It is particularly distinguished as a school of medicine. The Josephinum, or Academy of Medicine, is celebrated for its anatomical and pathological museum; and the public hospital is an admirably organized institution, with accommodation for 3000 patients. The Polytechnic Institution for affording instruction in practical science, industry and commerce, has 80 professors and teachers, and about 1400 pupils, with collections of industrial products, models of machinery, laboratories, &c. The Technological Museum in connexion with it, contains about 60,000 specimens of articles in different stages of manufacture, and about 5000 species of raw materials. The Academy of Fine Arts, founded in 1705, and reorganized in 1865, has valuable collections of engravings, drawings, paintings and casts of ancient and modern sculpture. It has 22 teachers, and 215 pupils. The Museum of Art was founded in 1864, on the plan of the South Kensington Museum, and installed in its present handsome building in 1872. The Art School in connexion with it has 13 teachers and 240 scholars. The Veterinary College is attended by upwards of 1000 pupils; and the Musical Conservatoire has 650 pupils. The Liechtenstein picture-gallery is the most extensive of the private collections—containing 1600 works by celebrated masters. The Archduke Albert collection of engravings and drawings is one of the finest in Europe—comprising about 300,000 specimens.

Of the ten theatres in Vienna, the best are the Court Theatre, the New Opera House, and the City or Stadt Theatre. The New Opera House, completed in 1869, is a magnificent edifice, externally and internally, and is seated for 3000 spectators. It is regarded as one of the finest theatres in Europe. A new Court Theatre is at present in course of construction; and among the other buildings in course of erection are the new Rathhaus, new University Buildings, Art and Natural History Museums, new Parliamentary Buildings, and new Palace of Justice. A new Exchange was erected in 1869-76.

Vienna is the great centre of the commerce of the country, and of the capital and enterprise necessary to maintain it. Six railways from different parts of the Monarchy have their termini here. It is also the leading manufacturing town of the empire. The principal manufactures are silk stuffs, shawls, gold and silver articles, hardware and cutlery, carriages, gloves and all kinds of fancy leather articles, musical and philosophical instruments, meerschaum pipes, paper, and chemical products. The northern arm of the Danube has been brought nearer to the city, and made more available for navigation, by means of a new channel about 4 miles in length and 300 yards wide, commenced in 1867, and opened in May 1875. Further extensions of this were completed in 1879, the entire cost being about 4,460,000*l*. Three railway bridges and two public bridges cross this channel. Vienna is well supplied with excellent water, brought by means of an aqueduct completed in 1873, from Schneeberg, 56 miles distant, at a cost of 2,300,000*l*.

The mean annual temperature of Vienna is 50° Fahr., the mean summer temperature being 71°, and the mean winter 30°. The weather, however, is variable, being subject to sudden changes. Formerly Vienna was considered unhealthy, but from the greater attention now given to sanitary matters, a great improvement has taken place. The death rate is from 25 to 27 per 1000.

The country around Vienna is very beautiful, and presents

many spots of interest. N.E. of the city is the Prater—one of the finest public parks in Europe, and much frequented by all classes of the people. The Great Exhibition of 1873 was held here, and the central portion of the main building,—the great Rotunda 344 feet in diameter, with the parts immediately connected with it,—have been preserved. The imperial summer palace of Schönbrunn, erected by Maria Theresa, is situated on the right bank of the Wien, about three miles S.W. of the city. The building is large and superbly furnished, the gardens are well laid out and very beautiful, and from the "Gloriette," a fine view is obtained of Vienna and the country around. At Laxenburg, nine miles S. of Vienna, are two imperial residences, one of which is a strict imitation of a baronial castle of the middle ages.

The Viennese are, as a rule, a contented, cheerful, and happy people. They enjoy much freedom, and possess many privileges. Their princes mix freely among them, and are regarded by them with affection. They are fond of pleasure, and the general tone of their character fits them for quiet enjoyment. Hence even the lower orders are characterized by mildness, gentleness, and goodhumour. They are uniformly kind and obliging, and ready to promote the pleasure of others.

Wiener Neustadt, or the *New Town of Vienna*, is the town next in size to Vienna, and contained, in 1869, 19,173 inhabitants. It lies twenty-eight miles S. of Vienna, with which it is connected by the Neustädter canal, and also by railway—being a station on the Vienna-Trieste line. It has an old ducal castle, built in 1168, and now used for a military academy, which has 48 teachers and 300 pupils. Important manufactures are carried on here, of machinery, cotton yarn, silk stuffs, ribbons, sugar, &c. The Emperor Maximilian I. was born and is also buried here.

UPPER AUSTRIA (Ger. *Oberösterreich* or *Oesterreich ob der Enns*) forms the western portion of the archduchy of Austria, and is bounded on the N. by Bohemia, W. by Bavaria,

S. by Salzburg and Styria, and E. by Lower Austria. It lies between lat. 47° 27′ and 48° 47′ N., and long. 12° 46′ and 15° E., and has an area of 4632 square miles, with (in 1869) 731,579 inhabitants.

Like Lower Austria, it is traversed by the river Danube, which enters it from Bavaria, below Passau, and divides it into two unequal parts, over a fourth part being to the N., and nearly three-fourths to the S. of that river. With the exception of a small portion on the borders of Bohemia, the whole of the province is drained by the Danube. Its principal affluents here are, on the right, the Inn, the Traun, and the Enns; and on the left, the Mühl. The Traun flows through the Hallstädter and Gmundner or Traun lakes, and, after leaving the latter, forms a beautiful waterfall. The upper valley of this river abounds in picturesque scenery. The Alpine lakes are numerous in Upper Austria,—the more important in addition to those mentioned being the Atter or Kammer lake, the Mond lake, and the Wolfgang lake.

The surface of the province is for the most part mountainous. The northern limestone range of the Alps enters it from Salzburg, and, together with its off-shoots, occupies the S. portion, while the N. portion is traversed by branches of the Bohemian mountain system. The loftiest summits are in the Dachstein group, which contains several glaciers, and whose highest point, Mount Dachstein, has an elevation of 9845 feet. The next highest elevation is the Great Priel, 8621 feet high. The higher mountain parts are generally bare and rugged, but lower down they are usually well wooded. The principal plains are the Welser Heath, and the Linzer Basin —neither of which are of great extent. The most fertile tracts lie along the Danube and the valleys that open into it. The climate is in general mild, but less so than in Lower Austria, owing to its greater elevation, and the proximity of high mountains.

About 90 per cent. of the surface is productive. Of the productive area, about 39 per cent. is arable, 37 per cent. in woods and forests, 20 per cent. in meadows and gardens, and 4 per cent. in pastures. The principal crops are oats, rye, barley, wheat, potatoes, turnips, beans, peas, lentils, hops, flax, and some hemp. The vine is no longer cultivated; but apples and other fruits are largely grown—the former being principally used in making cider. The rearing of horses and cattle is extensively carried on. The horses are noted for their strength and endurance, and the cattle and sheep are also distinguished. The chief mineral products are salt and coal. The salt works are at Ischl and Hallstadt, in the district of Salzkammergut, and produce annually over 1,000,000 cwt. of salt. There are also granite, millstone, grindstone, and gypsum quarries. The manufactures are not extensive, the principal being hardware and cutlery; linen, cotton, and woollen goods; leather, paper, and beer. A considerable trade is carried on along the Danube.

The inhabitants are almost without exception Germans, and are all Roman Catholics, except about 1600 Protestants. More than 56 per cent. of the adult population are engaged in agriculture, nearly 20 per cent. in manufactures, $2\frac{1}{2}$ per cent. in trade and commerce, and $7\frac{1}{2}$ in domestic service.

Linz, the chief town of the province, is beautifully situated on the right bank of the Danube, 100 miles W. of Vienna, and contains 33,394 inhabitants. It is the seat of various provincial and other courts, the see of a bishop, and carries on an active trade. Among the principal public buildings are the Cathedral with two towers, the church of St. Matthew and that of the Capuchins, the Landhaus, Rathhaus, and the old castle now used as a barracks. It has an interesting museum, a public library of 32,000 volumes, a gymnasium, real school, and a number of other educational, as well as a number of charitable, institutions. It is an important seat of traffic on the Danube, and has a dock for the building of ships. Various branches of manufacture are also actively carried on, particularly those of woollen, linen, silk, and cotton goods, leather and tobacco. On the opposite side of the Danube stands the suburb **Urfahr**, which is connected with it by an iron bridge. Linz was formerly defended by 32 towers, named after their founder, Maximilian of Este, Maximilian's towers, but most of these have now disappeared. One is still standing on the Pöstlingberg.

Steyr, Steyer, or *Steier* is situated at the confluence of the river Steyr with the Enns, 22 miles S.E. of Linz. It is chiefly celebrated for its manufacture of iron and steel goods; and is sometimes called the "Austrian Birmingham." It has a beautiful Gothic church after the model of St. Stephen's in Vienna. Population 13,392.

SALZBURG, *Duchy of*, is bounded on the N. by Upper Austria and Bavaria, W. by Bavaria and Tyrol, S. by Tyrol and Carinthia, and E. by Styria and Upper Austria. It lies between 46° 57′ and 48° 2′ N. lat., and 12° 6′ and 14° E. long., and has an area of 2767 square miles, with (in 1869) 151,410 inhabitants.

The surface is mountainous, forming a continuation of the Tyrolese Alpine land; only in the N., the valley of the Salzach belongs to the elevated plain of Bavaria. The Noric Alps stretch along the S. border of the province, and are covered with numerous glaciers, having as their highest points the Dreiherrenspitze (11,434 feet), Gross Venediger (12,053), and the Wieszbachhorn (11,737). The Northern Limestone Alps traverse the interior of the province, and are divided into several groups by the Saala and the Salzach, the most eastern of which, the Tännengebirge, is connected with the Dachstein group. Many of the summits are between 8000 and 9000 feet in height. Parallel ranges of less elevation lead by degrees to the flat tract of country in the N.

The principal river of the province is the Salzach, which rises in the S., and in the first part of its course forms the Pinzgauer swamps. After receiving, from the right, several mountain streams, the most important of which is the Krimmler Ache, it breaks through the Limestone Alps by the Lueg Pass; becomes navigable at Hallein; and after passing Salzburg, receives the Saala, and forms the boundary between Austria and Bavaria, to its mouth in the Inn. The Krimmler Ache forms the finest waterfall in the Monarchy. The rivers Enns and Mur have also their sources within the province—the former rising in the Pongau, and breaking through the Mandling pass, enters Styria, the latter rising in the Lungau, after a short course, also flows into Styria. The Alpine lakes are numerous, the largest being the Zeller lake. There are also numerous mineral springs, the most famous being those of Gastein, which enjoy a European reputation.

About 20 per cent. of the entire area of the province is unproductive, and only about 10 per cent. arable; the rest being chiefly woods and pastures. The chief agricultural products are oats, rye, wheat, potatoes and cabbages. The rearing of cattle is extensively carried on. The most important mineral product is salt; of which about 400,000 cwt. are annually obtained at Hallein. Iron, copper, nickel, cobalt, arsenic, and some gold and silver are also found. Marble of a fine quality is obtained from a quarry on the Untersberg. The manufactures are unimportant, and are chiefly chemical products, and wooden, earthen, and ironwares.

The inhabitants are mostly all Germans and Roman Catholics. About 51 per cent. of the adult population are engaged in agricultural pursuits or in the forests, 14 per cent. in the manufactures, 9 per cent. in domestic service, and 2 per cent. in trade and commerce.

Salzburg, the chief town of the province, is beautifully situated on both sides of the Salzach, in a valley between the Mönchsberg (Monk's Hill) on the left, and the Kapuzinerberg (Capuchiner Hill) on the right. The greater part of the old town stands on the left bank of the river, here crossed by four bridges. Stately quays have lately been erected on both sides of the river, forming pleasant promenades. It is the seat of a prince archbishop, and of various provincial and other courts, and contains numerous educational and benevolent institutions; among the former being a theological seminary. The town has very much the appearance of an Italian city, with its flat-roofed houses, its numerous public squares with fountains and monuments, and its many churches and chapels, whence it is sometimes called the "German Rome." The Cathedral is a large and splendid edifice of marble and freestone, in the style of St. Peter's at Rome, erected in the 17th century. St. Peter's church contains numerous monuments, among which is one to Haydn the composer. In the Residenzplatz is a beautiful marble fountain, 45 feet in height, and considered to be one of the finest in Germany. In Mozartplatz is a bronze statue of the composer of that name, who was born here. Among the principal buildings are the imperial summer palace of Mirabell, the old archbishop's palace, and the Rathhaus. On the Nonnberg (Nun's Hill) above the town, stands the old castle of Hohensalzburg. The town has an excellent museum of natural history and antiquities, and several extensive libraries. The manufactures comprise cotton goods, leather, hardware, earthenware, glass, pianos, and organs. The trade is considerable, particularly in goods on transit. Population (1869), 20,336. A Roman town, *Juvavia*, stood here as early as the first century of our era; and the locality is rich in Roman remains. It was made the see of a bishopric in 716, soon afterwards raised to an archbishopric. The archbishops in time became very powerful, holding temporal sway over a large district of country, and being princes of the empire. The territory was secularized in 1801, when it comprised 3500 square miles, and 250,000 inhabitants. In 1806, it was united to Austria, and in 1809 transferred to Bavaria, but in 1816 it was again conveyed to Austria.

STYRIA (Ger. *Steiermark*), *Duchy of*, is situated between 45° 49' and 47° 49' N. lat., and 13° 34' and 17° 1' E. long., and is bounded on the N. by Lower and Upper Austria, W. by Salzburg and Carinthia, S. by Carniola, and E. by Croatia and Hungary. It has an area of 8669 square miles, and a population (in 1869) of 1,131,309.

Styria belongs to the Alpine region of Austria, and is distinguished for its richness in picturesque scenery, and in magnificent Alpine views, while the valleys and plains are noted for the fulness and luxuriance of their vegetation. The N. and W. parts are especially mountainous, while, in the S. and E., fruitful valleys and plains intermingle with the mountainous and hilly portions. The mountains belong to all the three ranges of the Alps. The Central Alps enter from Salzburg, and the principal chain ends near the mouth of the Liesing in the Mur. A second chain forms the separation between the basins of the Mur and the Drave, and divides into two branches. The N.E. branch goes to Bruck, and, continuing its course from the left bank of the river, ends in the Wechsel. The S.E. branch tends towards the Drave, and at length, passing to the other side of that river, terminates in the Bachergebirge. Between the Wechsel and the Bachergebirge, the country is filled with off-shoots and inferior branches of the greater chains. The Northern Limestone Range of the Alps commences from the Dachstein and the Priel groups on the borders of Upper Austria, and passes by means of the long group of the Hochschwab to the Schnee and Rax Alm. The Southern Limestone Range begins from the Sulzbach Alps, on the borders of Styria, Carinthia, and Carniola, and spreading itself out between the Save and the San, is broken through by the latter, and afterwards, as the Matzelgebirge, passes into Croatia. In the Central Alps, several of the summits rise to the height of between 8700 and 9000 feet, and in the limestone ranges, several attain to the height of 7500 feet. The latter, in particular, abound in narrow passes, wild mountain defiles, and picturesque valleys.

The land is well watered by numerous streams, which are all tributaries of the Danube. The four principal streams—the Mur, Drave, Save, and Enns—have neither their sources nor their mouths within the territory. The most important of these is the Mur, which rises in Salzburg, and has a course of about 200 miles within the province, becoming navigable at Judenburg. The Drave is already navigable when it enters the territory from Carinthia, and has a course here of about 75 miles. The Save comes out of Carniola, and for some distance forms the boundary between that province and Styria. The Enns is, for the most part of its course here, only a rapid mountain stream; after receiving the Salza at Altenmarkt, it becomes navigable. The Traun and the Raab rise in Styria. There are, relatively, fewer waterfalls and lakes here, than in the other Alpine provinces; but, on the other hand, it possesses numerous mineral springs. The most distinguished are those of Gleichenberg and Rohitsch.

About 90 per cent. of the land is productive; and of this about one-half is in wood, 22 per cent. arable, 1 per cent. vineyards, 16 per cent. garden and meadow, the rest pasture-land. The differences in the elevation of the surface, and the differences in the climate occasioned thereby, give rise to great varieties in the vegetable kingdom. In Lower Styria, agriculture is the principal occupation of the inhabitants, and the well-cultivated soil yields abundant crops of all kinds of grain, particularly rye, wheat, oats, maize, and buckwheat. Flax, hemp, and some hops are also grown. Special care is bestowed on the cultivation of the grape and other fruits. The vineyards occur chiefly in the circles of Gratz and Marburg; and a considerable quantity of cider is made. The silk-worm is also cultivated to some extent. In Upper Styria, owing to the less genial climate, the less extent of arable land, and the sparser population, agriculture is but little practised, and the rearing of cattle receives the chief attention. The horned cattle and sheep of this province are distinguished, as are also the horses. The principal mining products are iron, coal, and salt. Styria is the greatest iron producing province in Austria, and yields annually an average of about 2,000,000 cwt. of wrought iron. Of brown coal, the annual produce is about 16,000,000 cwt., and of salt 280,000 cwt. Its chief industries are connected with the working of iron, and the manufacture of iron and steel goods, for which it is justly distinguished. Its wares are exported to Germany, France, Italy, and Russia.

The other industries are mostly of small extent and unimportant, and confined chiefly to Gratz and the neighbourhood. An active trade is carried on by road and rail with different parts, particularly Vienna and Trieste.

About 63 per cent. of the population are Germans, and 37 Slovens; and about 99 per cent. are Roman Catholics. Agriculture and the forests afford employment to 72 per cent. of the adult population, and about 13 per cent. are employed in the manufactures, of which 8 per cent. are in the various kinds of iron works.

Gratz (Ger. *Graz*), the chief town of the province of Styria, is situated in a charming valley on both sides of the river Mur, here crossed by 5 bridges, at the height of 1094 feet about the level of the sea, and 140 miles S.S.W. of Vienna. It consists of an old town or city proper, on the left bank of the river, and five suburbs, having in all a population of 86,369 in 1876. The streets in the old town are mostly narrow and irregular, but the suburbs contain many fine streets and elegant houses. In the neighbourhood are many beautiful walks and objects of interest. On the Schlossberg stands the ruins of the old castle, destroyed by the French in 1809. The cathedral is a Gothic building erected by the Emperor Frederick III., in 1462, and containing many monuments, and some fine paintings. Near it stands the mausoleum of the Emperor Ferdinand II. and his family. Among the other principal buildings are the citadel, the Landhaus—where the estates meet and which contains a large collection of old arms and armour—and the Rathhaus. It is the seat of the provincial and other courts, and of the bishop of Seckau, and contains numerous educational and charitable institutions. Among the former are the university, having, in 1876, 99 professors and teachers, and 878 students; and the technical high school, with 44 teachers and 246 pupils. The Johanneum, founded by the Archduke John, in 1811, contains collections of objects in natural history and technology, and a library of about 70,000 volumes. Its chief manufactures are iron and steel goods, chemicals, sugar, paper, leather, glass, and earthenware. Being in the line of railway between Vienna and Trieste, it carries on a considerable trade with these places, and also with Hungary and Croatia.

Marburg is situated on the left bank of the Drave, 36 miles S. of Gratz, and with its three suburbs contains a population of 12,828 persons. It is the seat of a bishop, and has a theological and other seminaries. The principal buildings are the cathedral and the castle. The manufactures are unimportant; but a considerable trade is carried on in iron wares, corn, fruit, and wine.

CARINTHIA (Ger. *Kärnthen*), *Duchy of*, is bounded on the N. by Styria and Salzburg, W. by Tyrol, S. by Italy, Görz, and Carniola, and E. by Styria. It lies between lat. 46° 20' and 47° 7' N., and long. 12° 40' and 15° 6' E., and has an area of 4005 square miles, with a population, in 1869, of 336,400.

The surface is for the most part mountainous, interspersed with numerous valleys, which sometimes open out into considerable plains. The mountains in the N.W. and N. belong to the Central Alps. In the extreme N.W. is the Grossglockner, rising to the height of 12,455 feet above the sea, with the great glacier of the Pasterze. Parallel ranges to the main chain run through the N. part of the province, some of the summits rising to the height of 9000 and 10,000 feet. In the S. is the Southern Limestone Range of the Alps—consisting of the Carnic Alps, which separate it from Italy, the Karawanko, between it and Carniola, and a portion of the Sulzbach Alps, dividing it from Styria. These rise, in some parts, to the height of 7000 and 8000 feet, and they also contain several important passes. The principal river is the Drave, which flows from W. to E. through the centre of the province, having a course here of about 90 miles. Its principal affluents are, from the left:—the Möll, the Lieser, the Gurk, and the Lavant; and from the right, the Gail. There are numerous lakes, the principal of which are the Wörther, the Ossiaker and the Milstätter. There are a number of mineral springs, but none are in high repute. In the N.W. the climate is severe, but in the lower parts it is milder and more genial.

About 12 per cent. of the surface is unproductive. Of the productive land about 61 per cent. is in woods and forests, 15 per cent. arable, 12 per cent. in meadows and gardens, and 12 per cent. in pasture-land. The chief grain crops are oats, rye, wheat, barley, maize, and buckwheat. The vine is cultivated only in a few favourable situations. The rearing of cattle is extensively carried on in the valleys and on the declivities of the mountains. It is however for its mineral products, and the industries depending thereon, that this province is most distinguished. The principal of these products are iron, lead, zinc, and coal. About 1,340,000 cwt. of wrought iron, 72,000 cwt. of lead, 20,000 cwt. of zinc, and 1,200,000 cwt. of brown coal, are annually obtained. The manufacturing industries are chiefly connected with the working of the metals, and, in particular, the iron and steel wares of Carinthia rank with the best in the Monarchy. A considerable trade is carried on.

About 71 per cent. of the population are Germans, and 29 per cent. Slovens, who live mostly to the south of the Drave. The Roman Catholics form about 95, and the Protestants 5 per cent. Over 68 per cent. of the adult population are employed in agriculture and the forests, 14 per cent. in manufacturing and mining industries (6 per cent. being employed in connexion with iron and lead alone), and $4\frac{1}{2}$ per cent. in trade and commerce.

Klagenfurt, the chief town of the province of Carinthia, is situated on the right bank of the river Glan, an affluent of the Gurk, 60 miles W.S.W. of Gratz. Population including the four suburbs 15,285. Among the principal buildings are the cathedral and the parish church, the Landhaus, the bishop's palace (with collections of natural history, antiquities, and art), the Rathhaus and the castle. It has manufactures of white lead and woollen stuffs, and carries on an active transit trade. The neighbourhood is rich in Roman and other remains.

CARNIOLA (Ger. *Krain*), *Duchy of*, is bounded on the N. by Carinthia, N.E. by Styria, E. and S. by Croatia, and W. by Görz, and Istria. It lies between 45° 18', and 46° 40' N. lat., and between 13° 44' and 14° 44' E. long., having an area of 3855 square miles, and a population in 1869 of 463,273.

The surface is for the most part mountainous. In the N. and N.W. occur portions of the Southern Limestone Range of the Alps. In the N.W. stands the Terglou group, the highest point of which, Mount Terglou, is 9371 feet above the sea. Further E. runs the Karawank range, common to Carniola and Carinthia, followed by the Steiner Alps, the name given in Carniola to the Sulzbach Alps, and having as their highest elevation Mount Grintouc, 8296 feet high. The valleys of the Izonzo, Idria, and Zeyer separate these Alps from the elevated plain region of the "Karst," which occupies the S.W. and S. The peculiarities of this region are broad, rocky ridges; troughs and funnel-shaped depressions; underground caverns and passages; few open river courses, but streams flowing underground, and waters that periodically disappear and reappear. Some of the caverns here are of great extent and famous, as the Adelsberg grotto, the Magdalena grotto, and the Planina grotto. Fertile spots, however, occur here and there in this region. In the E. the Karst passes into a hilly district, rich in vineyards, which towards the N. spreads itself out into the Gurker plain, and in the S. rises into the Uskoken mountains. Carniola has more and larger plains than Carinthia, the principal being the Gurker plain (the most fertile), and the plain of Laibach (the most unproductive, chiefly moor).

The principal river of the province is the Save, which is formed by the union of two small streams, the Wurzner Save, and the Wocheiner Save, and has a course here of about 120 miles. It receives most of the other streams, the Zeyer, Laibach, Feistritz, Gurk, and Kulpa. The most remarkable of these is the Laibach, which rises as the Poik, and after a course of 13 miles, disappears in the Adelsberg grotto. After receiving there several streams, it reappears as the Unz, flows through the valley of Planina, and again disappears to reappear at Upper Laibach, when it takes the name of Laibach, becomes then navigable, and at length empties itself into the Save below the town of Laibach. The principal mountain lakes are the Wocheiner, Wurzner, and Veldes. The Zirknitzer lake in the Karst, is subject to periodical ebbs and flows, and sometimes almost entirely disappears. Carniola only possesses two mineral springs of any note, at Teplitz and Veldes.

About $5\frac{1}{2}$ per cent. of the surface is unproductive. Of the productive land 46 per cent. is in wood, 14 per cent. arable, 17 per cent. in meadows and gardens, 1 per cent. vineyards, and 22 per cent. pastures. The chief grain crops are wheat, rye, oats, barley, maize, millet, and buckwheat. The produce, however, does not equal the home consumption, and a considerable quantity is annually imported, chiefly from Hungary. The rearing of cattle is not so extensively nor so successfully carried on here, as in most of the other provinces. The principal mineral product is quicksilver at Idria, the richest source in Europe after Almaden in Spain, yielding annually about 6400 cwt. Of wrought iron about 100,000 cwt. are annually produced, of brown coal about 3,000,000 cwt., and of copper 1800 cwt., besides small quantities of lead, zinc, and a few other metals. The manufactures are considerable, but are chiefly conducted on a small scale. The principal of them are carried on in and around the capital Laibach. They include hardware, cotton and woollen goods, sugar, paper, leather, cigars, and chemicals. A considerable trade is also carried on.

Of the inhabitants of Carniola 91 per cent. are Slovens, and only $5\frac{1}{2}$ per cent. Germans, chiefly in Upper Carniola, while the remaining $3\frac{1}{2}$ per cent. are Croatians who inhabit the south. In Laibach, the chief town, however, $40\frac{1}{2}$ per cent. of the inhabitants are Germans, and not more than 59 per cent. Slovens. They are almost all Roman Catholics, the Protestants numbering only 350. About 69 per cent. of the adult population are employed in agriculture and the forests, 10 per cent. in the manufactures, and 1½ per cent. in trade and commerce.

Laibach, the chief town of the province of Carniola, is situated in a valley on both sides of the river of the same name here crossed by six bridges, 78 miles S.S.W. of Gratz, and 52 miles N.E. of Trieste. Population with eight suburbs (1869), 22,593. It is built partly round a steep hill, the Schlossberg, the old castle on which is now used as a prison. It is a bishop's see, and among the principal buildings are the cathedral of St. Nicholas with a number of beautiful paintings and monuments, the citadel, Rathhaus, bishop's palace, Auersberg palace, lyceum, and theatre. It has a number of educational institutions, a museum, and a library of 35,000 volumes. Its manufactures are unimportant, chiefly cotton goods, and refined sugar; but it carries on an active transit trade, being on the line of railway between Vienna and Trieste. It occupies the site of the ancient Æmona, and is noted for a congress held here in 1821.

MARITIME DISTRICT, *the*, (Ger. *Küstenland*), comprehends the princely county of Görz and Gradisca, the Margraviate of Istria, with the Quarnerian Islands, and the free imperial city and district of Trieste. It lies between lat. 44° 29' and 46° 28' N., and long. 13° 25', and 14° 50' E.; and is bounded on the N. by Carinthia and Carniola, E. by Carniola and Croatia, S. by the Adriatic, and W. by Italy. It has an area of 3082 square miles, and a population in 1869 of 582,079; as follows, Görz and Gradisca, area 1139 square miles, population 204,076, Istria and the islands, area 1907 square miles, population 254,905, and Trieste and district 36 square miles, population 123,098.

The N.W. portion of the country is occupied by branches of the Southern Limestone Range of the Alps, the main chain of which extends along its border. The highest point here, Mount Canin, rises to the height of about 7300 feet. The rest of the country is mostly occupied by the region of the

Karst, the S.W. portion of which is here, while the N.E. portion is in Carniola. In Istria the elevated country descends gradually to the sea by a series of terraces, which are broken up into plateaus by deep water-courses running E., S., and W. The district at the mouth of the Isonzo is low-lying and flat. The hilly country in the S.W. is fertile, but otherwise the dry and sterile Karst is little productive. As in Carniola it abounds in caverns, many of which are of great extent, and have remarkable stalactitic formations. Among the principal are the grottos of Corgnale and San Servolo.

The principal river is the Isonzo, which rises on the W. side of the Terglou, flows generally S., with many windings, in a mostly narrow mountain valley, receives the Idria and the Wippach, takes the name of Sdobba, and falls into the bay of Monfalcone. The rivers Quieto and Arsa in Istria, have only very short courses.

About $6\frac{1}{2}$ per cent. of the surface is unproductive. Of the productive land about 41 per cent. is pasture-land, 25 per cent. in wood, 19 per cent. arable, $12\frac{1}{2}$ gardens and meadows, and $2\frac{1}{2}$ vineyards. Olive and chestnut-trees occupy about 0.6 per cent. The principal grain crops are maize (43 per cent.), wheat (30 per cent.), barley, rye, oats, and rice (in the Isonzo plain). Among the fruits are figs and almonds. About 8,500,000 gallons of wine are annually produced, and a considerable quantity of olive oil. The silkworm is also cultivated. The pasture-land though of great extent, is generally poor, and the cattle, sheep, and horses, are of inferior qualities.

There are no metals found here, but coal is worked in several places. Istria contains abundance of building stone and marble, in which an active trade was formerly carried on with Venice. The manufactures are unimportant. Trieste is more of a commercial than a manufacturing city. Some silk manufactures, cotton spinning, and sugar refining, are carried on in Görz and Gradisca. On the coast fishing is actively carried on, and ship-building, as also the manufacture of sea salt. The salt works of Capo d'Istria and Pirano, produce annually about 600,000 cwt. of salt. The bays and harbours here are of great importance to Austrian navigation.

In Trieste and its district more than one-half of the inhabitants are Slovens, about 34 per cent. are Italians, 8 per cent. Germans, and 4½ per cent. Jews. In Görz and Gradisca ⅔ of the people are Slovens, ¼ Friulians, 7 per cent. Italians, and 1 per cent. Germans. In Istria 56 per cent. are Serbo-Croatians, 31 per cent. Italians, 12 per cent. Slovens, and 1 per cent. Roumanians. Over 6 per cent. of the adult population are engaged in trade and commerce, 13 per cent. in the manufactures, and 42 per cent. in agriculture and the forests.

Trieste (Ger. *Triest*, Ital. *Trieste*), the chief town of the Maritime District, and also the principal seaport of the Monarchy, is beautifully situated at the foot of the declivities of the Karst, on a gulf of the same name, at the head of the Adriatic Sea, 230 miles S.W. of Vienna, and 73 miles E.N.E. of Venice; lat. (of observatory) 45° 38′ 50″ N., long. 13° 46′ 30″ E. The neighbouring heights, once naked and barren, have been, at great cost, covered with earth and rendered fruitful, so that they now present gardens, orchards and vineyards, with many elegant villas.

Trieste occupies the site of the Roman colony *Tergeste*, but in the middle ages it was only an inconsiderable seaport. In 1719 it was made a free port by the Emperor Charles VI., and thus freed from many of the restrictions that then interfered with the growth of commerce; but even in the middle of the 18th century it only contained about 6400 inhabitants. Maria Theresa greatly improved the harbour, and conferred upon the town many privileges, and from this time it began to rise into importance. In 1810 its population amounted to 29,908, in 1830 to 42,913, in 1840 to 57,519, and in 1869 to 70,274. The establishment of the Austrian Lloyd's Company, whose head-quarters are here, and the opening up of communication by railway with Vienna, have done much to advance the prosperity of the town. In 1849 it was made a free imperial city.

It consists of an old and a new town or Theresienstadt, with the more recently formed parts — Josephstadt and Franzensvorstadt. The old town is built partly on the slopes and partly at the foot of the Schlossberg, a hill which overlooks the town, and is crowned by an old castle with fortifications. The streets here are generally narrow and crooked, and the houses small; but it also contains a number of public squares. The new town is regularly laid out with wide and spacious streets, crossing each other at right angles, and lined with handsome houses. A spacious canal extends through the centre of the new town, dividing it into two parts. The cathedral of St. Just is a very ancient edifice, originally founded in the fourth century. It is in the Byzantine style, consists of a nave and four aisles, and contains many relics. The tower is believed to stand on the remains of an ancient temple of Jupiter. The Tergesteum is a vast quadrangular building containing the exchange, the Austrian Lloyd's offices, a bazaar, concert and ball rooms, a reading-room, &c. Among the other principal buildings are the new Rathhaus, the old exchange, large opera-house, and railway station. It has also a meteorological and astronomical observatory, natural history and archæological museum, public library, large hospital, three theatres, and an imperial academy with departments for commerce, navigation, and shipbuilding. The manufactures are secondary to the shipping, and are chiefly of articles required by ships. Besides shipbuilding, there are carried on rope and sail-making, the making of machines, and soap, oil, candles, beer, rosoglio, &c. The Lloyd's Company have extensive works here for shipbuilding, the making of engines, and other important works. This company was formed in 1833, and in 1878 it had a fleet of 71 steamers of 15,985 horse-power and about 85,000 tons' burden. The railway company have constructed a spacious harbour to the N. of the town for the convenience of their traffic. In 1877, 8522 vessels, having in all 1,089,272 tons, entered; and 8511 vessels, with 1,077,953 tons, left the port. The total value of the imports during that year was 14,027,700*l.*, and of exports, 10,588,100*l*. The imports are chiefly from England, Turkey, Italy, and Egypt; the exports chiefly to Italy, England, Turkey, and Egypt. A considerable trade is also carried on with America, and especially Brazil. The harbour is on the whole good, and is well protected except on the N.W. It is bounded on the S. by the Mole of St. Theresa, on the extremity of which is a lighthouse, and opposite to it is the New Lazaretto, with a basin capable of holding 60 or 70 vessels in quarantine. The harbour is semicircular in form, lined with spacious quays, and deep enough to admit large vessels, while vessels of the largest size can anchor in the roadstead outside.

Görz, the chief town of the county of Görz and Gradisca, is situated on the Isonzo, 26 miles N.N.W. of Trieste. It is the see of a bishop, and the seat of various provincial and other courts. Among the principal buildings are the cathedral, the castle—formerly occupied by the Counts of Görz, now used as a prison—the bishop's palace, and the Landhaus. The manufactures are inconsiderable; but an active trade is carried on in the productions of the district. Charles X. of France died here in 1836, and is buried in the Franciscan cloister of Castagnovizza in the vicinity. Population (1869), 16,659.

Pola, a fortified seaport town of Istria, situated near the S. extremity of the Istrian peninsula, 54 miles S. by E. of Trieste. It was made the chief naval station of the Monarchy in 1850, and since that time its population has increased from 1100 to 16,324 in 1869. It is strongly fortified, both towards sea and land, and the harbour is very commodious and safe, being capable of accommodating the entire fleet. It has a great naval arsenal, docks, wharves, and other establishments. As a trading port, it ranks next after Trieste and Fiume, a chief article of export being building stones. It has a cathedral dating from the fifteenth century, two other churches, an hospital, theatre, &c. There are also remains of a Roman amphitheatre, temple, triumphal arch, &c.

Pirano is a seaport town of Istria, situated on a peninsula, in

PIRANO.

the Gulf of Trieste, 15 miles S.W. of the town of that name. It has an old castle whose walls and towers appear amid olive-groves, an interesting gothic parish church, and a Rathhaus. The inhabitants are chiefly engaged in navigation, fishing, and the salt works in the vicinity. Population, 10,811.

TYROL (Ger. *Tirol*) and VORARLBERG, a princely county, lying between 45° 38' and 47° 45' N. lat., and 9° 32' and 12° 39' E. long., and bounded on the N. by Bavaria, E. by Salzburg, Carinthia, and Italy, S. by Italy, and W. by Italy, Switzerland, and Liechtenstein. Area, 11,320 square miles. Population (1869) 878,907. Of Vorarlberg alone, area 1004 square miles, population 102,624.

Tyrol is the most mountainous province of Austria and contains several of the loftiest summits in the Monarchy. In many respects it resembles Switzerland, and may be regarded as a continuation of that country. Here, too, there are mountains of great elevation, immense fields of snow, glaciers, avalanches, waterfalls, and precipices. About $\frac{9}{10}$ of the surface is mountainous. The three great chains of the Alps—the Central, and the Northern and Southern Limestone Alps pass through the country. Three principal valleys lie between these—the valleys of the Inn and the Adige, and the Pusterthal. The northern limestone chain passes through Vorarlberg, and then stretches along the northern border of Tyrol from W. to E. It is divided into four distinct groups by the valleys of the Lech, the Isar, and the Inn. Northward it descends gradually to the high plain of Bavaria, while towards the south its descent is mostly rapid and precipitous. The Central Alps or the Tyrolese Alps Proper separate the valleys of the Inn and the Adige, and extend through the country in an easterly direction, giving off branches to the N. and S. It has numerous glaciers, and its principal summits rise to the height of from 9000 to 12,000 feet. The southern limestone range stretches mostly along the southern border of the province, and is divided by the Adige into two groups. It contains the Ortlerspitze, the highest point in Austria, being

12,814 feet in height. From all these principal chains branches go off in different directions and cover most of the surface of the country.

The waters of Tyrol are conveyed in three different directions, into three distinct seas—into the North Sea by the Rhine, the Black Sea by the Danube, and the Adriatic Sea by the Adige, &c. The Rhine flows along the W. border of Vorarlberg for about 18 miles, and receives from that part a few streams, the principal of which is the Ill. More extensive is the portion of country drained by the Danube, which receives the Lech, Isar, Inn, Drave, and several other streams. But the largest portion of the province is drained into the Adriatic by the Adige with the Eisak and Lavis, the Sarca afterwards the Mincio, and the Brenta. A portion of Lake Constance, and a large part of Lago di Garda lie within the borders of Tyrol, but the other lakes are all of small size.

The climate varies greatly in different parts. To the S. of the Alps it is much milder than to the N., and is milder in those valleys that are open towards the S. than in those which are exposed to the N. At Innsbruck the mean annual temperature is 45°, at Meran 50.7°, and at Roveredo 51.2°. The average annual fall of rain at Innsbruck is 34 inches.

About 17.4 per cent. of the surface is unproductive. Of the productive land only about 6.9 per cent. is arable, 1.2 per cent. vineyards, 13.4 per cent. meadows and gardens, 31 per cent. pasture-land, and 47.5 woods and forests. In none of the other provinces of Austria is there so much unproductive land as in Tyrol. Agriculture here, too, is generally attended with difficulties, particularly in the higher regions, so that it is mostly in a very backward state. In S. Tyrol, and in the lower valley of the Inn, the principal grain crop is maize. In other parts the chief grain crops are rye, barley, wheat, and oats. Among the other products are flax, hemp, and tobacco. Fruit is extensively cultivated, and much of it is of very superior quality, including apples, peaches, almonds, figs, lemons, oranges, &c. Wine is a principal product of S. Tyrol; and here, too, the mulberry-tree is largely cultivated,—about 20,000 cwt. of cocoons being annually produced. The forests, also, are valuable, and produce annually a large amount of timber, much of which is sent into Italy. The rearing of cattle is extensively carried on, and large quantities of butter and cheese are made, the latter especially being distinguished for its excellence. Among the wild animals found here are the chamois, red deer, hare, and wild fowl. Tyrol was formerly rich in the precious metals, but at present its principal mineral products are salt, coal, and iron, but only the first is largely obtained. The salt-mines at Hall produce annually about 450,000 cwt. of salt. Among the metals obtained here, besides iron, are gold, silver, copper, lead, and zinc. There are also important marble quarries in S. Tyrol.

Tyrol is not a great manufacturing province, and generally the manufactures are on a small scale. Vorarlberg, particularly the valley of the Rhine, is a great seat of the cotton manufacture. In other parts linen and woollen stuffs are largely manufactured, but chiefly as domestic industries. In S. Tyrol the principal manufacture is silk. Among the other manufactures are iron-ware and machinery, wooden-wares, paper, leather, sugar, tobacco and beer. An active trade is carried on by Tyrol with other parts of the Monarchy, and also with Germany, Italy, and Switzerland. The most important railway is that from Kufstein on the borders of Bavaria, by Innsbruck, through the Brenner Pass, to Botzen and Verona. The exports are chiefly wine, silk, cattle, wood, salt, and cotton goods; the imports, corn, colonial produce, and various industrial products.

About 60.7 per cent. of the population of Tyrol are Germans, of the Bavarian stock; 38.7 per cent. are Italians; and 1.6 per cent. Ladins. Of the adult population, 54 per cent. are engaged in agriculture and the forests; 15.5 per cent. are employed in the manufactures; 3 per cent. in trade and commerce; and 6.8 per cent. in domestic service. The inhabitants are all Roman Catholics, with the exception of some Protestants and Jews in Innsbruck and Vorarlberg.

The German Tyrolese are a handsome, strong, and hardy race of men, good-natured, sprightly and gay, fond of outdoor exercises, and distinguished as marksmen. They are trustworthy and brave, but somewhat superstitious; and have an intense love of country, and a strong attachment to the imperial house. Formerly, many of the Tyrolese travelled abroad over Europe as pedlars, selling the wares of their country, to afterwards return with their savings to their own land; and even now it is calculated that over 30,000 of the grown population are abroad in this way. In German Tyrol the means of education are abundant, and are largely taken advantage of; so that in no other part of the Monarchy is the school attendance so high. The Italian Tyrolese very much resemble other Italians in appearances as well as in manners and pursuits. By them education is by no means so highly valued or taken advantage of as by their German neighbours.

Innsbruck, the chief town of Tyrol, is beautifully situated on both sides of the river Inn, in a valley enclosed by mountains rising to the height of 7000 or 8000 feet. The river is here crossed by three bridges, one of which is a handsome iron bridge, constructed in 1871-2 on the site of an old wooden one, which gave name to the town. There is a modern chain bridge below the town, and between the two is a wooden bridge. The town is 1870 feet above the sea, and consists of an old and a new town, with several suburbs. The houses are mostly in the Italian style, with flat roofs, and frequently ornamented with frescoes. Many of them have arcades below, with shops. The principal church is the Franciscan or Court Church, which contains a beautiful monument to the Emperor Maximilian I., reckoned one of the finest works of the kind in Europe. It consists of a marble sarcophagus, the sides of which are covered with 24 reliefs, representing the principal actions of his life, and around it are 28 colossal bronze statues, representing relatives of the emperor and other distinguished persons It also contains the mausoleum of the Archduke Ferdinand of Tyrol, and his spouse; and the tomb of the patriot Hofer, surmounted by a marble statue. The imperial palace, erected by Maria Theresa, is an extensive building with gardens extending along the Inn and forming an agreeable promenade. The university founded here in 1673, by Leopold I., has faculties of theology, law, medicine, and philosophy, 86 professors and teachers, and 614 students (in 1876). It has also a library of 61,000 volumes, anatomical museum, botanic garden, &c. The city museum, or Ferdinandeum, is rich in objects of natural history, art, antiquities, &c., connected with Tyrol. The chief manufactures are silk, woollen, and cotton stuffs, leather, gloves, glass, and cutlery. A very active transit trade is carried on. Population (1869), 16,324.

Trent (Ger. *Trient*, Ital. *Trento*, the ancient *Tridentinum*), the principal town of Southern Tyrol, is pleasantly situated on the left bank of the Adige, here crossed by a stone-bridge 130 feet long, 92 miles S.W. of Innsbruck. It consists of the town proper and two suburbs, is surrounded by high walls, and built in the Italian style. The cathedral is a fine marble edifice dating from the 5th century. The church of St. Maria Maggiore is noted as the place where the celebrated Council of Trent held its sittings (1545-63), and it has a painting with portraits of all the 278 members. The principal of the other buildings are the old castle, the bishop's palace, the theatre, and Rathhaus. Trent has also a museum, rich in local antiquities, and a library of 35,000 volumes. The manufactures are not considerable, but an active transit trade is carried on. Population (1869), 17,073.

BOHEMIA (Ger. *Böhmen*), *Kingdom of*, is situated between 48° 34' and 51° 3' N. lat. and 12° 21' and 16° 47' E. long., and is bounded on the N. by Prussia and Saxony, W. by Bavaria, S. by Upper and Lower Austria, and E. by Moravia. Area 20,119 square miles. Population (1869), 5,106,069, of whom 2,433,629 were males, and 2,672,440 females.

Bohemia is almost entirely surrounded by chains of mountains, the principal of which are the Riesengebirge, on the N.E., separating it from Prussia and Silesia, and having as its highest point the Schneekoppe, 5248 feet above the sea; the Erzgebirge, on the N.W., dividing it from Saxony, but with no elevation rising to the height of 4000 feet; the Bohemian Forest on the S.W., between it and Bavaria, having its loftiest summit only 4550 feet above the sea; and the Moravian Mountains on the S.E., separating it from Moravia, but of no great elevation. The surface of Bohemia therefore forms a kind of basin shut in on all sides by mountain ranges, and hence it is believed to have in ancient times formed a great lake, until the waters found an outlet for themselves in the N. along the course now taken by the Elbe, which drains almost the whole of the interior of the country. The lowest part of the land therefore is at the point where the Elbe leaves it, 350 feet above the sea, and from this the surface rises on all sides in the form of terraces interspersed with ranges of mountains usually of no great elevation, and with broad rounded summits. Bohemia as a whole has an average elevation of about 1000 feet above the sea. The whole of the southern portion is over 1250 feet and the highest summits in the interior rarely rise to more than 2300 feet. The lowest land is in the N. in the valley of the Elbe. A considerable stretch of low-lying country here, extending from Leitmeritz to Königgrätz, has an elevation of from 500 to 800 feet, and few of the mountains in the neighbourhood rise to more than 1150 feet. Bohemia has no extensive plains nor any large valleys, the rivers generally flowing through narrow valleys and ravines.

Bohemia is well watered. The principal rivers are the Elbe and its affluents, the Iser, Moldau, and Eger (see *ante*). The chief affluents of the Moldau are the Wotawa, Sazawa, and Beraun. Some small streams on the borders flow towards the Oder and some towards the Danube. Bohemia possesses no lakes of any size, but many small mountain lakes occur in the Bohemian Forest. On the other hand, it has numerous ponds, particularly in the S., amounting in all to several thousands, and occupying an area of more than 150 square miles. It possesses an immense number of mineral springs, several of which are of world-wide fame, and attract numerous visitors from all parts, their waters also constituting an important article of export. The most famous of these are Carlsbad, Marienbad, Franzensbad, Teplitz, Bilin, Püllna, Saidschitz, and Sedlitz.

The climate of Bohemia varies greatly according to the elevation of the surface. In the mountainous regions it is cold, the higher peaks being covered with snow during a great part af the year. In the valleys it is mild and genial, and on the whole salubrious. In Prague the average annual temperature is 46° 8′ Fahr., being for January 29° 6′, and for July 63° 2′. The average annual rainfall in Prague is only 15.7 inches, and in many parts it does not exceed 20 inches. The prevailing wind in Prague is the S.W.

Of the entire area of Bohemia only about 3.1 per cent. is unproductive; not less than 48.1 per cent. is arable; 29 per cent. in wood, 12.1 in meadows and gardens, and 7.7 per cent. in pasture. The principal grain crops are rye, oats, barley, and wheat. The wheat districts lie principally in the N. and W., and the rye districts in the E. and S. The amount of grain annually produced exceeds the home consumption, and usually affords over 1,700,000 bushels for export. Potatoes are extensively grown and form a chief article of food with the poor in the Erzgebirge, the Riesengebirge, and other parts. The beet-root is also largely cultivated, for the manufacture of sugar. Among the other products are flax, hemp, and hops—the chief hop districts being the circles of Eger, Saaz, and Leitmeritz. The low lands along the Eger, and the middle and lower valleys of the Elbe, are the most fertile parts of the country. Fruits, especially plums, are largely grown and exported. Vineyards are only found in a few favoured localities, and altogether do not occupy 1000 acres. The forests furnish annually a large amount of timber for building purposes and also firewood. The rearing of cattle is extensively carried on in certain parts, but the cattle generally are of inferior kinds. About one-half of the sheep, however, are of superior breeds, and produce large quantities of excellent wool. Many of the horses, too, are of improved races.

Bohemia is particularly rich in minerals. About 329 cwt. of silver are annually obtained, chiefly at Pribram and Joachimsthal, 1,340,000 cwt. of iron, 4600 cwt. of copper, 7500 cwt. of lead, 630 cwt. of zinc, 6450 cwt. of sulphur, 154,000 cwt. of vitriol, 27,000 cwt. of alum, and in lesser quantities bismuth and antimony. The amount of coal annually obtained is about 2,000,000 tons, besides about 1,700,000 tons of brown coal; and there also occur in certain parts extensive layers of peat. Precious stones are likewise found in the N.E. mountains, as garnets, sapphires, chalcedonies, opals, &c.

Bohemia ranks as the first manufacturing province in the Monarchy. The density of the population, the fertility of the soil, the abundance of water-power, and the presence of coal and timber, have all contributed to this result. The chief seats of manufacturing industry are in the northern parts of the province, although certain branches of industry extend over the whole country. The value of the manufactured products must at least exceed 22,000,000*l.* annually. The chief manufactures are woollen, linen, and cotton stuffs, and glass. The most important of these is the woollen manufacture, of which there are about 150 establishments in the province. In the Reichenberg district alone, which includes the circles of Leitmeritz, Bunzlau, Jiczin, and Königgrätz, it employs more than 25,000 hands, and the value of the goods annually produced exceeds 1,800,000*l.* These goods are not only sold throughout the Monarchy, but are also largely exported to Italy, the Levant, and North America. In the linen manufacture Bohemia excels all the other provinces. It employs over 52,000 hands, and the value of the goods produced exceeds 3,000,000*l.* annually. Its principal seat is Rumburg, and the surrounding district. There are over 80 spinning-factories for the manufacture of cotton, with more than 540,000 spindles, and producing annually over 120,000 cwt. of yarn. Its principal seat is Reichenberg and its neighbourhood.

Bohemia is particularly distinguished for its glass manufactures, the chief seats of which are Haida, Gablonz, Steinschönau, &c. The annual value exceeds 1,100,000*l.* The iron industry is also considerable, and the value of wrought and cast iron annually produced exceeds 150,000*l.* Machinery is largely made in and around Prague, the annual value being about 450,000*l.* Among the other industrial products, for some of which Bohemia ranks first among the provinces of the Monarchy, are beetroot sugar, leather, paper, porcelain and earthenware, beer, and chemicals.

The productiveness of its soil and the extent of its manufactures naturally give rise to an active trade, which is farther favoured by excellent roads and a number of railways running in different directions. The river navigation, however, is not considerable, being confined to the Elbe and the Moldau. The annual value of the exports amounts to about 2,200,000*l.*, and of the imports to 2,000,000*l.*, while the value of the goods in transit is not much less than the two together. The principal imports are salt, from Upper Austria, colonial produce, and raw materials for manufacture; and the chief exports are its various articles of manufacture, corn, and other agricultural products, and timber. Almost all the colonial and foreign products that come into the Monarchy, through Hamburg, and Bremen, pass through Prague.

Of the population about 61 per cent. are Czechs, 37 per cent. Germans, and 2 per cent. Jews. About 96 per cent. are Roman Catholics, and 2 per cent. Protestants. Of the adult population over 41 per cent. are engaged in agriculture and in the forests, $25\frac{1}{4}$ per cent. in the manufactures (10 per cent. in the textile fabrics, and 6 per cent in the metals), nearly 3 per cent. in trade and commerce, and $6\frac{3}{4}$ per cent. in domestic service.

Bohemia takes its name from the Boii, a Celtic people

who inhabited the country at an early period. They were subdued by the Marcomanni, and these in turn were displaced by the Czechs, a Slavonic race, in the 5th century. In the latter part of the 9th century the King of Moravia subdued Bohemia and introduced Christianity. In 895 it became a state of the German empire, and in 1061 the Emperor Henry IV. conferred the title of King of Bohemia on the then Duke of Prague. On the extinction of the male line of this dynasty the country came to be governed by members of the House of Luxemburg, from 1310 to 1437. During the reign of Wenzel IV. (1378—1419), the religious movement under John Huss and Jerome of Prague took its rise. The imprudent measures adopted by the Emperor Sigismund, led to a war in Bohemia, which lasted for 16 years (1419-34) and ended in its becoming an elective kingdom. In 1458 George of Podiebrad, a Protestant nobleman, ascended the throne and reigned 13 years. His successor, Ladislaus (1471—1516) was elected (1490) to the throne of Hungary and removed his residence to Buda. He was succeeded by his son Lewis, after whose death in 1626 Hungary and Bohemia passed into the hands of Ferdinand I. of Austria who in 1547 declared Bohemia to be a hereditary possession, and from that time it has formed a part of the Austrian empire.

Prague (Ger. *Prag*, Czech, *Praha*), the capital of Bohemia, is situated nearly in the centre of the province, on both sides of the river Moldau, 154 miles N.W. of Vienna, and 75 miles S. by E. of Dresden, with both of which cities it is connected by railway. For extent and population it is the third city in the Monarchy, and for beauty of situation, quaintness of architure, and historical associations, it is unrivalled by any other city of Germany. It stands in a valley surrounded on all sides by hills, along the slopes of which it ascends in such a way as to appear to rise from the water's edge, with building towering above building and spire above spire. It contains numerous magnificent edifices, and more than 60 singularly formed spires. It consists of five divisions or parts—the *Altstadt* or old town, *Neustadt* or new town, Josephstadt, Kleinseite, and Hradschin. The two last are on the left, the others on the right bank, of the river. The most populous is the old town, in which business is principally carried on, while the Kleinseite is the aristocratic quarter, the seat of the courts and government officials. The river is here crossed by seven bridges; the oldest and most frequented is the Karlsbrücke, founded by the emperor Charles IV. in 1357. It is 1596 feet long, and 32 feet wide, with a tower at each end, and rests on 16 arches. It is adorned with 28 statues, among which is one of St. John of Nepomuk, the patron saint of Bohemia, who is said to have been cast into the river from this bridge by order of the King Wenzel in 1383. Thousands of pilgrims from all parts of Bohemia, Moravia, and Silesia, assemble here annually on St. John's day (16th May). Above this is an iron suspension bridge, 1508 feet long and 21 feet wide, erected in 1841, leading from Kleinseite over the beautiful island of Schützen to the new town. The Franz-Joseph-Brücke, also a suspension bridge, leading from the old town to the grand new promenade on the left bank was opened in 1868, and is 938 feet long, and 36 feet wide. Along the right bank of the river extends a magnificent quay, on which stands a bronze equestrian statue of the emperor Francis I. Among the principal buildings are the imperial palace erected by the emperor Charles IV. in 1333, after the plan of the Louvre in Paris, and several times restored; the magnificent cathedral of St. Vitus, somewhat resembling that of Cologne, begun in 1343, and still unfinished, containing many beautiful monuments, among which a splendid mausoleum of the Kings of Bohemia, and a silver monument to St. John of Nepomuk; the beautiful church of St. Nicholas; the Teinkirche, with a monument to Tycho Brahe, who is buried here; the Loretto chapel, an exact copy of the famous Santa Casa in Italy; the old town Rathhaus, rebuilt in 1840 in the old German style on the site of an older edifice, of which the great tower, with a curious old clock, still remains; the new town Rathhaus erected in 1370, and greatly altered 1806; the archiepiscopal palace; the Czernin palace, one of the largest in Germany, now used as a barracks; the Nostitz palace, with a library, picture-gallery, and collection of coins; the Fürstenberg palace, with a large library and art collections; the palace of Wallenstein; the Schwarzenberg palace; and several others. There are in all 62 Roman Catholic and 3 Protestant Churches, and 10 synagogues, one of which is very old; and there is also a curious old Jewish burying-ground. The rich abbey of Strahow contains many interesting objects, and has a valuable library of 90,000 volumes. The university of Prague was founded by the Emperor Charles IV., in 1348, after the model of that of Paris, and endowed with many important privileges. In the beginning of the 15th century it numbered over 20,000 students, but it soon after declined. In 1876 it had 172 professors and teachers, and 1885 students. It has a library of 142,000 volumes, a mineralogical and zoological museum, botanic garden, observatory, pathological museum, chemical laboratory, &c. There are a great many other educational institutions, and a number of literary and scientific societies. The Polytechnic Institution has lately been completely reorganized, and has now a Czech and a German division, the former having 47 teachers and 708 scholars, the latter 41 teachers and 567 scholars. The national museum has collections of natural history and antiquities, and a library of 30,000 volumes. Prague has two theatres, a German and a Bohemian. The grand new National Bohemian theatre, the foundation-stone of which was laid in 1867, will, when finished, be one of the finest edifices in the city. The principal promenades within the city are the people's garden, the imperial pleasure-garden, and the Schützen and Sophia Islands in the river. The old city walls and fortifications are now being removed.

Prague is one of the principal manufacturing cities, and one of the most important places of trade in the Monarchy. Among the principal manufactures are cotton, linen, and woollen goods, leather, gloves, chemicals, mathematical and musical instruments, machinery, cabinet-work, carriages, &c. It is the centre of almost the whole trade of Bohemia, for here a number of different railways meet and the River Moldau, is navigable. The population in 1869 amounted to 157,713, of whom about three-fifths were Czechs; but the capital, enterprise, and learning, are chiefly among the Germans.

Pilsen, which after Prague is the largest town in Bohemia, is situated at the influx of the Mies into the Beraun, 60 miles W.S.W. of Prague. It is generally well-built, and has several handsome churches, a Rathhaus, theatre, and other public buildings. It is an active manufacturing town, having coal-mines and iron-works, breweries and chemical works, and carries on a very important trade. Four large yearly fairs are held here. Population, 23,681.

Reichenberg, an important manufacturing centre, is situated on the Neisse, 56 miles N.N.E. of Prague. The streets are generally narrow and irregular, but it contains a number of good buildings. The great manufacture of the town and neighbourhood, for which they are widely known, is woollen stuffs, the annual value of which exceeds 1,200,000*l*. Cotton spinning is also largely carried on. Population, 22,394.

Budweis, the capital of a circle of the same name, and the see of a bishop, is situated at the mouth of the Malsch in the Moldau, 75 miles S. of Prague. Among the principal buildings are the cathedral, bishop's palace, Rathhaus, and theatre. It has a diocesan school of theology, gymnasium, and other schools; and a number of benevolent institutions. It carries on an active trade in coal, salt, and corn, the Moldau being navigable up to this point; and it is also connected with Linz by railway. Population, 17,413.

Eger, the capital of a circle of the same name, stands on a rocky eminence on the right bank of the Eger, 94 miles W. of Prague. It consists of a town proper and three suburbs, and has several handsome buildings, including a fine parish church and a spacious town hall. It was formerly strongly fortified, and the ruins of a strong royal castle still exist. In the burgomaster's house, which is still to be seen, Wallenstein was assassinated on 25th February 1634. It is the centre of several railways, and carries on an active trade. The chief manufactures are woollen and cotton goods. Population, 13,463.

MORAVIA (Ger. *Mähren*), *Margraviate of*, is bounded on the N. by Austrian and Prussian Silesia, E. by Austrian Silesia and Hungary, S. by Hungary and Lower Austria, and W. by Bohemia. It lies between lat. 48° 40' and 50° 15' N., and long. 15° 9' and 18° 34' E., and contains an area of 8582 square miles, with 1,997,897 inhabitants.

It is surrounded on three sides by mountains, having the Bohemia-Moravian mountains on the W., the Sudetes with the Gesenke and the Odergebirge on the N. and the Little Carpathians and Beskides on the E. The highest mountains in Moravia are the Sudetes in the N., where some of the summits rise to the height of more than 4500 feet. Of the Carpathian chain on the E. some of the summits exceeds 4000 feet, while of the Bohemia-Moravian mountains in the W., only a few exceed 2000 feet. The interior is generally hilly, sloping gradually towards the S. to the valley of the March, by which almost the whole surface of the province is drained. Moravia thus bears a considerable resemblance to the adjoining province of Bohemia, except that the slopes of Bohemia are directed towards the N., while those of Moravia are towards the S. In this respect Moravia has the advantage of being exposed to the genial influences of the S., and shut in by high mountains on the N. The principal river is the March, which rises in the Spieglitzer Schneeberg, in the N., and flows in a winding course, from N. to S., through the province. Its principal affluent is the Thaya which flows through the southern portion of the territory. Several small streams in the N. flow into the Oder. Moravia has no lakes, but, on the other hand, contains numerous ponds. The climate is on the whole mild and genial. At Brünn, the capital, the average annual temperature is 46.2° Fahr., being in July 63.2°, and in January 27.2°. The average annual fall of rain is 19 inches.

About 96 per cent. of the surface of Moravia is productive, and of this about 53 per cent. is arable (a greater proportion than is found in any of the other provinces), 27 per cent. woods, 10.5 per cent. pastures, 9 per cent. gardens and meadows, and over 1 per cent. vineyards. Its chief wealth lies in its agricultural products. The principal grain crops are oats and rye, but barley and wheat are also largely grown. Although considerably behind in improved agricultural methods, the quantity of grain produced greatly exceeds the home consumption, and is largely exported. Potatoes, peas, beans, beet-root, cabbages and other vegetables, are also largely grown. Flax and hemp are likewise produced. The most fertile tracts are in the centre, particularly the district of Hanna, S. of Olmütz and the low-lying lands on the March and Thaya. Among fruits, the plum is largely grown, and the chestnut-tree flourishes in the S. The vine is mostly confined to the S., and the quantity of wine produced is not large, but some of it is of good quality. Moravia is particularly distinguished for its superior races of sheep, the wool being of the finest quality, and in great demand. Sheep's cheese too, and sheep's whey, are here articles of trade. Cattle and horses are also numerous, and of good qualities. Geese exist in great numbers. Bee culture is extensively carried on, and Moravian wax is noted for its excellence. The mining products are confined to coal, iron, graphite, and alum. None of the precious metals are found here, neither is salt found. Upwards of 15,000,000 cwt. of coal, however, is raised annually, and about 500,000 cwt. of wrought iron, and 250,000 cwt. of cast iron, are annually obtained.

As regards manufactures Moravia ranks high, being surpassed only by Bohemia and Lower Austria. The principal seat of manufacturing industry is the capital, Brünn. The chief manufactures are woollen, linen, and cotton goods, and beet-root sugar. For woollen goods—whether we regard the quantity or varieties, from the coarsest to the finest—Moravia is unequalled by any other province. The annual value is estimated at over 3,000,000*l*. The principal seats of this industry are Brünn, Iglau, Zwittau, and Namiest. The linen manufacture is carried on principally on the borders of Bohemia and Silesia, and between Wischau and Olmütz, and is mostly a domestic industry. The cotton manufacture is carried on principally on the borders of Bohemia, between Zwittau and Schildberg, but likewise in other parts. The manufacture of sugar from beet-root is largely carried on, and is constantly extending. Among the other manufactures are iron and cast-iron wares and machinery, earthenware, glass, leather, paper, beer, brandy, chemicals, and tobacco.

The trade of Moravia is very considerable. It exports its manufactured articles and its natural products, particularly grain, cattle, and wool; and it imports salt, colonial products, and raw materials for manufacture. Important markets are held at Brünn, which are among the most frequented in Austria. There is also a considerable through-traffic carried on, the province being traversed by several lines of railway and having also good roads. The March is navigable to Göding.

Of the population about 72 per cent. are Slavs (Czechs, Slovaks and Wallachians), $25\frac{3}{4}$ per cent. Germans, and $2\frac{1}{4}$ per cent. Jews. About 95 per cent. are Roman Catholics, and 3 per cent. Protestants, the rest being Jews. Of the adult population 48 per cent. are engaged in agriculture and the forests, 21 per cent. in the manufactures, $2\frac{1}{2}$ per cent. in trade and commerce, and over $7\frac{1}{2}$ per cent. in domestic service. Education is very generally diffused among the people.

Brünn, the capital of Moravia, is situated on rising ground between the Schwarzawa and the Zwittawa, just before their confluence, 70 miles N. of Vienna, and 115 miles S.E. of Prague, with both of which cities it is connected by railway. To the west of the town stands the hill of Spielberg, on which is a castle of the same name, formerly used as a State prison, in which the Austrian Baron Trenck and Silvio Pellico were confined. The town is generally well built, and from its elevated position commands extensive views. It has 17 churches, the principal of which are the recently restored Gothic church of St. Jacob, with a monument to Marshal von Souches, the defender of Brünn against the Swedes in 1645; the cathedral church of St. Peter; the beautiful church of the Minorites; the church of the Capuchins, with the tomb of Baron Trenck; and the Gothic parish church erected in the 15th century. Among the principal of the other buildings are the bishop's palace, the Landhaus, Rathhaus, theatre, polytechnic, German gymnasium, and the government upper real school. Its educational institutions are numerous, and include the polytechnic with 35 teachers and 167 scholars, 2 gymnasia, 3 real schools, 3 commercial schools, and several schools for special subjects. It has also a museum with several interesting collections, and a library of 26,000 volumes. It is the seat of the chief legal and administrative courts of the province, of a bishop, and a Protestant consistory, and contains a number of benevolent institutions. The old Jesuits' college is now a barracks.

Brünn is one of the most important manufacturing towns of Austria, and a great seat of the woollen manufacture, whence it is sometimes termed the Austrian Leeds. The woollen goods annually produced are estimated at over 1,750,000*l.* Among its other manufactures are linen and cotton goods, leather, gloves, &c. It is likewise the centre of a very important trade. Of late years this town has been rapidly extending. In 1846, the population amounted to 45,189, in 1857 to 58,809, and in 1869 to 73,771.

Iglau, the town next in size to Brünn, is situated not far from the Bohemian frontier on the river Iglawa, here crossed by a stone bridge, 46 miles W.N.W. of Brünn. It consists of the town proper and three suburbs, and has a large public square and several handsome churches. The great staple manufacture is woollen cloth, which employs a great number of hands within the town and in its vicinity, and forms an important article of trade. It also manufactures leather and tobacco, and four large annual fairs are held here. Population, 20,049.

Prossnitz, stands in a wide and pleasant valley on the brook Romza, in the fertile district of Hanna, 60 miles S.W. of Olmütz. It consists of the town proper and four suburbs, and the inhabitants are principally engaged in the manufacture of woollen cloths; also cotton goods, sugar, and leather. There are likewise a number of distilleries of brandy and rosoglio. Large markets are periodically held here for corn and cattle, this being the principal town of the Hanna district. Population, 15,787.

Olmütz, a strongly fortified town, formerly the capital of Moravia, is situated on the river March, 44 miles N. by E. of Brünn. It is surrounded by walls and ditches, and entered by four gates, and is reckoned one of the strongest places in the Austrian dominions. It was taken by the Swedes during the thirty years' war, but was besieged in vain for seven weeks by Frederick the Great in 1758. The cathedral is a fine Gothic edifice founded in the 14th century by Wenzel III. of Bohemia. The parish church of St. Maurice dates from the 15th century, and contains the largest organ in Moravia. Among the other principal buildings are the archbishop's palace, the Rathhaus, the old university buildings, and the theatre. The university was removed in 1855, but the library, which is here, contains 55,000 volumes. Its chief manufacture is that of woollen stuffs, but linen and cotton goods, and leather are also manufactured. Large cattle markets are held here periodically. Population, 15,229.

SILESIA (Ger. *Schlesien*), *Duchy of*, is the smallest of the provinces of Austria, and is all that remains to it of the former duchy of Silesia, the greater portion of which was seized by Frederick the Great in 1740, and now forms part of Prussia. It is bounded on the N. by Prussian Silesia, E. by Galicia, S. by Hungary and Moravia, and W. by Moravia and Prussian Silesia. It lies between lat. 49° 28' and 50° 26' N., and long. 16° 54' and 19° 1' E., and has an area of 1986 square miles. Population (1869), 511,581.

The surface is for the most part mountainous, particularly in the W. portion, which is traversed by the Gesenke, a branch of the Sudetes. The smaller E. portion lies on the northern declivities of the Beskides. The Gesenke have usually broad bases and rounded summits, while the Beskides generally rise more abruptly and have sharper outlines. Several of the elevations attain the height of 4000 feet above the sea. The Jablunka Pass occurs here and affords communication between Silesia and Hungary. The mountains occur principally in the S., and the land declines towards the N. The lowest portion of the surface is at the outflow of the Oder, where it is 610 feet above the sea. There are no plains of any extent. The principal rivers by which the country is drained are the Oder and Vistula, both of which discharge themselves into the Baltic, but neither of which is here navigable. The chief affluents of the Oder are the Oppa and Olsa, and of the Vistula, the Biela.

About 96 per cent. of the soil is productive, and of this 47 per cent. is arable, 32 per cent. in wood, 10 per cent. in pasture, and 7 per cent. meadows and gardens. Though agriculture is pursued with diligence and with considerable skill, yet owing to the unfavourableness of the climate and backwardness of much of the soil, the quantity of grain produced is not equal to the wants of the people. The principal grain crops are oats and rye, but barley is also grown, and some wheat. Flax is grown in certain parts. The vine is not cultivated, and fruits are not abundant. Silesia, like Moravia, is distinguished for its fine races of sheep, and for the excellence of the wool which they produce. The principal mineral products are coal and iron. As regards coal it is one of the richest provinces of the Monarchy, yielding annually over 20,000,000 cwts. The amount of wrought and cast-iron annually produced, is about 120,000 cwt.

As in Moravia the manufactures of Silesia are principally connected with the working up of its products of wool, flax, and iron. The chief centres of the woollen manufacture are Bielitz, Troppau, Wagstadt, and Jägerndorf, and the value is estimated at over 2,000,000*l*. annually. The linen manufacture is chiefly a domestic industry carried on by the peasants in the Sudetes. The chief seats of the cotton manufacture are around Freudenthal and Wigstadt. The principal centre of the iron manufacture is Ludwigsthal in the Sudetes. Among the other manufactures are beet-root sugar, leather, glass, beer, brandy, chemicals. The trade is chiefly confined to the importation of corn and raw materials for manufacture, and the exportation of manufactured articles. A considerable transit trade is likewise carried on.

Of the population, 51 per cent. are Germans, 20 per cent. Czechs, 28 per cent. Poles, and 1 per cent. Jews. As to religion, 84.5 per cent. are Roman Catholics, and 14 per cent. Protestants. Of the adult population, 43 per cent. are engaged in agriculture and the forests, 25.5 per cent. in the manufactures, 2 per cent. in trade and commerce, and 5.5 per cent. in domestic service. The Silesians are a peaceful, unostentatious, contented people, distinguished by industry and frugality.

Troppau, the capital of Silesia, is pleasantly situated on the right bank of the river Oppa, near the borders of Prussia, and 82 miles N. by E. of Brünn. It has two handsome squares, a fine Gothic parish church built of basalt, a castle, and a tasteful city tower. There are a number of educational and benevolent institutions, a museum with several excellent collections of objects, and a library of 36,000 volumes. The manufacture of woollen stuffs is actively carried on, also those of sugar, paper, rosoglio, &c. Population, 16,608.

GALICIA (Ger. *Galizien*) comprises the kingdom of Galicia and Lodomeria, with the Grand Duchy of Cracow, and the Duchies of Auschwitz and Zator. This territory formerly formed part of the kingdom of Poland, and came to Austria by the partitions of 1772 and 1795, while the Grand Duchy of Cracow was annexed in 1846. It is bounded on the N. by Russian Poland, E. by Russia and Bukowina, S. by Hungary, and W. by Austrian and Prussian Silesia. It lies between lat. 48° and 50° 40' N. and long. 19° 11', and 26° 31' E., and has an area of 30,306 square miles, with a population in 1869 of 5,418,016, being the most extensive and having the largest population of the provinces of Austria Proper.

The whole S. border of Galicia is traversed by the Carpathians which with their branches occupy about one-third of the territory. The Beskides enter the country from Silesia and spread themselves out between the Sola and the Skava. They are separated from the Central Carpathians by the valley of the Dunajec. A small portion of the Tatra range belongs to Galicia, its highest summit here being about 7800 feet. E. of the Poprad begins the Carpathian Waldgebirge, a steep precipitous mountain chain, with some cross valleys and mountain passes, which extends through the rest of the province. Between the Carpathians and the Podolian Highland (an undulating plateau in the neighbourhood of Lemberg) rise the Mazurian hills, which cover the territory from the declivities of the Beskides at Bochnia to the Dniester. The Tarnowitzer or Polish Plain, only extends into Galicia, in the neighbourhood of Cracow. Beyond the Dniester and the Podolian Highland stretches the Plain of Galicia forming part of the Great Plain of N.E. Europe. Galicia is a well-watered country. The principal streams are the Vistula, which receives the rivers of W. Galicia, and empties itself into the Baltic, and the Dniester which conveys the waters of E. Galicia, into the Black Sea. The chief affluents of the Vistula are the Skava, Sola, Dunajec (with its affluent the Poprad), Wisloka, San, and Bug; and of the Dniester, the Stry, Lomnica, Sered, and Podhorze. The Pruth, an affluent of the Danube is an insignificant stream in Galicia. There are no lakes of any size, but numerous small mountain lakes among the Carpathians. There are also numerous ponds abounding in fish. Extensive swamps occur in the upper courses of the San and the Dniester. The climate is severe, particularly in the S., and it also presents the greatest extremes of heat and cold. The winters are long and severe, and the summers short but very warm. At Cracow, the average annual temperature is $45.6°$, being for January, $24.8°$, and for July $61.7°$.

The principal pursuit of the inhabitants is agriculture. About 87 per cent. of the surface is productive, and of this 47 per cent. is arable, 15 per cent. meadows and gardens, 9.5 per cent. pasture-land, and 29 per cent. forests. The soil is in general favourable for agriculture, particularly on the plains in the N. and especially the N.E. The principal grain-crops are oats, barley, and rye, also buckwheat. The produce varies greatly, in bad years not being equal to the home consumption, and in good years affording a large surplus. Much of this, owing to distance from markets and bad means of communication, is used in the manufacture of spirits. In the N.E., wheat, maize, tobacco, and melons, are produced, but the vine fails. Flax and hemp are largely grown, and some hops. The Carpathians are rich in timber, and quantities of it are sent down the Vistula and Dniester, to Danzig and Odessa. The great extent of pasture-land is favourable to cattle-rearing, and young cattle are brought from Russia and Moldavia, to be fattened here, and then sent westward. The rearing of sheep is also actively carried on. The horses are numerous, and though small, are strong and hardy. The most important mineral product of Galicia is salt, of which it possesses almost inexhaustible stores, extending along the outer chain of the Carpathians from Wieliczka to Bukowina. It is found in great abundance at Wieliczka in the W. and Solotwina and Delatyn in the E. In the W. about 1,400,000 cwt. of rock salt are annually obtained, and in the E. about 600,000 cwt. of salt are made from brine. Galicia furnishes about 40 per cent. of the whole salt obtained in the Monarchy. After salt is coal, which is obtained in the district of Cracow and yields annually about 3,350,000 cwt. Among the other mineral products are iron, lead, zinc, sulphur, petroleum, chalk, marble, alabaster, &c.

The linen manufacture is extensively carried on, favoured by the abundance of flax and hemp. In the W. not only the ordinary kinds of linen are made, but also damasks and other finer sorts. In the E. in general only the ordinary kinds are made. In the country parts the peasantry, during the winter season, mostly employ themselves in weaving. Next to linen comes the manufacture of brandy, which, although less largely carried on now than formerly, is still an extensive industry. The leather manufacture is also important, and is extensively carried on. The manufacture of beet-root sugar is likewise an important industry, and some of the works here are among the largest in the Monarchy. Among the other manufactures are woollen cloth (on the borders of Silesia), cotton goods, glass, paper, earthenware, hardware, beer, potash, &c.

The trade of Galicia is mostly in the hands of the Jews. The exports are chiefly the raw products of the country,—corn, salt, cattle, wood, also textile fabrics; the imports chiefly colonial goods and manufactured articles. A considerable transit trade is also carried on through it, between Russia on the one side, and the western provinces of Austria on the other,—in cattle, skins, wool, tallow, &c., from Russia, and manufactured articles from Austria. A chief market for exports and imports is the town of Brody. Galicia is still very deficient in means of communication, the roads are not many, the railways are few, and the only navigable river of consequence is the Vistula.

The population of Galicia is divided into two principal races, the Poles and the Ruthenians, the former being most numerous in the W. portion, the latter in the E. In W. Galicia the Poles number 86 per cent. of the population, the Ruthenians 4, Germans 3, and Jews 7; while in E. Galicia the Ruthenians are 67 per cent., Poles 20, Germans 2, and Jews 11. In the entire province the Ruthenians reckon 45 per cent., and the Poles 43 per cent. In W. Galicia 89 per cent., and in E. Galicia only 21.5 per cent. are Roman Catholics, while in W. Galicia only 4 per cent., and in E. Galicia 66.5 per cent. are Greek Catholics. In Lemberg the Jews form four-tenths of the population, and in Cracow not much less, while in other parts the proportion varies from 5 to 15 per cent. Education is very much neglected here, and of the children of school age only 26.3 per cent. are at school.

Lemberg, the capital of Galicia, is situated in a narrow valley on the Peltow, a small tributary of the Bug, 368 miles E.N.E. of Vienna, and 184 E. of Cracow. It was founded by Leo, prince of Halicz in 1259, and was formerly an important fortress, but its fortifications have been destroyed, and their site laid out in public walks. The town itself is small, containing only about 300 houses, but it is surrounded by 7 suburbs, most, if not all, of which are larger than itself. In the town the streets are generally narrow and irregular, but the suburbs are well laid out and contain many elegant streets. It is the seat of the higher courts and government offices of the province, and also of 3 archbishops, a Roman Catholic, a Greek Catholic, and an Armenian Catholic. Among the principal buildings are the Dominican Church, built on the model of St. Peter's at Rome, and containing a monument to the Countess Borkowska, by Thorwaldsen; the Greek Catholic Metropolitan Church of St. George, a magnificent building in the Italian style; the Latin Cathedral, a Gothic structure, erected in 1344; the New Jewish Synagogue, a handsome edifice, of large size, erected in 1847; the new Rathhaus, a very elegant building, with a lofty tower; the palace of the Roman Catholic Archbishop; the university buildings; and the theatre built by Count Skarbek. The university was founded here by the Emperor Joseph II. in 1784, and reorganized by Francis I. in 1817. In 1876 it had 49 professors and teachers, and 918 students. It has a library of 55,000 volumes, botanic garden, museum, &c. The Polytechnic Institute has 29 teachers, and 260 scholars. The Ossilinski National Museum contains valuable collections of objects, and a library of 62,000 volumes. Lemberg is the principal manufacturing and commercial town in the province. Its moie important manufactures are woollen and cotton stuffs, leather, hardware, rosoglio, vinegar, and candles; and in the vicinity is a large government tobacco factory. A great part of the trade of the province centres here, but much of it is merely transit, and it is principally in the hands of Jews. Three annual fairs held here are much frequented. Lemberg has risen into importance chiefly since it came into the hands of Austria. In 1772 the population little exceeded 20,000, in 1808 it had risen to 41,493, and in 1869 it was 87,109.

Cracow (Ger. *Krakau*), formerly the coronation city, and a frequent residence of the Polish kings, afterwards capital of the republic of the same name, and now the chief town of W. Galicia, is pleasantly situated in a fertile valley, on the left bank of the Vistula, and connected with the opposite bank by the Francis-Joseph Bridge, 266 miles N.N.E. of Vienna. It has lately been strongly fortified, being surrounded by ramparts and ditches, and protected by detached forts on the neighbouring heights. It contains numerous interesting buildings, among which are the former residence castle of the Polish kings, erected in the 14th century, but several times restored, and now used as a barracks and military hospital; the magnificent cathedral, containing numerous beautiful monuments; the Gothic church of the Virgin Mary, founded in 1226; the church of St. Peter, built after the model of that at Rome; the church of St. Anne, with a monument to the Astronomer Copernicus; the Rathhaus; university buildings; government offices, &c. The university was founded in 1549, and in 1876 had 75 professors and teachers, and 587 students. It has a library of 140,000 volumes, a botanic garden, observatory, &c. Cracow has also a polytechnic academy, and a number of other educational, as well as scientific and benevolent institutions, and is the seat of a bishop. The principal manufactures are cloth and leather; and a very large trade is carried on in corn, wood, salt, wine, &c. Two large annual fairs are held here, and the neighbourhood is very interesting. Population, 49,835.

Brody, a free commercial town, is situated near the borders of Russia, 52 miles E.N.E. of Lemberg. The town is ill-built and dirty, and the houses mostly of wood. It has a castle, one Roman Catholic and two Greek churches, three synagogues, and a theatre. Since 1779 it has enjoyed the privilege of being a free commercial town, but a law has just passed (1879) by which it is to be brought within the customs limits. The manufactures are chiefly linen and leather; and it carries on a very extensive transit trade with Russia, Moldavia, Wallachia, and Turkey, on the one side, and Austria and Germany on the other. Population 18,733, more than three-fourths of whom are Jews, whence it is sometimes called the German Jerusalem.

BUKOWINA, *Duchy of*, formerly the most S.E. portion of Galicia, but now a separate province of Austria, is bounded on the N. by Galicia, E. by Russia and Moldavia, S. by Moldavia and Transylvania, and W. by Transylvania, Hungary, and Galicia. It lies between lat. 47° 14' and 48° 40' N., and long. 24° 34' and 26° 22' E., having an area of 4034 square miles, and (in 1869) 511,964 inhabitants.

The territory of Bukowina is for the most part mountainous. The W. portion is traversed by the Carpathians, which send their branches eastward, between the courses of the principal rivers, where they form undulating plateaus. The highest summits are in the adjacent lands, but here some of the peaks rise to the height of 6000 feet. There are no plains of great extent, but some of the river valleys are of considerable size. The lowest land is on the Dniester and Pruth. The country is for the most part densely wooded, and the river valleys are in many parts covered with swamps. The most important river is the Dniester, which forms the boundary on the N. After it is the Pruth, and then the Sereth, which after leaving the province receives the Suczawa, Moldawa, and the golden Bistritz, all rivers of Bukowina. In summer they usually contain little water, but in spring or after much rain they frequently overflow their banks, and cause much damage. The climate is milder than in Galicia, but is still severe, though salubrious. At Czernowitz, the capital, the average annual temperature is 45.2°, being for January 24.8°, and for July 64°. In summer violent thunder-storms and heavy rains are common, but autumn is usually dry and pleasant.

About 11.5 per cent. of the land is unproductive, 39.7 in

woods and forests, 24.9 arable, 11.7 meadows and gardens, and 12.2 pastures. The soil is in general good, particularly in the valley of the Suczawa, in the Sereth plain, and in the low-lying parts between the Pruth and the Dniester, but in general there is much room for improvement in the methods of cultivation. The principal grain crop is maize, which constitutes an important article of food. Besides this, oats, rye, wheat, buckwheat, potatoes, and some flax and hemp are grown. The rearing of cattle and sheep is extensively carried on, and at Radautz is a government military stud. The principal mineral products are iron, copper, and salt. Gold is found in the sands of the Bistritz, and silver and lead were formerly obtained. The manufactures are all on a limited scale, and are chiefly for the supply of the home demand. They include woollen and linen goods, wooden iron and copper wares, machines, brandy, beer, paper, glass, and leather. A considerable trade is carried on with Moldavia and Bessarabia, and a still more important transit trade favoured by the railway which passes through the country from Lemberg, through Czernowitz, to Jassy and Odessa. The population is a very mixed one. Exclusive of the gipsies, who are pretty numerous, there are reckoned 8 distinct nationalities, and as many religions. About 41 per cent. are Ruthenians, 38 per cent. Roumanians, 8 per cent. Germans, 1 per cent. Poles, 1.7 per cent. Magyars, 9.5 per cent. Jews, .5 per cent. Armenians, and less than .5 per cent. Czechs. As to religion, 10.5 per cent. are Roman Catholics, 3.2 Greek Catholics, 73 per cent. Oriental Greeks, 2.2 per cent. Protestants, .5 per cent. Armenians, and 9.5 Jews. No fewer than 78.5 per cent. of the adult population are engaged in agriculture and the forests, 5.5 per cent. in manufacturing and industrial pursuits, 2.2 per cent. in trade and commerce, and 3 per cent. in domestic service.

Czernowitz, the capital of Bukowina, is pleasantly situated on an elevation on the right bank of the Pruth, which is here crossed by a bridge, 472 feet long, 165 miles S. by E. of Lemberg. It consists of the city proper and four suburbs, and is the seat of an Oriental Greek archbishop, and the chief courts of the province. The principal buildings are the new Greek cathedral, and the archiepiscopal palace. In 1875 a new university was established here which in 1876 had 29 professors and teachers; and 209 students. The theological faculty is for the Oriental Greek church. There are likewise a gymnasium, real school, and other educational institutions. The manufactures are not considerable, but it carries on a large trade. Population, 33,884.

DALMATIA (Ger. *Dalmatien*), *Kingdom of*, is the most southern province of Austria, lying between 42° 10′ and 44° 10′ N. lat. and 14° 46′ and 18° 59′ E. long. It extends along the E. shore of the Adriatic, and is about 345 miles in length, while its greatest breadth does not exceed 45 miles. It is bounded on the N. by Croatia, E. by Bosnia, Herzegovina, and Montenegro, S. by Turkish Albania, and W. by the Adriatic. Area (including the adjacent islands), 4938 square miles. Population (1869), 442,796.

The surface is for the most part mountainous or hilly. A mountain range in the N. separates it from Croatia, and rises to the height of 5700 feet. Along the E. border running parallel with the coast are the Dinaric Alps, of which Mount Dinara is 5956 feet high. The highest mountain in the country however, is Orien in the neighbourhood of the bay of Cattaro, 6226 feet high. The mountains are for the most part composed of limestone, and present a bleak and barren aspect. Many other parts of the country are in like manner rugged and barren, being of a similar nature to the Karst country. The coast is steep and rocky, and is intersected by numerous bays forming excellent havens. The islands present the same leading features as the mainland. The rivers are few in number, have short courses, are rapid, and form frequent waterfalls. The principal are the Zermagna, Kerka, Cettina, and Narenta. The lakes are numerous, but with the exception of lake Vrana which is near the coast and whose waters are brackish, they are mostly dry in summer. There are also numerous swamps

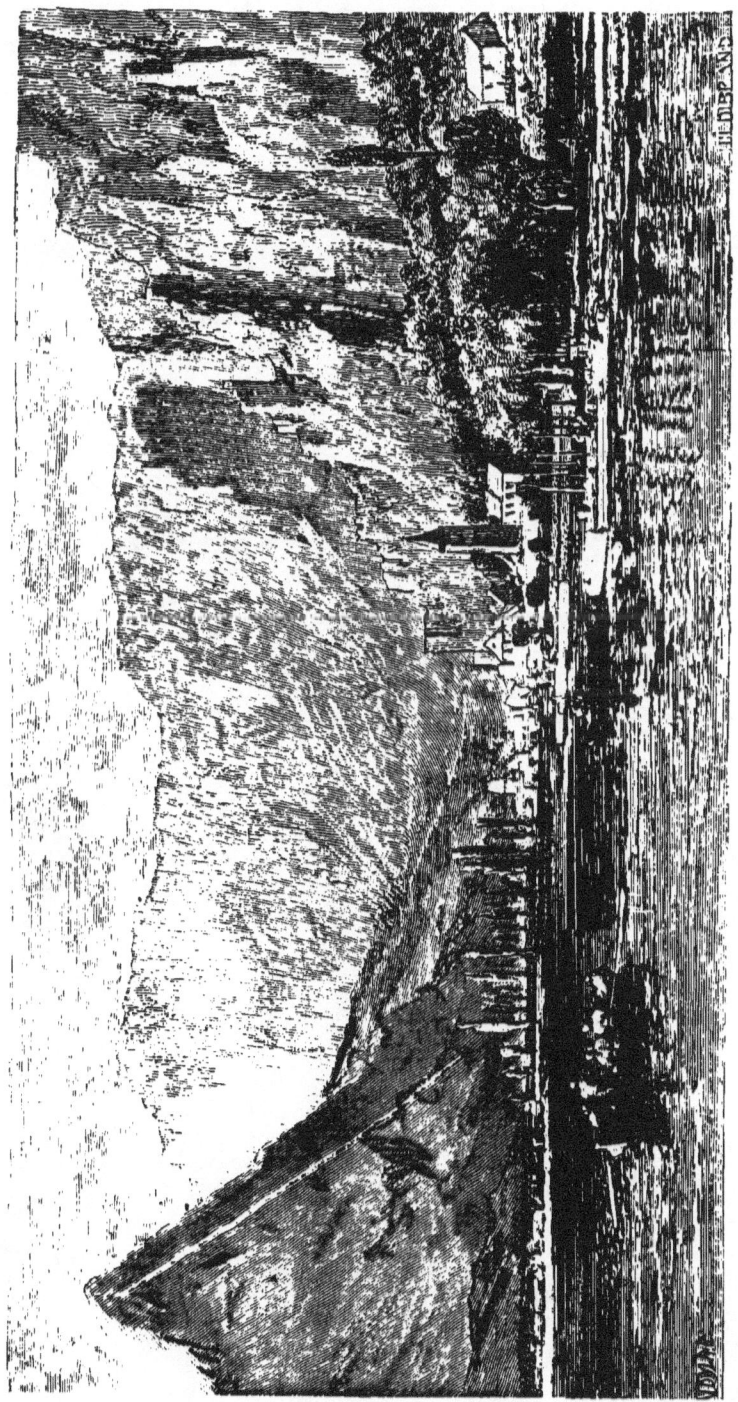

THE ADRIATIC COAST.

and marshes. The climate of Dalmatia is in general warmer than that of any other part of the Monarchy, and except in the neighbourhood of the swamps it is salubrious and favourable to long life, the heat being tempered by the mild sea breezes. The average annual temperature at Zara is $55.5°$, being in January $41.7°$ and in July $70°$. The African sirocco however, makes itself occasionally felt here. The people are principally engaged in agriculture, cattle-rearing, fishing, and navigation. Only about 3.6 per cent. of the land is reckoned as unproductive, but much of the pasture-land, which amounts to 56.5 per cent. is little better than waste. The arable land is 10.9 per cent., vineyards 5.4, gardens and meadows 1, and woods and forests 22.6 per cent. Agriculture is in a very backward state, and the amount of grain produced is not equal to the home consumption. The chief grain-crops are barley and maize, but wheat, oats, and rye, are also grown. About 16,000,000 gallons of wine are annually produced, and a considerable quantity of olive oil. The principal fruits are apples, pears, plums, peaches, apricots, figs, almonds, lemons, oranges, pomegranates. The cattle and sheep are numerous but of inferior qualities, and none of the other provinces have so many goats. The rearing of the silkworm has of late years been making rapid progress, favoured by the government causing to be distributed, free, annually, hundreds of thousands of mulberry-trees. Fish are numerous on the coast, and afford employment to many of the inhabitants. The mineral products of Dalmatia are unimportant. The principal are brown coal and asphalt, but neither in large quantities. In some places, however, a considerable quantity of salt is obtained by evaporation from sea-water, amounting annually to about 100,000 cwts.

The manufactures are few and unimportant. The most important is the distillation of spirits and liqueurs, of which the most famous is Maraschino. Manufactures of coarse woollen stuffs, leather, and soap, are also carried on. In several of the ports ship and boat-building is actively pursued.

The trade of Dalmatia is very considerable, the chief exports being olive oil, wine, figs, liqueurs, raw hides, wool, fish, and sea salt; and the imports corn, flour, various kinds of woven and manufactured goods, tobacco, cattle, &c. In 1876 the exports amounted to 816,000*l*., and the imports to 1,377,200*l*. A large overland trade is carried on with Bosnia, Herzegovina, Montenegro, &c. At present Dalmatia forms a customs district by itself, but it is about to be included within the general customs limits.

Of the population 89 per cent. are Morlaks—a Servian race inhabiting the interior—and 10.5 per cent. Italians, living on the coast, the rest being Albanians and Jews. About 82 per cent. are Roman Catholics, and 17.7 per cent. belonging to the Oriental Greek Church. Of the adult population 50 per cent. are employed in connexion with the land, 3.7 in the manufactures, 2.5 per cent. in trade and navigation, and 7.5 per cent. in domestic service. The Dalmatians are a tall and handsome race of men, bold and brave as seamen and soldiers, hospitable to strangers, and great lovers of freedom. They are however also said to be lazy, dissipated, deceitful, addicted to robbery.

Zara, the capital of Dalmatia, is situated on a long narrow tongue of land, so that it is surrounded on three sides by the sea, and on the E. side, where it is connected with the land, a canal has been cut, and thus it actually stands upon an island. It is 129 miles S.S.E. of Trieste, and prior to 1873 was strongly fortified. Of the gates, the sea-gate has been constructed out of the remains of an ancient Roman triumphal arch, and the land-gate is adorned with columns. The principal streets are wide and regular, but the others are mostly narrow, unpaved, and dirty. The cathedral is a handsome building in the Byzantine style, erected in the beginning of the thirteenth century. Zara is the seat of the principal courts of the province, of a Roman Catholic archbishop, and a Greek bishop. It has a Roman Catholic theological seminary, gymnasium, real school, hospital, theatre, people's garden, &c. It is, however, ill-supplied with water. The manufactures are unimportant, but there are several distilleries producing large quantities of Maraschino. A considerable trade is carried on, and fishing is actively pursued. The harbour on the N.E. of the town is spacious and secure, able to receive ships of war of moderate size. In 1877, 1324 ships of 200,838 tons entered, and 1316 ships of 200,734 tons left the harbour. Population, 20,849.

Spalato is situated on a small peninsula, on the N.E. side of the strait which seperates the Islands of Solta and Brazza from the mainland, 82 miles S.E. of Zara. It consists of an old and new town and several suburbs. The old town occupies the place of the vast palace built for himself by the Emperor Diocletian after he resigned the reins of government, A.D. 304. It was quadrangular in form, covering nearly eight acres, and contained within its precints temples, theatres, and other edifices. When the neighbouring town of Salona, then large and populous, was destroyed by the Avars in 640, the inhabitants fled for refuge into the palace, and settled there, forming a small town. Hence the name *Palatium*, afterwards *Spalatium*, now *Spalato*. Considerable portions of the old palace still exist. The temple of Jupiter has been turned into a cathedral, and that of Æsculapius is now the baptistery of St. John. It has a museum of antiquities, and the neighbourhood is rich in Roman remains. A considerable trade is carried on both by sea and land, in corn, wine, oil, fruit, cattle, &c. The harbour is safe and commodious. The principal manufactures are woollen cloth, leather, silk, candles and rosoglio. Population, 18,261.

Sebenico is situated on a bay of the same name, at the mouth of the Kerka, 42 miles S E. of Zara. It is built in the form of an amphitheatre, on the side of a hill, and its principal building is the cathedral, a Byzantine Gothic edifice of the fifteenth century, the interior of which is much admired. Excellent wine is produced in the neighbourhood, and the inhabitants are actively employed in fishing. A considerable trade is carried on. Population, 15,115.

Ragusa, formerly the capital of a small republic of the same name, is picturesquely situated at the foot and on the steep slopes of Mount Sergia, on a peninsula 216 miles S.E. of Zara. It is surrounded by old walls with towers and bastions, and is protected by several forts. The streets are mostly very narrow, but the houses are substantially built of stone. Among the principal buildings are the government palace, custom-house, cathedral, and church of the Jesuits. The harbour at the town is very small, the proper harbour, which is excellent, being at Gravosa, where an important trade in wine, oil, silk, &c., is carried on. The manufactures are inconsiderable, being chiefly silk and woollen goods and leather. The town has repeatedly suffered from earthquakes, particularly in 1667, when 5000 persons are said to have lost their lives, and a great part of the town was reduced to ruins. Ragusa was originally founded in the middle of the seventh century by fugitives from the neighbouring Epidaurus or old Ragusa, when that city was destroyed by the Slavonians. In 1358 it was the capital of a small republic under the protection of Hungary. It was taken possession of by Napoleon in 1806, and incorporated in the Kingdom of Illyria in 1811. In 1814 it became a part of Austria. Population, 8678.

HUNGARY (Ger. *Ungarn;* Magyar, *Magyar-Orszag*), *Kingdom of,* is bounded on the N. by Silesia and Galicia, E. by Bukowina and Transylvania, S. by Servia, Slavonia, and Croatia, and W. by Styria, Lower Austria, and Moravia. It lies between 44° 41' and 49° N. lat., and 16° 20' and 25° 8' E. long.; has an area of 87,044 square miles, and a population (in 1869) of 11,117,623.

The surface forms part of the great basin of the Middle Danube, and is partly mountainous, partly flat territory. The most mountainous part is Northern Hungary. The Carpathians commence on the Danube near the mouth of the March, and describe a great curve along the borders of Hungary, so as to bound it on the N.W., N., and N.E. On entering Transylvania they form several branches, one of which bounds Hungary on

A STREET IN RAGUSA.

the E., and overruns that part of the country lying E. of the Theiss. In like manner, in other parts, branches of the Carpathians spread themselves over the country lying adjacent to the main chain. The mountains, which are rich in ores of all kinds, and in rock salt, are well wooded and enclose numerous beautiful fertile and vine-growing valleys. In the W. of Hungary prolongations of the Noric and Carnic Alps enter the country and extend as far as the Danube, forming the Leithagebirge, Bakony Forest, Vertesgebirge, &c. Few of the elevations here rise to the height of more than 2000 feet; S. of this, beyond the Platten lake, and between the Drave and the Szarviz, is a hilly country, which attains its highest elevation in the Fünfkirchen group (1300 feet), partly richly wooded, partly occupied by vineyards and fertile fields, interpersed with numerous towns and villages.

The interior of the country is for the most part composed of extensive plains, of which the principal are the Little or Upper and the Great or Lower Hungarian Plains. The Little Hungarian Plain extends on both sides of the Danube, between Pressburg and Komorn, having an area of about 3400 square miles, and a general elevation of 360 feet. It is surrounded on all sides by mountains, and is, no doubt, the bed of an ancient lake, the remains of which we find in the Neusiedler lake, with its marshy borders. The plain is, for the most part, very fertile, particularly the island of Schütt, in the Danube, which is sometimes called the "Golden Garden of Hungary." To the N. and W. there also extend flat and hilly tracts presenting the most varied and fertile aspect—cultivated fields interspersed with vineyards, gardens, and orchards. These tracts extend along the river valleys, even to the Carpathians, the Alps, and the Bakony Forest. Very different from this is the great Hungarian Plain, which lies to the E., extending from the Bakony Forest on the W., to Transylvania on the E., and from the Carpathians on the N. to the Danube on the S. It has an area of about 38,000 square miles, and a general elevation of from 150 to 200 feet, rising in some parts to

400 or 500 feet above the sea. This too is no doubt the bed of an ancient lake. It is traversed by the rivers Danube and Theiss, the former flowing very slowly and forming numerous islands, the latter pursuing a very winding course, and both having on their banks numerous swamps and marshes. Much of this region is a dry and arid desert, covered with drifting sand; in other parts are wide expanses of moor and moss; yet there are not wanting in parts fertile fields and good pasture-land. It is remarkably destitute of trees and stones.

The principal rivers of Hungary are the Danube and Theiss. The former receives from the left, the March, Waag, Gran, Eipel, Theiss and Temes; and from the right the Leitha, Raab, Szarviz, and Drave. The Theiss receives from the right the Borzova, Hernad, Eger, and Zagyva; and from the left the Szamos, Körös and Maros. The more important of these rivers have been already described. The principal lakes are the Balaton or Platten, and the Neusiedler Lake already noticed. The mineral springs are numerous, some being hot, others endowed with important medicinal qualities. Among the best known and most frequented, are those at Teplitz near Trentschin, Füred, Bartfeld, Parad, Buda, Grosswardein and Mehadia.

The climate varies greatly in different parts of the country. In the N. among the Carpathians, the winter is long and cold, snow beginning to fall in September, and continuing to May or June; whereas in the S. the trees blossom as early as March, and in June the heat becomes oppressive, reaching its culminating point in July. At Buda, near the centre of the kingdom, the average annual temperature is 49.4° Fahr., being for January 29.8°, and for July 67.5°. The annual rainfall here is about 16 inches, but in some parts it exceeds 30 inches. In general the climate is subject to great and sudden changes, the thermometer sometimes rising or falling 30° or 40° in two or three hours.

The unproductive land of Hungary amounts to about 16 per cent. of the whole. Of the productive land 40.5 per cent. is arable, 27 per cent. woods and forests, 17 per cent. pastureland, 14 per cent. meadows and gardens, and about 1.6 vineyards. Agriculture has made great improvements of late years, and is now much more carefully prosecuted than formerly, especially on the large farms. The principal corn-producing districts are in the two plains, particularly the part of the great plain lying beyond the Theiss, and the Banat, which produces the finest wheat in the country. In some parts, however, the crops frequently suffer from drifting sand and the overflowing of the rivers. The principal grain crops are wheat, rye, maize, oats and barley. Rye is everywhere cultivated, especially in the N. by the Slavs, and maize especially in the E. and S. The quantity of grain annually produced is estimated at more than 200,000,000 bushels, which affords a considerable amount for exportation, after meeting the home wants. Among the other products, tobacco occupies an important place, and much of it is of superior quality. It is estimated that about 1,000,000 cwt. are annually produced. Hemp of good quality and in large quantity is grown in the S. Flax is also grown, but not to the same extent. The hops grown do not come up to the home demand for that article. The culture of rape-seed and beet-root is extending. The quantity of fruit produced, although large, is not equal to what might be expected, looking at the favourable conditions of soil and climate. The principal fruits are apples, pears, and cherries in the N., and figs, almonds, and olives in the S. Plums, apricots, walnuts, and chestnuts are generally grown. The country is particularly noted for its melons, which are extensively cultivated.

Hungary in proportion to its extent is a great wine producing country, and much of it is of very superior quality. The amount annually produced is estimated at over 220,000,000 gallons; and among the best sorts are Tokay, Menescher, Ruster, Schomlauer, Szexarder, Ofner, Visontaer, &c. According to the last census, Hungary contained 1,700,000 horses, small indeed, but active and hardy; 3,600,000 cattle; 12,500,000 sheep; and 3,200,000 swine; besides goats, asses, and mules.

The sheep yield 235,000 cwt. of wool, besides which the silkworm produces 6400 cwt. of cocoons, and bees about 196,000 cwt. of honey and wax. Many of the rivers and lakes afford excellent fishing, and good shooting is also to be had.

Hungary is particularly rich in minerals of various kinds, being in this respect, one of the most favoured countries in Europe. Gold and silver ores are obtained chiefly at Schemnitz, Kremnitz, and Schmöllnitz in the W. Carpathians, and Nagy-Banya and Oravicza (in the Banat) in the E. and S. Carpathians. About 21,862 oz. of gold, and 964,500 oz. of silver are annually obtained from the mines, besides small quantities of gold obtained from the sand of certain rivers by washing. The principal copper-mines are in the neighbourhood of Schmöllnitz, and the quantity annually obtained exceeds 40,000 cwt. Upper Hungary is rich in iron, which ranks next in quality to that of Styria. It is principally obtained in the countries of Sohl, Gömör and Zips; and the annual amount is 1,700,000 cwt. of wrought, and 670,000 cwt. of cast iron. In 1855 the quantity of coal raised was 3,500,000 cwt., and it now exceeds 14,000,000 cwt. The principal coal-mines are at Fünfkirchen and Oravicza. Salt is obtained in the Marmaros to the amount of about 1,000,000 cwt. annually. Among the other metals and minerals are lead, cobalt, nickel, soda, saltpetre, alum, Glauber salts, &c. Various kinds of precious stones are found, the opals (in Saroser county) being especially famous.

Hungary does not rank high as a manufacturing country. Indeed in this respect it is far behind, although of late years it has been making considerable advances, and will no doubt continue to do so, for it enjoys many facilities for carrying on flourishing manufactures. At present the manufactures do not meet the wants of the people. The principal seats are in the W. and N., and industry is more directed to the preparation of the raw materials than to the production of finished articles. The most extended industry is the preparation of leather. The linen industry has its chief seat among the Slovaks of Upper Hungary, but it is only on the W. borders that good fabrics are made. The woollen manufacture, notwithstanding the quantity and excellence of the wool produced is of small extent. The iron manufacture flourishes chiefly in N. Hungary and is rapidly progressing. Among the other manufactures the chief are paper, glass, porcelain, beet-root sugar, brandy, beer, tobacco, and chemicals.

The external as well as the internal trade of Hungary is very considerable. The surplus products of the country, particularly corn, wine, wool, and cattle, are exported, while various sorts of manufactured goods and colonial products are imported. The external trade has very much increased since the removal of the customs restrictions by which it was hampered, and the improved means of communication. At the end of 1876, Hungary (including Transylvania, Croatia, and Slavonia) had 4142 miles of railway in operation, and 87 miles in course of construction. The navigable length of the rivers and canals was 1876 miles, and there were 14,000 miles of made roads. Still the trade of Hungary suffers much from want of more adequate means of communication, and with the extension of these the trade will be improved. At present the principal trade of the country is carried on at the numerous fairs, which are from time to time held in different parts of the country. There are more than 900 places where these fairs are held, but the most important are in Pesth, Debeczin, Arad and Szegedin. Many of these fairs are for special objects, as horses, cattle, wool, granite, &c.

Of the population 43 per cent. are Magyars $16\frac{1}{4}$ Slovaks, 13 Germans, $11\frac{1}{4}$ Roumanians, $6\frac{1}{2}$ Serbians, $4\frac{1}{4}$ Ruthenians, and $4\frac{1}{2}$ Jews. The remainder are made up of various nationalities, Slovens, Croatians, Gipsies, &c. As regards religion 53 per cent. are Roman Catholics, 15.4 Calvinists, 7.8 Lutherans, 10 Oriental Greeks, 8.8 Greek Catholics, and 4 Jews. The rest are Armenians, Unitarians, &c. Of the adult population $\frac{2}{3}$ are employed in agriculture, the forests and the mines, scarcely $\frac{1}{10}$ in manufacturing industry, 2 per cent. in trade and commerce, and over $17\frac{1}{2}$ in domestic service.

The history of the country begins with its conquest by the Magyars in the last decade of the ninth century. At that time it was inhabited chiefly by Slavonians, Bulgarians, and Wallachians under petty princes. The leader of the Magyars was Duke Arpad, and his descendants ruled the country for several centuries. One of the most renowned of these was Duke Stephen, who in 1000 assumed the title of king, and is regarded as the founder of the political and administrative institutions, and the organization of the country. One of his successors, Andrew II., engaged in a contest with his nobles, which ended in his granting in 1222 the *Aurea Bulla*, or Golden Bull, which has been called the Magna Charta of Hungary. Among its provisions are that the estates be henceforth annually convoked; that no nobleman be arrested without being previously tried and legally sentenced; that no contribution or tax be levied on the property of the nobles; that high offices be neither heriditary, nor given to foreigners without the consent of the Diet; and that every noble had the right to resist with arms any attempt at the infringement of his privileges by the king. This charter, except the last clause, which was abolished in 1687 is still valid, and is sworn to by each successive king at his coronation. In 1301 the race of Arpad became extinct, and several candidates came forward for the crown, but at length it was settled on the head of Duke Charles Robert of Anjou, a nephew of the King of Naples, and by his mother, a descendant of the extinct dynasty. Under this king and his son Lewis, who succeeded him, the power of Hungary was very much extended and consolidated. Moldavia, Wallachia, and other territories were added to it, and in 1370 on the death of Casimir the Great, the kingdom of Poland came to Lewis. He was succeeded by his son-in-law, Sigismund of Brandenburg, afterwards Emperor of Germany. He engaged in wars with the Turks, a revolt of his subjects in Hungary for a time deprived him of his liberty, and he prosecuted the Hussite war in Bohemia. During the reigns of Ladislaus III. and IV., the wars with the Turks continued, and brought out the hero John Hunyady,

PESTH.

Page 113.

whose son, Matthias Corvinus, subsequently came to the throne in 1458. He was the ablest monarch that had ruled over Hungary. He vanquished in numerous campaigns the Turks, the Poles, and the Austrians, quelled his rebellious nobles, restored law and order in the country, promoted science and art, fostered industry and commerce. He was succeeded by Wladislaus II., of Poland, in whose reign broke out the peasant war, which was suppressed with dreadful bloodshed by John Zapolya, and the peasantry reduced to a state of serfdom. He was succeeded by his son Lewis II., who lost his life in the battle of Mohacs in 1526. The crown then fell to his brother-in-law, Ferdinand of Austria, and since that time the emperors of Austria have been the rulers of Hungary.

Buda-Pesth (Ger. *Budapest*, or *Ofen-Pest*), the capital of Hungary, the seat of the government and chief courts of justice, consists of two towns, Buda on the right, and Pesth on the left bank of the Danube, formed into one city in 1872, and communicating by means of a magnificent suspension bridge, 1272 feet in length, erected in 1842-49 by the English architect, Mr. Clark, who built Hammersmith Bridge. In 1875 a new iron bridge was opened, for railway and passenger traffic, and another has been opened since. The city is 171 miles E.S.E. of Vienna by railway. In 1836 Buda contained 34,893, and Pesth 70,278 inhabitants; in 1857 Buda had 55,240, and Pesth 131,705; and in 1869 Buda 53,998, and Pesth 200,476, making together 254,474 inhabitants.

Buda (Ger. *Ofen*), the old capital of Hungary, stands partly on, partly around, a rocky eminence, on the summit of which is the fortress. In the neighbourhood are the loftier hills of Blocksberg and Schwabenberg, the former of which is strongly fortified. The royal palace, completed by Maria Theresa in 1771, is the most conspicuous building within the fortress, and having been partially destroyed in 1849 it has since been restored with great splendour. In a small chapel here are preserved the crown and regalia of Hungary. In the garrison church repose the remains of Andrew III., the last of the

Arpads. A tunnel has been made through the hill, 1115 feet in length, in connexion with the chain bridge. Buda consists of the city proper and six suburbs, one of which is Old Buda, or Alt-Ofen, where are the docks and building-yards of the Danube Steam Navigation Company. Here, too, are remains of a Roman aqueduct, and a Jewish synagogue, formerly considered the largest and finest in Hungary, but now surpassed by the one recently erected in Pesth. At the foot of the Blocksberg are some hot sulphureous springs, in good repute, and from which the German name of the town is taken, *Ofen* (i. e. oven). Here is the grave of the Mohammedan saint, Gül Baba, to which pilgrims from Turkey still repair. Buda contains a number of churches, and many handsome edifices. It has a polytechnic institute, a gymnasium, a real school, and a number of other educational institutions.

Pesth, unlike Buda, is built on a low, sandy plain, having nothing in its situation to recommend it; and yet, from the number of its fine streets and squares, its magnificent public buildings and elegant shops, in general appearance it is not far behind Vienna. In 1780 it contained only 16,746 inhabitants, so that it is mostly of recent erection; and it is regularly and handsomely built, the streets being wide, straight, and well-paved, and lined with handsome edifices. It consists of the *Innere* Stadt or old town, and four suburbs, called Leopold, Theresa, Joseph, and Francis Towns respectively. The Innere Stadt and the Leopoldstadt lie along the bank of the river, the former below, the latter above the bridge. The Innere Stadt is the most fashionable quarter of the town. It contains many palaces of the aristocracy, the university, law courts, county hall, town hall, the best shops, and the most frequented streets. Leopoldstadt, however, has larger and handsomer houses, and is better laid out. Along the bank of the river extends a broad and handsome quay, about a mile and a half in length, and lined by lofty and elegant buildings. Among the principal edifices of Pesth are the chief parish church (St. Leopold's); the Jewish synagogue, erected in 1857, and considered the finest in Hungary; the National Museum, with large collections of antiquities, natural history, and art; the palace of the Hungarian, Academy, with a library of 150,000 volumes; the university buildings; the Redoute buildings for assemblies and concerts; the new opera-house (1878); the National or Hungarian theatre; the German theatre; the Neugebäude, a large edifice erected by Joseph II. in 1786, now an artillery depôt; the large invalid hospital, now a barracks; the Ludoviceum, now a military hospital; new custom-house; Rathhaus; Landhaus, or hall of the Hungarian estates; exchange, &c. The university was founded in Tyrnau in 1635, transferred to Buda in 1777, and to Pesth in 1784. In 1875 it had 149 professors and teachers, and 2566 students. There are also a technical high school, with 56 teachers and 818 scholars, a military academy, commercial academy, three real schools, five gymnasia, and a number of other educational institutions. There are likewise a number of literary and scientific associations, which meet at stated times and publish proceedings. The celebrated Esterhazy Gallery, consisting of 800 pictures, 50,000 engravings, and 12,000 drawings, was removed from Vienna in 1865, and is established in the palace of the Academy here. The principal promenades are the Stadtwäldchen, a small park with ornamental water, on the outskirts of the town, and the Margaret Island in the Danube.

Buda-Pesth is, after Vienna, the most important city on the Danube; and it is also connected by railway with all the more important towns in the country. It is therefore a place of very considerable trade, particularly in corn, flour, wine, brandy, timber, cattle, wool, and various manufactured articles. Its manufactures include silks, velvets, cloth, leather, oil, tobacco, flour, brandy, carriages, machinery and iron wares, gold and silver articles, and meerschaum pipes. The wine produced in the neighbourhood is excellent, particularly the "Ofner" wine. Besides weekly markets, there are four annual fairs held here, which are visited by upwards of 30,000 strangers. Of the population about 48 per cent. are Germans, 32 per cent. Magyars, and 15 per cent. Jews.

Szegedin, the largest city of Hungary after Buda-Pesth, is situated on the bank of the Theiss, nearly opposite the point where the Maros flows into it from the E., and also on the railway from Pesth to Temesvar, 117 miles S.S.E. of the former. It consists of the town proper and five suburbs, and has six Roman Catholic churches, a Greek church, a Piarist College, gymnasium, town hall, theatre, &c. It carries on a very important trade, and has the principal docks for vessels navigating the Theiss. The chief manufactures are cloth, tobacco, and soap. In March, 1879, the town was partially destroyed by an overflow of the river. Population, 70,179.

Pressburg, the capital of a county of the same name, formerly capital of Hungary, and down to 1784 the place where its kings were crowned, stands on the left bank of the Danube, and on the railway between Vienna and Pesth, 42 miles E. of the former, and 130 W.N.W. of the latter. It is pleasantly situated on the river bank, and rises gradually up the lower slopes of the Little Carpathians. On a height overlooking the town are the remains of the royal palace, accidently destroyed by fire in 1811. Among the principal buildings are the cathedral of St. Martin, where the kings were crowned, a large Gothic edifice with a lofty tower; the Landhaus, in which the meetings of the Diet were held; Rathhaus; archiepiscopal palace; and theatre. The educational institutions include an academy of law, gymnasium, and real school. A new university for Hungary is about to be established here. The chief manufactures are silk and cotton goods, tobacco, and leather; and an active trade is carried on in wine and the other products of the district. Population, 46,540.

Debreczin stands on a sandy plain, 141 miles E. of Pesth by railway. It resembles more a large village than a town, being straggling and ill-built, the houses mostly of one storey and thatched, and the streets unpaved and dirty. The principal building is a large Protestant church, in connexion with which is a Protestant college, with a library of 20,000 volumes. The inhabitants are mostly Calvinists, and the great majority are Magyars, whose character may here be most advantageously studied. The manufactures are considerable, and include coarse woollen cloth, leather, soap, tobacco pipes, cutlery, and wooden wares. An active trade is also carried on in the products of the district, and four large fairs are held here annually. Population, 46,111.

Temesvar, the capital of a circle of the same name in the Banat, is situated in a marshy plain on the Bega canal, 188 miles S.E. of Pesth, with which it is connected by railway. It is fortified by walls, moats, and outworks; and consists of a town proper, and four suburbs. The streets are generally wide and regular, and the houses well-built. The principal buildings are the Roman Catholic cathedral, a fine Gothic edifice; handsome Greek cathedral; Roman Catholic parish church; Jewish synagogue; old castle of John Hunyady; county hall; two episcopal residences; and large barracks. It is the seat both of a Roman Catholic, and a Greek bishop, and has a gymnasium and other schools. It has considerable manufactures of cloth, silk, paper, leather, and oil; and carries on an important trade, particularly in corn. Population, 32,223.

Grosswardein (Magyar, *Nagy-Varad*), the capital of the county Bihar, is situated in a beautiful but somewhat marshy and unhealthy plain, on the river Körös, 154 miles E. of Pesth, with which it is connected by railway. It is the seat of a Roman Catholic, a Greek Catholic, and an Oriental Greek bishop, and has several handsome edifices, the finest of which is the cathedral. Among the educational institutions are an academy of law, theological seminary, and two gymnasia. It has extensive manufactures of earthenware, and carries on a considerable trade in wine, tobacco, cattle, &c. Several large annual fairs are held here. In the neighbourhood are warm sulphureous springs, well frequented, and valuable marble quarries. Population, 28,698.

TRANSYLVANIA (Ger. *Siebenbürgen*, Magyar *Erdely*), *Grand Duchy of*, no longer forms an independent province, having been united with Hungary under one administration in 1868; yet it is of sufficient importance, and sufficiently distinct in character from Hungary, to entitle it to some separate notice. It is bounded on the N. by Hungary, E. by Bukowina and Moldavia, S. by Wallachia, and W. by Hungary. It lies between lat. 45° 18' and 47° 38' N., and long. 22° 30' and 26° 20' E., and has an area of 21,214 square miles, with a population in 1869 of 2,101,727.

Transylvania, as we have seen, is a mountainous country, rising from plains on all sides, and only connected at the N.E. extremity with the main chain of the Carpathians. It is surrounded on all sides by lofty mountain ranges from 4000 to 6000 feet in height, while some elevations rise to 7500 and 8000 feet. In the E. are the Transylvanian High Carpathians, S. the Transylvanian Alps, W. the Transylvanian Erzgebirge, and N. the Nagy-Banha Mountains. The principal passes in these chains, affording communication with the neighbouring districts, are the Rodna Pass into Bukowina, the Gymes, and the Ojtos Pass into Moldavia, the Törzburger, Nothenthurm, and Vulcan Pass into Wallachia, and the Pass of the Iron Gate into the Military Frontier. In the interior are numerous mountain ranges and groups of mountains, with river valleys running in different directions. The general elevation of the country is about 1200 feet above the level of the sea. The principal rivers of the country are the Szamos in the N., the Maros, with its affluents, the Kokel, Aranyos, and Strehl, in the middle, and the Aluta in the South. There are few lakes, and they are all of small size, but there are numerous mineral springs. The climate varies considerably in different parts. In the higher regions the winter is generally severe, and often protracts itself far into the spring, while in the lower parts the summer heat is often extreme. At Hermannstadt the average annual temperature is 45.7°. Fahr., being for January 25.8°., and for July 63°.

Of the entire area about 86 per cent. is productive, and of this about 26 per cent. is arable, 18 per cent. meadows and gardens, $\frac{1}{2}$ per cent. vineyards, 11 per cent. pasture-land, and

43 per cent. woods and forests. The principal grain crops are maize, oats, rye, and wheat, but owing to the want of proper cultivation, the amount produced is frequently below what is required by the people. Wine of good quality, and in considerable quantity, is produced in the valley of Szamos, and the lower valleys of the Kokel and Maros. Fruit is extensively cultivated, as are also tobacco, hemp, and flax. The rearing of horses and cattle receives more attention than agriculture. The horses are numerous, and are distinguished for their beauty, nimbleness, and endurance. The cattle and sheep are also numerous, and many of them are of superior breeds. Among the former are a number of buffaloes; and swine are particularly abundant. Among the wild animals found here are bears, wolves, foxes, also deer, hares, chamois, &c. The country is particularly rich in minerals. More than one-half of the gold obtained in the Monarchy is found here, the amount averaging 35,000 oz. annually. The principal gold-mines are at Zalathna, Abrudbanya, and Vöröspatak; and it is also obtained by washing in the Maros, Szamos, Aranyos, and other streams. Silver is extracted, to the amount of about 86,000 oz. annually, mostly in the same districts where gold is found. Quicksilver (at Zalathna), copper, and lead, are also obtained, but not in large quantities. Iron and coal are found in various parts; but at present they are not worked to any great extent. An important source of wealth are the salt-works at Maros-Ujvar and other parts, the amount of rock-salt annually raised being over 950,000 cwt. There exist large beds of clay suitable for earthenwares, and excellent building stones are everywhere found.

The manufactures are chiefly confined to the production of such articles as are necessary for the simple wants of the people. Not much is done in the way of working up or improving the raw products of the country. Of the entire adult population only $1\frac{1}{2}$ per cent. are employed in the working of the metals, or of stone, or wood, and only about $\frac{3}{4}$ per cent. in weaving, which is chiefly a domestic industry. The principal manufacturing products are linen and woollen stuffs, leather, beer, brandy, earthenware, glass, and paper. The trade consists chiefly in the export of the natural products of the country, and the import of the manufacturing products of the West. A considerable transit trade is likewise carried on, particularly in corn and cattle, between Roumania and Hungary. The principal towns of Transylvania are connected with Pesth and the other towns of Hungary by railway.

The inhabitants of Transylvania belong to several nationalities, speaking distinct languages, and of different religious beliefs. The most numerous are the Roumanians, who constitute more than one half of the population; the Magyars and the Szeklers (a kindred people), form about $\frac{1}{4}$ and the Germans or Saxons, about $\frac{1}{10}$ of the whole. Among the less numerous races are about 80,000 Gipsies and 20,000 Jews. Over 12 per cent. are Roman Catholics, 28 per cent. Greek Catholics, 31 per cent. Oriental Greeks, 10 per cent. Lutherans, 14 per cent. Calvinists and $2\frac{1}{2}$ per cent. Unitarians. Of the adult population about $\frac{3}{4}$ are employed in agriculture, the forests, and the mines, 6 per cent. in manufacturing industry, 1 per cent. in trade and commerce, and 15 per cent. in domestic service.

Kronstadt, the largest and most populous, as well as the principal manufacturing and commercial town of the province, is situated near the S.E. extremity, in a narrow well-watered valley hemmed in on three sides by hills. It consists of an inner town surrounded by walls, and three suburbs, and is protected by a castle of some strength. The principal buildings are the old Gothic parish church (Lutheran), with a large organ, Roman Catholic church, Rathhaus, Kaufhaus, gymnasium, and theatre. The chief manufactures are woollen and linen stuffs, leather, paper, and refined wax. Dyeing is also carried on. A very active trade is carried on in cattle, corn, wine, salt, &c., which is now favoured by the extension of the railway system to this part. Population, 27,766.

Klausenburg (Magyar, *Kolosvar*), the capital of Transylvania, is pleasantly situated in a beautiful and fertile valley on the Szamos, 72 miles N.N.W. of Hermannstadt. It was founded by German colonists in 1178, but it is now mostly a Magyar city. It consists of the city proper and six suburbs, and is well built, having large substantial houses, and wide, open, and well paved streets. A large portion of the old walls which once surrounded the town are still standing, with some of the towers and gateways. Among the principal buildings are the fine old Gothic Catholic church and several of the other churches, Rathhaus, theatre, and numerous palaces of the nobility. It has a number of institutions for higher education, among which are an academy of law, and three gymnasia, and in 1872 a new university was established here, which in 1875 had 23 professors and teachers, and 178 students. There is also an interesting museum of natural history and antiquities and a large library. The principal manufactures are tobacco, spirits, leather, paper, and beet-root sugar. Population, 26,382.

Hermannstadt (Magyar, *Nagy Szeben*), the capital of the German portion of Transylvania, is pleasantly situated on an irregular eminence of no great elevation, in an extensive valley on the Zibin, an affluent of the Aluta, 70 miles W.N.W. of Kronstadt. It consists of an upper and lower town and three suburbs. The houses here are smaller, and the streets less regular or spacious and worse paved, than in Klausenburg. Considerable portions of the old walls still remain, but in a very dilapidated condition. The Gothic parish church is a handsome edifice surmounted by a lofty tower. The Bruckenthaler palace contains a natural history museum, picture-gallery and library. Hermannstadt is the seat of several courts and of a Greek Catholic and an Oriental Greek bishop. There are a number of educational and benevolent institutions, and various literary and scientific associations. The manufactures are chiefly woollen and linen goods, hats, leather, paper, candles, earthenware, and tobacco-pipes. Population, 18,998.

CROATIA-SLAVONIA (Ger. *Kroatien-Slavonien*), *Kingdom of*, is bounded on the N. by Styria and Hungary, E. by Hungary, S.

by the principality of Servia, the territories of Bosnia and Herzegovina, and Dalmatia, and W. by the Adriatic Sea, Istria, Carniola and Styria. Including the Military Frontier, it has an area of 16,172 square miles, with a population in 1869 of 2,197,977.

The Military Frontier (Ger. *Militärgrenze*) originally comprised a long tract of country extending along the S. boundary of the Monarchy, from the Adriatic to Transylvania, and intended as a protection against Turkey. It was originally formed by Ferdinand I. about the middle of the 16th century, and subsequently underwent repeated changes. The inhabitants were at once cultivators of the soil, and soldiers, holding their lands under conditions of military service. Every male between the ages of 18 and 60 was liable to military service, and was occupied in such duties for about eight months in the year. They formed 14 regiments of infantry, 1 of hussars and 2 battalions of boatmen, amounting in all to about 45,000 men in time of peace. In 1851 the Transylvanian Military Frontier was abolished, and in 1869 the then existing Military Frontier, had an area of 7308 square miles, with 699,228 inhabitants. In 1872 the Hungarian Military Frontier was incorporated with Hungary, and the next year a royal order was issued for the incorporation of the Croatian and Slavonian Military Frontiers with Croatia and Slavonia under the name of the Croatia-Slavonian Boundary District, with a new organization.

Croatia forms the W. and Slavonia the E. portion of this territory. The prevailing character of the surface of Croatia, is mountainous and that of Slavonia flat. The N. portion of the former is traversed by the Warasdiner range, a branch of the Carnic Alps constituting the watershed between the Drave and the Save. The S. and larger portion is generally covered with lofty mountains forming a continuation of the Julian Alps, and bearing the general name of the mountains of Velebich. They consist of two principal chains called the Great and Little Kapella, and rise to the height of over 5000 feet. This mountainous portion of Croatia belongs to the region of the

Karst, and has numerous cavern and underground passages, in which streams disappear to afterwards reappear. The prolongation of the Carnic Alps is continued from Croatia into Slavonia, traversing the latter territory between the Drave and the Save and terminating somewhat abruptly on reaching the banks of the Danube. The loftiest summit here is Mount Papuk, 3130 feet high, but generally they are of much less elevation, and are covered to their summits with excellent timber.

With the exception of some small coast streams which fall into the Adriatic, the rivers are all affluents of the Danube. The principal of these are the Drave, and the Save with its tributaries the Kulpa and Unna. The Drave enters the country from Styria, flows generally in an E.S.E. direction along the N. boundary, separating it from Hungary, to its mouth in the Danube below Essek. The Save after forming the boundary between Styria and Carniola, enters Croatia, and, after receiving the Unna, forms the boundary between this territory and Bosnia and Servia to its mouth in the Danube between Semlin and Belgrade. Its course is generally E.S.E. but with numerous turnings and windings. Both these streams are navigable for their entire length in this territory. Between the mouth of the Drave and the Save the Danube flows along the border and separates it from Hungary. The coast-line is about 86 miles in length, but is for the most part steep and rocky, and presents few safe harbours. There are numerous lakes, but they are all of small size. There are also a number of mineral springs, some of which are in good repute, as those at Krapina, Toplice near Warasdin, Stubica near Agram, Daruvar, &c. The climate varies greatly in different parts. The high lands are very much exposed to the action of certain winds, which, notwithstanding their S. position, sometimes render them intensely cold, while the low-lying parts generally enjoy a moderately warm climate. The temperature is mildest towards the coast, becoming by degrees less so as we proceed inwards. Thus at Fiume the average temperature for January is 41.6°, and for July 72°; while at Agram for January it is 31.2°, and for July 67.7°, the average annual temperature being 50°.

Of the civil portion of the territory about 87 per cent. is productive, and of this 31 per cent. is arable, 43 per cent. woods, 13 per cent. meadows and gardens, 11 per cent. pasture-land, and 2 per cent. vineyards. In the Military Frontier, 80 per cent. is productive, and of this 30 per cent. is arable, 35 per cent. woods, 18 per cent. meadows and gardens, 16 per cent. pastures, and 1 per cent. vineyards. The agricultural products of the two parts also differ. In the Military Frontier considerably less wheat, oats, and rye are cultivated, and consequently more maize, barley, and millet than in the other part. Taken together the principal grain crops are maize, wheat, oats, rye, barley, and millet. Croatia does not produce enough of corn for the wants of its population, while Slavonia has annually a considerable quantity for export. The flat portion of Slavonia is mostly of great fertility, producing abundant crops; only on the banks of the Drave are many swamps and marshes, and the land is subject to frequent inundations. The amount of wine annually produced in the civil district is about 28,000,000 gallons, and in the Military about half this quantity. Large quantities of fruit are grown, particularly plums from which a spirit is distilled. The rearing of cattle is not extensively carried on and the breeds are not generally distinguished for excellence. Horses are more numerous in Slavonia than in Croatia but are not remarkable except as being strong and hardy. Sheep on the other hand are more numerous in Croatia, and some of them are of superior excellence. Swine are very numerous, particularly in the neighbourhood of the forests. Bees and the silk-worm are common, about 600 cwt. of cocoons being produced annually. The rivers abound in fish; and leeches form an article of export, obtained chiefly in the lakes and marshes about Essek. The mineral productions of this province are inconsiderable. Iron, copper, sulphur, and brown coal are found, but not in any large quantities. There are also marble, building-stone and millstone quarries, but altogether in mining, quarrying, and smelting, scarcely 400 persons are employed.

The manufactures are still in a very backward state, and are generally conducted on a very limited scale. Their principal seats are the larger towns as Fiume, Agram, Essek, &c. They include linen and woollen stuffs, leather, paper, glass, porcelain, earthenware, hardware, wooden wares, brandy, rosoglio and other spirits, sugar, soap, tobacco, and chemical products. At Fiume and a few other places, ship and boat-building and sail-making are carried on. The trade is considerable, consisting in the export of corn and other natural products of the country, and the import of manufactured goods of various kinds and colonial and other products. Slavonia in particular exports largely corn, wine, timber, cattle, swine, hides and skins, honey and wax. The export of timber, on the coast, is rapidly increasing. Croats and Serbs form about 97 per cent. of the entire population; and are chiefly distinguished from each other in that the former are Roman Catholics, and the latter belong to the Oriental Greek church. The Croats constitute 74 per cent. of the population of the whole territory, and are distinguished by difference of dialect into Sloveno-Croats and Serbo-Croats. The Serbs form 23 per cent. of the population, so that there is only 3 per cent. of other nationalities, of which the Germans, (chiefly in Slavonia) form 1 per cent., and the Magyars (also mostly in Slavonia) only 0.6 per cent. The Jews are not numerous. There are a few Italians dwelling on the coast and some Albanians chiefly in Slavonia. As regards religion about $\frac{6}{10}$ are Roman Catholics, and about $\frac{1}{3}$ belong to the Oriental Greek church, about $\frac{1}{2}$ of the small remainder being Protestants. About 80 per cent. of the adult population are engaged in agriculture and the forests, 7 per cent. in the civil and 4 per cent. in the military portion in the manufacturing industries, and little more than 1 per cent. in trade and commerce. In the military division there are no less than 13 per cent. domestic servants (to officers, &c.), and in the civil division 6 per cent. Education is here very much neglected, and the people in general are very ignorant. This is more the case in the civil than in the military division. While in the latter ⅔ of the population can neither read nor write, in the former the proportion is as high as 6/7.

Agram, the capital of the province and a royal free-town is pleasantly situated on a wooded slope, near the left bank of the Save, 290 miles S. of Vienna and 106 E. of Trieste. It consists of the upper or free town, the lower or chapter town, and the bishop's town; and is the seat of an archbishop and the principal courts of the province. The first is the most fashionable part of the town, and the streets here are regular and well built, but in the lower town, chiefly inhabited by the poorer classes, the streets are generally irregular and dirty, and the houses mean. The principal buildings are the cathedral, a fine Gothic edifice with a lofty tower, the archiepiscopal palace, Rathhaus, Landhaus, National museum, &c. There are a university having 25 professors and teachers, and 205 students, a gymnasium, real school, and several literary and scientific societies, among which is a Southern Slav historical society. The chief manufactures are silk and porcelain; and an active trade is carried on in grain, potash, tobacco, and honey. Population, 19,857.

Essek, a royal free town and the chief town of Slavonia, as Agram is the chief town of Croatia, stands in a marshy district on the right bank of the Drave, thirteen miles above its mouth in the Danube, and 120 miles E. by S. of Agram. It was strongly fortified by the Emperor Leopold I., and consists of the fortress or town proper and the Upper, Lower, and New towns. It has three Roman Catholic and one Greek parish churches, Rathhaus, Landhaus, arsenal, and barracks. The inhabitants are chiefly engaged in the spinning of silk. It is a steamboat station, and a place of considerable trade, particularly in corn, cattle, raw hides, and leeches. Population, 17,247.

Fiume, a royal free town and free port, the only seaport of Hungary, is situated on the Adriatic near the head of the Gulf of Quarnero, where it receives the small stream Fiumara, 115 miles W.S.W. of Agram, and 38 miles S.E. of Trieste. It consists of an old and a new town, the former standing on a hill, and consisting of steep and narrow streets, with old and mean houses; the latter extending along the shore, and having wide, clean, and well-paved streets, and many handsome edifices. The old high church is adorned with a beautiful front after the style of the Pantheon at Rome. The church of St. Veit is a very fine building in imitation of that of St. Maria della Salute at Venice. The Casino is a handsome edifice containing coffee and ball rooms and a theatre. Fiume carries on important manufactures, especially of paper, tobacco, sailcloth, chemicals, ship biscuits, and maccaroni. Shipbuilding is also actively carried on. Being the principal seaport for a large district of country behind it, it has a very considerable trade. The chief exports are corn, wine, tobacco, timber, fruit, and salted provisions. The harbour is accessible only to vessels of small size, but the largest vessels can lie in the roadstead within a short distance of the town. Fiume, though situated in Croatia, is not subject to the provincial authorities, but with a small district round it, amounting in all to about seven square miles, is directly under the administration of the Hungarian Government, and its governor is a member of the House of Magnates. Population, 13,314.

BOSNIA and HERZEGOVINA, which are at present occupied and administered by Austria-Hungary in terms of the Berlin Treaty of 1878, previously formed the most N.W. province or eyalet of European Turkey. They lie immediately S. of Croatia and Slavonia, from which they are separated by the rivers Unna and Save, and E. of Dalmatia, having on the E. Servia, and S. Prisrend, Albania, and Montenegro. They extend from lat. 42° 30' to 45° 15' N., and from long. 15° 40' to 21° 10' East, and have an area of 24,247 square miles.

With the exception of the valley of the Save in the north, the surface of the country is generally mountainous, being traversed in different directions by mountain ranges of various elevations, from 3000 to over 8000 feet. A branch of the

Dinaric Alps runs from N.W. to S.E. through the territory, and forms the watershed between the rivers flowing northward into the Save and those which flow southward. The valleys are well watered, the principal rivers being the Save, with its affluents the Unna, Verbas, Bosna, and Drina, and the Narenta, which falls into the Adriatic. The mountains consist chiefly of limestone, with sandstone and shales of the carboniferous system; and beds of coal are said to be general throughout the country. The great mineral wealth of this region, however, is still undeveloped, though a few mines of iron, lead, quicksilver, and coal, are worked. Gold and silver are also found in some parts. The slopes of the mountains are for the most part densely covered with forests of oak, beach, pine, lime, chestnut, and other trees, which furnish almost inexhaustible stores of timber for building purposes and fuel. The forests occupy nearly one-half of the entire area of the country. Over 5000 feet in elevation the trees cease, and are succeeded by an Alpine vegetation.

The climate is variable and severe, but not unhealthy. The winter lasts long, and the spring is short, while the summer is extremely hot. The country is generally better adapted for feeding cattle than for agriculture, and it is only in the valleys and low-lying parts that any cultivation is carried on. The arable land occupies about one-fourth of the entire area. The principal grain crops are maize and wheat, but barley, oats, and even rice, are also produced. Plums are largely grown, and the vine, olive, fig, and pomegranate flourish. Sheep, goats, swine, and poultry, are raised in great numbers, but cattle and horses receive less attention. Game and fish abound, as well as wild animals, such as bears, wolves, lynxes, &c. Industry and trade are in a very low state, and are only carried on to any extent in the towns and larger villages. The manufactures are chiefly coarse cutlery and fire-arms, leather, ropes, and woollen goods chiefly for home use. The exports include agricultural products, fruit, timber, cattle, hides, wool, honey, and wax. The principal imports are colonial goods, cloth, cotton, salt, and cutlery.

The inhabitants are almost entirely Southern Slavs, and with few exceptions Serbs. In character they are rude and barbarous, insolent, and repellent to strangers, lazy and dissipated, but at the same time daring and brave, though cruel and treacherous. In their domestic relations they are simple and primitive, and in religious matters bigoted and superstitious. According to the census of 1879 the total population amounted to 1,142,147, of whom 487,022 belonged to the Oriental Greek Church, 442,500 were Mohammedans, 208,950 Roman Catholics, and 3426 Jews. The Mohammedans are nearly all descendants of Slavs who embraced Islamism in order to preserve their estates. The Turks in the country are few.

Bosnia, in early times, was governed by princes of its own, who afterwards became dependent on Hungary. In the beginning of the 15th century, Turkey laid claim to the province, and at length it was annexed to the Ottoman Empire in 1522 by Solyman the Magnificent. Many efforts have been made by the Bosnians to regain their independence. In 1849 a rebellion broke out, which was quelled by Omar Pasha in 1851. In 1875 the people were again in revolt, and were only subdued in 1877. After the treaty of Berlin was concluded, the Austrian troops crossed the river Save in July, 1878, but everywhere met with the most determined resistance from the people, supported, it was said, by Turkish soldiers. The Austrians, however, were generally successful, and entered the capital, Bosna-Serai, on 10th August. In April, 1879, a convention was concluded between Turkey and Austria, with reference to the occupation of Bosnia and Herzegovina, in which the latter recognized the suzerainty of the Sultan, and the rights of the Porte in regard to religious matters and real property.

Bosna-Serai, or *Seraievo* (Ital: *Seraglio*), the capital of the province of Bosnia, occupies a romantic position on both sides of the Migliazza, near its confluence with the Bosna, 250 miles S. of Buda-Pesth. It is 1700 feet above the level of the sea, and is surrounded on three sides by lofty mountains. The walls which surrounded the town have fallen into decay, and the citadel is a place of no strength. The houses generally are mean, but there are numerous mosques, and several Roman Catholic and Greek churches, which give the town a striking appearance. It is a great centre of trade between Turkey, and Dalmatia and Croatia. The principal manufactures are iron, copper and tin-wares, fire-arms, cutlery, leather, and cotton and woollen clothes. There are iron-mines in the vicinity. Population (1879), 21,577.

Novi-Bazar, the capital of a Sandjak of the same name in the province of Bosnia, is situated on the Rashka, an affluent of the Morava, 130 miles S.E. of Bosna-Serai. It is meanly built, the houses being mostly of mud, but is a place of considerable trade, and large fairs are held here periodically. Population about 10,000.

CHAPTER X.

HISTORY.

THE present Austro-Hungarian Monarchy took its rise in a Margraviate founded by Charlemagne towards the close of the eighth century in that fertile tract of country lying along the S. bank of the Danube, E. of the river Enns, and now included in Lower Austria. It was called *Ostreich* or *Oesterreich*—the eastern country, from its position relatively to the rest of Germany; and its governor received the title of Margrave or lord of the Marches.

This territory was in early times inhabited by the Taurisci—a Celtic race who were afterwards better known as the Norici. They were conquered by the Romans in B.C. 14, and thereafter a portion of what is now Lower Austria and Styria, with the municipal city of Vindobona, now Vienna, and even then a place of considerable importance, were formed into the province of Pannonia; and the rest of Lower Austria and Styria, together with Carinthia and a part of Carniola, into that of Noricum. Tyrol was included in Rhætia; while N. of the Danube, and extending to the borders of Bohemia and Moravia, were the territories of the Marcomanni and the Quadi. These were not unfrequently troublesome to the Romans; and during the greater part of the reign of Marcus Aurelius, from 169 to 180 A.D., they maintained with varying success a harassing war against them. In 174 the Roman army was so nearly cut off by the Quadi, that its safety was attributed to a miracle. The emperor died at Vindobona when on an expedition against these troublesome neighbours, and his successor Commodus was glad to come to terms of peace. On the decline of the imperial power, the Roman provinces here became a prey to the incursions of barbaric tribes. During the fifth and sixth centuries, the country was successively occupied by the Boii, Vandals, Goths, Huns, Lombards, and Avari. About 568, after the Lombards had settled in Upper Italy, the river Enns became the boundary between the Bajuvarii—a people of German origin, and the Avari, who had come from the East. In 788 the Avari crossed the Enns and attacked Bavaria—then a part of the Frankish empire, but were subsequently driven back by Charlemagne, and forced to retreat as far as the Raab, their country from the Enns to that river being then made a part of Germany. It was taken by the Magyars in 900, but was again annexed to Germany by Otto I. in 955. In 983 the emperor appointed Leopold I. of Babenberg or Bamberg Margrave of Austria, and his dynasty ruled the country for 263 years. He died in 994, and was succeeded by his son Henry I., who governed till 1018. In 1156, Austria received an accession of territory W. of the Enns, and was raised to a duchy by the Emperor Frederic I. The first duke was Henry Jasomirgott, who took part in the second crusade. He removed the ducal residence to Vienna, and began the building of St. Stephen's cathedral. His successor, Leopold V., in 1192 obtained Styria as an addition to his territory; and Frederic II. received possession of Carniola. This last in the latter years of his life contemplated the raising of Austria to a kingdom, but his death in a battle against the Magyars in 1246 put an end to the project, and with him the line became extinct.

The Emperor of Germany now declared Austria and Styria to have lapsed to the imperial crown, and appointed a lieutenant to govern them. But a claimant came forward in the person of Margrave Hermann of Baden, who was married to a niece of the late duke; and after his death, the states chose Ottokar, son of the king of Bohemia, who was duly invested with the government. In 1269 he succeeded to Carinthia and a part of Carniola and Friuli, but he lost all by refusing to acknowledge the Emperor Rudolph of Hapsburg, and eventually fell in battle in an attempt to recover them in 1278.

The emperor now took possession of the country, and appointed his oldest son governor; but, subsequently, in 1282, having obtained the sanction of the electors of the empire, he conferred the territories of Austria, Styria, and Carinthia on his sons Albert and Rudolf, and thus introduced the Hapsburg dynasty. Albert afterwards obtained the sole rule; and he extended his possessions considerably by wars with his neighbours, but was murdered in 1308 by a nephew whom he had deprived of his hereditary possessions. He was succeeded by his five sons, the last of whom, Albert, died sole ruler in 1358, and was succeeded by his son Rudolf II., who finished the church of St. Stephen's, and founded the University of Vienna. On his death, in 1365, he was succeeded by his two brothers Albert and Leopold, who, in 1379, divided their possessions between them, the former taking Austria, the latter Styria and other parts. Leopold fell at Sempach in 1386, but his descendants continued to rule in Styria. Albert acquired Tyrol and some other districts, and died in 1395. He was succeeded by his son Albert IV., who was poisoned at Znaim in 1404, when on an expedition againt Procopius, Count of Moravia. Albert V. succeeded his father, and, having married the daughter of the Emperor Sigismund, he obtained the thrones of Hungary and Bohemia, and became Emperor of Germany in 1438. He died the following year, and was succeeded by his posthumous son Ladislaus, who dying without issue in 1457, the Austrian branch of the family became extinct. It was succeeded by that of Styria, but the crowns of Hungary and Bohemia passed for a time into other hands.

The possession of Austria, which in the last reign had been raised to an archduchy, was for some years a subject of dispute between the Emperor Frederic III. and his brothers; but, at length, on the death of Albert in 1464, the emperor obtained sole possession. His son Maximilian succeeded his father as Emperor of Germany in 1493. He added Tyrol and some parts of Bavaria to his ancestral possessions, and advanced claims on Hungary and Bohemia. Maximilian died in 1519, and was succeeded by his grandson Charles V., who, a few years later, resigned all his hereditary possessions in Germany to his brother Ferdinand. The latter, by his marriage with Anna, sister of the king of Hungary, acquired right to the kingdoms of Hungary and Bohemia, together with Moravia, Silesia, and Lausatia. His right to Hungary, however, was contested by John Zapolya, who, obtaining the aid of the Sultan, Soliman II., in 1529, advanced with a large army to the very gates of Vienna, but after several ineffectual attempts to take it, he raised the siege and returned to Buda. At length, in 1535, an agreement was come to, allowing John to retain half of Hungary with the title of king, but his descendants only to have Transylvania. John died in 1540; but the people of Lower Hungary were opposed to Ferdinand, and set up the son of their late king in opposition to him. The aid of the Turks was again invoked, and eventually Ferdinand had to agree to pay an annual tribute of 30,000 ducats to the Sultan for this part of Hungary. On the abdication of Charles V. in 1556, Ferdinand succeeded to the imperial throne. He died in 1564, leaving his possessions to be divided between his three sons. The eldest, Maximilian II., received the imperial crown together with Austria, Hungary, and Bohemia. The second, Ferdinand, obtained Tyrol and Upper Austria. And the third, Charles, was made master of Styria, Carinthia, Carniola, and Görz. Maximilian was more fortunate in Hungary than his father. The sudden death of Soliman before Szigeth in 1566 led to a truce, and peace was subsequently concluded with his successor. In 1572 Maximilian caused his eldest son Rudolf to be crowned king of Hungary; in 1575 he was crowned king of Bohemia, and was also elected king of Rome. Maximilian II., under whose wise and tolerant reign Protestantism made great progress in the Austrian territories, died in 1576, and was succeeded in the imperial throne by Rudolf II. During his reign the possessions of the Archduke Ferdinand of Tyrol reverted to the other two lines. This monarch was little fitted to rule, and left the management of affairs very much to others. He was entirely under the power of the Jesuits, set at nought the ancient laws of the country, and persecuted the Protestants. In 1608 he was compelled to cede Hungary, and in 1611 Bohemia and Austria, to his brother Matthias, who, on his death, in 1612, was crowned emperor. His reign was full of promise, but, unfortunately, it was only of short duration.

Being an old man and childless, he chose as his successor his cousin Ferdinand, Archduke of Styria, whom he caused to be crowned King of Bohemia in 1616, and of Hungary 1618. He died the following year, but lived long enough to witness the commencement of the great struggle between Roman Catholicism and Protestantism, known as the thirty years' war (1618—1648). Ferdinand had manifested himself as an ardent supporter of Romanism, and a determined enemy of Protestantism; and the Bohemians declined to acknowledge him as king, but chose instead the Elector Palatine, Frederic V. The latter was supported by all the Protestant princes, except the Elector of Saxony, while Ferdinand was assisted by the Catholic princes and the King of Spain. At first, success attended the arms of the insurgents, but at length Frederic was totally defeated at White Hill, near Prague (1620), and in a short time the country was reduced to subjection. The inhabitants suffered the most cruel persecutions, and many thousands of them were driven into exile. At length they were compelled again to take up arms, and Christian IV. King of Sweden, put himself at their head. The war waged for some years with varying success, but at last the king was compelled to conclude a humiliating peace at Lubeck, in 1629. The Protestants were now subjected to even greater hardships, but a new champion appeared in the person of Gustavus Adolphus,

King of Sweden. The Elector of Brandenburg, and afterwards the Elector of Saxony joined Gustavus, and the combined army engaged the imperialists under Tilly, at Breitenfeld, near Leipsic, and defeated them with great slaughter (17th Sept., 1631). Again Tilly was beaten at the passage of the river Lech on 5th April, 1632, and the next day he died of his wounds. Wallenstein was now placed in command of the imperialists, and the eventful struggle between the two great generals took place at Lutzen on 6th Nov. 1632. The greatest skill and bravery were displayed on both sides, and the issue was long doubtful, but at length victory declared for the Swedes, though dearly purchased with the loss of their brave commander, who fell mortally wounded. Nor did Wallenstein long survive, for being suspected of treacherous designs against the empire, and having many enemies in the army and at court, he was on 25th Feb., 1634, assassinated by some of his own officers, who were afterwards rewarded by the emperor. Saxony and the Lutheran states soon after concluded peace with the emperor, leaving the Calvinists to their fate. Sweden, no longer able to carry on the war alone, called to her aid France, to whom she resigned the direction of operations. The emperor died in 1637, and was succeeded by his son Ferdinand III. The war was continued for eleven years longer, but at length the emperor, pressed on all sides, was glad to agree to terms of peace, which were signed at Westphalia, 24th Oct., 1648. France acquired Alsace; Sweden Upper Pomerania, the Isle of Rugen, and some other parts; and the Calvinists were placed on the same footing as the Lutherans. This religious war and persecution cost the House of Austria the flower of its possessions. In Bohemia, of 732 towns, only 130 remained, and of 30,700 villages, scarcely 6000; while of 3,000,000 inhabitants, only 780,000 were left.

Ferdinand died in 1657, and was succeeded by his son Leopold I., who by his harsh treatment of the Hungarians, drove that people into revolt. Unable to cope single-handed with the empire, they called in the aid of the Turks, who under Kara Mustapha, in 1683, besieged Vienna, and the city was only saved by the arrival of an army of Poles and Germans, under John Sobieski. The imperial army then reduced the whole of Hungary into subjection, uniting to it Transylvania, which had hitherto been governed by its own princes, and the whole was declared to be an hereditary kingdom. In 1699 Prince Eugene compelled the Turks, by the peace of Carlovitz, to cede to Hungary the country lying between the Danube and Theiss, and by the peace of Passarovicz in 1718, to yield up other important provinces. The death of Charles II. of Spain, without leaving issue, led to the war of the Spanish Succession, between Leopold and Louis XIV. Leopold died in 1705, and was succeeded by his oldest son, Joseph I., by whom the war was continued. The latter died childless, in 1711, and was succeeded by his brother Charles VI. By the peace of Utrecht, 11th April, 1713, Austria received the Netherlands, and the Spanish possessions in Italy—Milan, Mantua, Naples, and Sardinia (in 1720 exchanged for Sicily). The Monarchy now comprised about 255,000 square miles, with nearly 29,000,000 inhabitants; it had an annual revenue of about 1,400,000*l.*, and an army of 130,000 men.

Charles, being without heirs-male, was desirous of securing the succession to his eldest daughter, Maria Theresa, and with this view he framed the celebrated Pragmatic Sanction, to which he eventually succeeded in getting the assent of the other powers of Europe. In 1733 he became involved in a war with France, which was carried on principally in Italy, and resulted in his being obliged to cede Naples and Sicily to Don Carlos of Spain, and part of Lombardy to the king of Sardinia, receiving only Parma and Piacenza in return. In a war with the Turks he was obliged to give up, by the peace of Belgrade (1739), nearly all that the arms of Eugene had gained—Belgrade, Servia, and the Austrian portions of Wallachia and Bosnia. He died 20th October, 1740, and was succeeded by his eldest daughter, Maria Theresa, who was married to the Duke of Lorraine or Lothringen, afterwards Archduke of Tuscany. Immediately counter-claims were advanced on all sides. The Elector of Bavaria claimed to be the rightful heir to the kingdom of Bohemia; the Elector of Saxony and King of Poland, and also the King of Spain, claimed the entire succession; the King of Sardinia laid claim to the Duchy of Milan; and Frederic the Great of Prussia, to the province of Silesia. France espoused the cause of Bavaria, while England alone came forward to the assistance of the queen, and the Hungarians, now united and loyal, willingly recruited her armies. Aided by France and Saxony, the Elector of Bavaria, took possession of Bohemia, and was proclaimed king in 1741, and the following year he was elected Emperor of Germany, as Charles VII. The King of Prussia marched suddenly into Silesia, and took possession of that country. The Elector of Bavaria, aided by French troops, next invaded Austria, and even threatened Vienna. The queen fled to Pressburg, and convoked the Hungarian Diet. Appearing in the midst of the assembly with her infant son in her arms, she appealed to them for protection and help, and a powerful Hungarian army was speedily at her service. The French and Bavarians were soon driven out of the Archduchy. Not so the Prussians, who having defeated the Austrians at Czaslau in May, 1742, were, by the peace of Breslau which followed, confirmed in the possession of Upper and Lower Silesia. In 1744 the King of Prussia again took the field, but the death of the emperor the following year, and the accession of the husband of Maria Theresa to the imperial throne under the title of Francis I., changed the aspect of affairs, and a peace was concluded at Dresden, which confirmed Frederic in the possession of Silesia. The war with France was continued for some time longer, but at length peace was concluded at Aix la Chapelle in 1748, when Austria ceded Parma, Piacenza, and Guastalla, to Don Philip of Spain, and several districts of Milan to Sardinia. Maria Theresa, still harbouring evil designs against Frederic, now set herself to strengthen and improve her army and to form alliances with foreign powers. In July, 1756, Frederic despatched a messenger to Vienna, to ascertain the meaning of the massing of troops in Bohemia and Moravia, and receiving an evasive answer, he at once marched an army of 60,000 men into Saxony, took Dresden, and made himself master of the country. This was the commencement of the *Seven Years' War*, in which Austria was assisted by the French, Russians, and Swedes, and Prussia by the English. The contest raged long with varying success. The Austrians were beaten at Prague, Rossbach, and Leuthen (1757) at Zorndorf (1758), at Liegnitz and Torgau (1760); and on the other hand were victorious at Collin, and Breslau (1757), at Hochkirch (1758), and at Kunersdorf (1759). The ablest general opposed to Frederic was Daun. The king was often reduced to great difficulties, and at last seemed on the verge of ruin, when in 1762 the Empress of Russia died, and her successor, Peter III., recalled his troops and made peace with Prussia. Sweden soon after followed this example, and at length peace was signed at the castle of Hubertsburg in Saxony, 15th February, 1763, confirming Prussia in the possession of Silesia. This war, disastrous alike to all concerned, and which brought no territorial advantage to either party, is believed to have cost not less than 853,000 actual fighting-men.

Maria Theresa now zealously devoted herself to improving the condition of her people and country. She established schools, removed feudal hardships, improved the condition of the serfs, reformed ecclesiastical abuses, and fostered industry and commerce. The Emperor Francis died in 1765, and was succeeded by his son Joseph II., who the year before had been elected King of the Romans. By the first partition of Poland (1772) Austria acquired Galicia and Lodomeria; and in 1777, Bukowina was ceded by the Porte. Maria Theresa died 29th November, 1780, at which time the Monarchy comprised 235,500 square miles, with a population of about 24,000,000, and a public debt of 16,000,000*l*.

The Emperor Joseph II., who had been joint regent of the hereditary states with his mother during her life-time, now became sole ruler, and gave full scope to his zeal for reform.

He sought to establish a system of central government and uniformity of legislation throughout his dominions; gave freedom of worship and civil rights to Protestants; extended toleration to the Jews; abolished numerous convents and monasteries; dismantled various fortresses; and revised and improved the system of education. His zeal for reform excited the opposition of those who were attached to the old state of things, and the energy with which he sought to Germanize every thing without regard to other nationalities, created great dissatisfaction in Hungary and the Netherlands. At length, in 1789, the people of the Netherlands broke out into open revolt, and this, together with an unsuccessful war in which he had been engaged against the Turks, is believed to have so preyed upon his over-sensitive mind, as to have caused his death in 1790. He was succeeded by his brother, Leopold, Grand Duke of Tuscany, who, by his moderation and firmness, succeeded in quelling the insurrection in the Netherlands, and in restoring peace to the country. He also made peace with the Porte. The misfortunes of his sister Maria Antoinette, and her husband Louis XVI. of France, led him to enter into an alliance with Prussia against the French Revolutionists, but he died before the war broke out (1st March, 1792). He was succeeded by his son Francis II., who had hardly ascended the throne, when he found himself involved in a war with France. This was prosecuted for some time with varying success, but at length a series of disasters overtook the allies, and in the beginning of 1795 Prussia concluded peace with the French Republic. The war was now carried on with redoubled vigour against Austria; the young general, Napoleon Bonaparte, by a series of brilliant exploits, made himself master of the whole of Lombardy; and at length peace was concluded at Campo Formio, 17th October, 1797, Austria giving up Lombardy and the Netherlands, and receiving as compensation the larger part of the territory of Venice. Two years previous to this she had received W. Galicia on the third division of Poland.

In the beginning of 1799, Francis having entered into an alliance with Russia and England, renewed the war against France, but after suffering severe losses, was obliged to agree to terms of peace, which was concluded at Luneville, 9th February, 1801. In 1804, after Napoleon had assumed the title of Emperor of France, Francis took for himself and his successors that of Emperor of Austria. The war was renewed in 1805, and Napoleon, after a series of successes, entered Vienna, and subsequently defeated the allies at Austerlitz. By the peace of Pressburg (26th December, 1805), Austria lost Tyrol, Vorarlberg, Venice and other possessions, amounting in all to about 28,000 square miles, and a population estimated at 3,000,000.

The formation of the Confederation of the Rhine was designed by Napoleon for the purpose of weakening the power of Germany, and the Emperor Francis, yielding to what he could not prevent, renounced the imperial throne, which his family had occupied for nearly 500 years, and declared himself the first Emperor of Austria. Francis now made every effort to strengthen and improve his army, and increase his military resources; and in 1809 entered on a new war with France, aided only by England. The capital was again taken by the enemy, and in its neighbourhood were fought two of the most glorious battles in the world's history, Aspern and Wagram, the French being commanded by Napoleon, the Austrians by Archduke Charles. "The campaign of Aspern and Wagram," says Sir A. Alison, "is the most glorious in the Austrian annals—one of the most memorable examples of patriotic resistance recorded in the history of the world. . . . . Austria is the only state recorded in history, which (without the aid of a rigorous climate like Moscow), fought two desperate battles in defence of its independence, after its capital had fallen." (*History of Europe*). By the peace of Vienna (1809), Austria lost some of her finest provinces, Salzburg with Berchtesgaden, the Innviertel, Carniola with Görz, Trieste, the circle of Villach, the greater part of Croatia, Istria, W. Galicia, and a part of E. Galicia, in all about 42,000 square miles of territory, and 3,500,000 inhabitants.

On 11th March, 1810, the marriage of Napoleon to Maria

Louisa, daughter of the emperor, was celebrated with great pomp at Vienna. In 1812 Austria was obliged to enter into an alliance with France against Russia, and to furnish an auxiliary force of 30,000 men for the invasion of that country. The disastrous result of this expedition induced Prussia to join with Russia, and declare war against France (17th March, 1813). At first Austria held aloof from this quarrel, notwithstanding the endeavours of both the contending parties to win her over to their side. At length she declared for the allies, and on 12th August, 1813, pronounced war against France. The battle of Dresden was fought on 28th August, that of Leipsic on 16th and 18th October, and the allies entered Paris on 31st March, 1814. By the peace of Paris Austria received the portion of Italy which afterwards formed the Lombardo-Venetian kingdom, and those portions of her hereditary territories which she had previously lost, together with Dalmatia. The Congress of Vienna in 1815, and the treaty with Bavaria in 1816, gave Austria about 3200 square miles of additional territory, and otherwise improved its position by making it more compact, and adding to its commercial facilities.

Austria now exercised an important influence in the affairs of Europe, and particularly in those of the German Confederation; and this influence was directed to the suppression of free institutions, and almost every form of liberty among the people. In Austria itself this system was strictly carried out under the direction of Metternich. A strict censorship of the press was established, and a system of secret police organized to observe and report what was said and done by the people in private. In the construction of the German Confederation, she used her influence to suppress the popular voice in all matters of government; her armies were employed in quelling the popular insurrections in Naples and Piedmont in 1822; and by diplomacy she aided in the suppression of the popular movement in Spain in 1823. During the insurrection in Greece the influence of Austria was exerted against it; and when it was established as a kingdom, under the protection of

England, France, and Russia, she kept aloof. When, however, Russia invaded Turkey in 1828, Austria joined with England in interfering to prevent the fall of Constantinople, and in bringing about peace. The emperor died 2nd March, 1835, and was succeeded by his eldest son Ferdinand I., an amiable but weak-minded prince, who left the government very much in the hands of his prime minister, Metternich. An insurrection in Galicia afforded Austria an excuse for annexing the small republic of Cracow, and thus extinguishing the last remnant of Polish independence.

The French revolution of 1848, which convulsed almost the whole of continental Europe, caused the Austrian empire to totter to its foundations. The insurrection first broke out in Vienna (13th March), when the populace, headed by the students, made their way into the imperial palace, and demanded a new constitution, and the dismissal of the present ministers. Metternich resigned, a new ministry was formed, and other measures taken to allay the disturbance, but without success; and on 17th May, the emperor and court secretly quitted the palace and fled to Innsbruck. In Italy a general rising took place throughout Lombardy and Venice, and the King of Sardinia took part with the insurgents. In Bohemia also the insurrectionary spirit manifested itself and broke out into open rebellion in Prague. The city was bombarded and taken, and the ringleaders dispersed or taken prisoners. In Hungary, the National Diet passed measures in favour of a responsible ministry, a perfect equality of civil rights, and the abolition of the privileges of the nobles,[1] religious toleration, the formation of a national guard, and abolition of the censorship of the press. The emperor gave his assent to these measures; but there was a strong party, chiefly Slavs, in favour of the imperial government, and Jellachich, the ban of Croatia, at the head of

[1] The nobles represent the original free conquerors of the land, and prior to 1848 enjoyed many important privileges. They enjoyed immunity from taxation and military conscription, and had exclusive possession of the freehold land. No degree of poverty or ignorance, nothing short of actual proved crime, could disfranchise a noble.

an army of Croats, entered the country to put down the Magyars, secretly encouraged thereto by the government. A committee of safety was organized, and Kossuth elected president. When the garrison in Vienna left that city to fight against the Hungarians, the inhabitants rose up in arms, stormed the arsenal, and murdered the war minister. The emperor, who had returned to Vienna, now fled to Olmütz. The people of the capital put themselves under the command of General Bem, and prepared to resist the impending attack of the army. This commenced on the 28th of October, and after a stout resistance of three days the city was taken. The Emperor Ferdinand was induced to abdicate the throne on 2nd December, and his brother, Francis Charles, who was his legal successor, having renounced his right in favour of his son, the latter was proclaimed emperor under the title of Francis Joseph I. The war in Hungary continued, and for a time the Hungarians were successful, but a Russian army being brought against them, they were unable to contend against greatly superior numbers, and after a gallant resistance, and being beaten in several engagements, their general, Görgei, surrendered on 13th August, 1849. Hungary was now treated as a conquered country, and the greatest cruelties were practised against the people by the Austrian General Haynau. In the meantime the insurrection in Italy had been suppressed, and the King of Sardinia, after being beaten at Novara (23rd March), abdicated in favour of his son, Victor Emmanuel.

Austria now made strenuous efforts to develope the resources of the country by encouraging agriculture, industry, and commerce. The land was freed from feudal burdens, taxes were removed, new roads formed, railways made, commercial treaties entered into with foreign powers, and the like. The liberal concessions, however, that had been extorted from the government were rapidly disappearing; a rigorous system of military rule was introduced; the censorship of the press was again in operation; and the influence of the clergy and Jesuits re-established. Sardinia had frequently remonstrated with

Austria concerning her policy in Italy, but without success, and at length war was declared in 1859. France took part with Sardinia, and marched an army into Italy. The battle of Magenta was fought on 4th June, and that of Solferino on 24th June, in both of which the Austrians were defeated. An armistice followed, and subsequently a peace was concluded at Zurich on 10th November, by which Austria gave up Lombardy, except the fortresses of Mantua and Peschiera.

The emperor now saw the necessity of establishing his government upon a more liberal footing; and a new constitution was promulgated, admitting the co-operation of the Reichsrath in all matters relating to the promulgation, alteration, or abolition of the laws; the Reichsrath was declared to consist of two bodies—a house of peers, and a house of deputies, and the functions of each were defined. On 1st May, 1861, the New Reichsrath was formally opened by the emperor, but Hungary, Croatia, Slavonia, and Transylvania declined to send representatives, claiming a constitution distinct from the empire.

In 1864 Austria joined Prussia in making war upon Denmark, on account of the duchies of Schleswig, Holstein, and Lauenburg. Scarcely had they attained their object, when they went to war with each other over the spoil. On 7th June, 1866, the Prussian troops entered Holstein, and compelled the Austrians to retire, which they did without bloodshed. Before this Prussia had secured Victor Emmanuel as an ally, by promising him Venetia. On the 16th of June the Prussians entered Saxony, and marched upon Dresden, the Saxon army retiring to join the Austrians. Various engagements took place, in which the Austrians were worsted, partly owing to the deadly execution effected by the needle-gun, then a new weapon, with which the Prussian infantry were armed. The final struggle took place at Sadowa or Koniggrätz, when the Austrians were defeated with great slaughter on the 3rd of July, and on the 26th of the same month preliminaries of peace were signed at Nikolsburg. The treaty was concluded at Prague on 23rd August, by which Austria gave up Venetia, Mantua, &c., to Italy; withdrew all claim to the duchies of Holstein and Schleswig; consented to the dissolution of the German Confederation, and the formation of a new confederation in which she should have no part; and agreed to pay a war indemnity of 6,000,000*l.*, less 3,000,000*l.* allowed her on account of the duchies. With the loss of Lombardo-Venetia (in 1859 and 1866), Austria was deprived of upwards of 17,500 square miles of territory, and over 5,000,000 of inhabitants.

The emperor, having obtained peace, now turned his attention to home affairs. Hungary was still in a very dissatisfied state, and clamorous for self-government; and at length in the beginning of 1867 the constitution of 1848 was restored to her, and a ministry was formed. In opening the Reichsrath on 22nd May, the emperor said, "To-day we are about to establish a work of peace and of concord. Let us throw a veil of forgetfulness over the immediate past, which has inflicted deep wounds upon the empire. Let us lay to heart the lessons which it leaves behind; but let us derive, with unshaken courage, new strength, and the resolve to secure to the empire peace and power." On June 8th, the emperor and empress were crowned king and queen of Hungary at Pesth, amid great public rejoicings, on which occasion full pardon was given for all past political offences, and liberty to return to all offenders residing in foreign countries. Many important and liberal measures were discussed and passed in the Reichsrath, several of which were directed to limiting the power of the clergy, and establishing equality among the professors of different creeds. In March, 1873, a law was passed taking the election of members of the Reichsrath out of the hands of the provincial diets, and transferring it to the general body of the electors in the several provinces, thus substituting direct for indirect election. On 1st May, a great exhibition of the industries of all nations was opened at Vienna, and attracted an immense concourse of people, among whom were the Prince of Wales, the

Czar of Russia, the Emperor of Germany, the King of Italy, and the Shah of Persia. The twenty-fifth anniversary of the emperor's accession to the throne was celebrated with great rejoicings on 2nd December, 1873, in Vienna and throughout the Monarchy. In 1874 the Concordat entered into with the Pope in 1855, extending the power of the clergy, was abolished, and measures were introduced greatly restricting the power of the Church. By the treaty of Berlin, 13th July, 1878, the small territory of Spica, having an area of 13 square miles, and a population of about 2000, was separated from Turkey, and incorporated with Dalmatia. It also stipulated that "the provinces of Bosnia and Herzegovina shall be occupied and administered by Austria-Hungary," and accordingly the government has entered upon the occupation of these provinces, and established administrators in them. On the 22nd of April, 1879, the silver wedding of the emperor and empress was celebrated, and the rejoicings that took place among all classes of the people and in all parts of the Monarchy were so enthusiastic and spontaneous that no doubt could be felt as to the fervent loyalty with which the people of Austria-Hungary regarded their sovereign. In October of that year the Czech representatives, for the first time after 14 years' absence, took their seats in the Reichsrath, an indication that they are becoming more reconciled to the government, though they still reserve their claims to a constitution of their own like Hungary.

We cannot better conclude the history, and with it this brief sketch of Austria-Hungary, than by an extract from a Report on the commercial and industrial progress of the country, prepared at the time of the Exhibition in 1873, and which clearly and forcibly contrasts the old and the new state of things. "The year 1848 parts old from new Austria. The former, the absolutely governed state, whose territory, barred to the foreign world by high duties, prohibitions of imports and exports, a troublesome passport system, and an anxiously-watched censorship, and traversed by customs frontiers within its own borders, fell to pieces, which, in spite of the great and radical reforms of Maria Theresa and Joseph, possessed no bond of organic connexion among their political and economical institutions. In the majority of the provinces the peasant population were degraded to a position that bordered on serfdom. Labour was trammelled by the privileges owned by guilds; education pitifully neglected; intellectual life paralyzed; literature and art, in their inability to evade the restraint of an executive hostile to thought, or to contract their energy to the representation of the insignificant, were devoid of any influence. In consequence of all this, the resource of capital was very small, the power of independence was stifled, and self-reliance supplanted by blind idolatry of the foreigner. New Austria, as the state after its changes in 1848 was rightly characterized .... appears in spite of the shortness of the time since elapsed as a new world. Henceforth a constant member of the international trading community, in lively commercial intercourse with the rest, Austria has freed her peasant population from the traditional burdens of feudalism, and her working industry from its trammels; while a system of education, worthy of a constitutional state, is bringing light to the lowest strata of society. The press is displaying its instructive and educational, deciding and guiding power; finally, the intelligent cultivation of the rich capabilities of the soil, as a sum of all the above, gives extraordinary strength to the power of raising capital."

INDEX.

Mt. and Mts. stand for Mountain and Mountains, L. for Lake, R., River, T., Town.

ABRUDBANYA T., 179.
Adelsberg Grotto or Cavern, 10, 128, 129.
Adigo R., 18, 25, 135, 136.
Ages of population, 36.
Agram T., 185, 186.
Agriculture, persons engaged in, 70; arable land, *ib.*; principal crops, 71; estimated produce, 72; horses, 73; cattle, 74; sheep, &c., 75; schools of, 67.
Aix la Chapelle, peace of, 198.
Albert, dukes I., II., III., IV., V., 193.
Alps, 4, 5, 29, 135; geology of, 16; Central Range, 6, 7, 16, 110, 123, 126, 135; Northern Range, 6, 7, 16, 110, 118, 120, 123, 135; Southern Range, 6, 7, 16, 123, 126, 128, 130, 135; Transylvanian, 178.
Alsace acquired by France, 196.
Altenburg, German, 27.
Aluta R., 23, 178.
Animal kingdom, 31.
Arable land, 70, 71.
Aranyos R., 178, 179.
Army, 104; liability to serve in, *ib.*; standing army, 105; reserve, *ib.*; landwehr, *ib.*; ersatz-reserve, *ib.*; landsturm, *ib.*; marines, *ib.*; total strength of army, 106; expenditure for, 107.
Arpad, duke, 172; dynasty, *ib.*
Art schools, Fine, 68.
Aspern, battle of, 201.
Asses, number of, 74.
Atter L., 26, 118.

Aurea Bulla, 172.
Aurelius Marcus, 191.
Auschwitz and Zator, Duchies of, 154.
Ausser T., 27.
Austerlitz, battle of, 201.
Austria, Empire of, 33, 34, 36, 37, 38, 39 *et passim*; Margraviate of, 191.
Austria-Hungary—name, position, extent, 1; boundaries, 2; divisions, 3; physical features, mountains, 4; plains, 14; geology, 16; minerals, 17; rivers, 18; lakes, 26; mineral springs, 27; climate, 28; flora, 30; fauna, 31; population, 33; races, 40; languages and literatures, 51; religion, 58; education, 62; agriculture, 70; mining, 77; manufactures, 81; means of communication, 91; trade and commerce, 93; banks, 97; post-office, 98; government, 100; army and navy, 104; finance, 106; history, 191; old and new contrasted, 207.
Austria Lower province, 30, 109.
Austria Upper province, 17, 117.
Austrian Lloyd's Co., 132, 133.
Austrian Steam Ship Co., 93.
Avari, 192.

BABIA-GORA, Mt., 13.
Baczer or Francis Canal, 23, 93.
Baden T., 27.
Bahar Mt., 14.
Bajuvarii, 192.
Bakony Forest, 167.
Balaton or Platten L., 26, 168.

P

Banat of Hungary, 169.
Banks, number, capital, and names of principal, 97; savings, *ib.*
Barley, 71; estimated produce of, 72.
Beer, 87.
Bees, 76, 149, 170.
Beet-root, 73, 141.
Bega R., 23; Canal, 23, 93.
Belgrade, peace of, 197.
Beraun R., 140.
Berlin treaty, 1, 189, 207.
Beskides Mts., 12, 148, 153, 155.
Biela R., 153.
Bilin T., 27, 141.
Births, average number of, 38.
Bistritz or Bistritza R., 23, 160.
Blind, number of, 37; schools for, 69.
Bodrog R., 23.
Bohemia, 11, 139, 143, 193, 194, 195, 196, 198, 203, 207.
Bohemia-Moravian Mts., 11, 140, 148.
Bohemian Forest Mts., 10, 16, 140.
Bohemians, *see* Czechs.
Boii, 143.
Books, number printed, 58.
Boots and shoes, 86.
Bosna R., 188.
Bosna-Serai T., 189.
Bosnia and Herzegovina, 1, 94 *n.*, 187, 189, 207.
Brahe, Tycho, 145.
Brandy, 88, 157.
Breitenfeld, battle of, 195.
Brenner Pass, 6, 7, 137.
Brenta R., 136.
Breslau, battle of, 199; peace of, 198.
Brody T., 94 and *n.*, 157, 159.
Brünn T., 148, 149, 150.
Buccari, 94.
Buda or Ofen, 27, 168, 173.
Buda-Pesth, 99, 173.
Budget, *see* Finance.
Budweis T., 147.
Bug R., 24, 155.
Bukowina, Duchy of, 160, 199.

CABBAGE, 72.

Calvinist church, 58, 59, 60.
Campo Formio, peace of, 200.
Canals, 93.
Canin Mt., 130.
Capo d'Istria, 131.
Carinthia, Duchy of, 126.
Carlopago, 94.
Carlovitz, peace of, 197.
Carnic Alps, 9, 126, 167, 182, 183.
Carniola, Duchy of, 128.
Carpathian Highlands, Hungarian, 12; Waldgebirge, 13, 155.
Carpathians, 4, 12, 29, 155, 160, 166; geology, 16; Little, 12, 148; Transylvanian High, 178.
Cattle, 74, 76; trade in, 95.
Cettina R., 162.
Charlemagne, 192.
Charles V., 194; VI., 197; VII., 198; II. of Spain, 197.
Chemicals, manufacture of, 88.
Chestnuts, 71, 131.
Christian IV. of Sweden, 195.
Cis-Leithania, 33, 34.
Climate, 28.
Clock and watch-making, 86.
Coal, 80, 124, 127, 129, 142, 142, 153, 156, 170.
Coffee imported, 95, 96.
Collin, battle of, 199.
Communication, means of, 91; roads, *ib.*; railways, *ib.*; river and canal navigation, 92; seaports, 93.
Concordat, the Papal, 207.
Confederation of the Rhine, the, 201.
Constance L., 26, 136.
Copper, 79, 142, 170; manufacture, 85.
Corgnale grotto, 131.
Corvinus Matthias, 173.
Cotton manufacture, 82; imported and exported, 95, 96.
Cracow, Grand Duchy of, 154; republic, 203; town, 99, 155, 157, 159.
Cretins, number of, 37.
Croatia-Slavonia, kingdom of, 181; Diet of, 104; people, 41, 44, 46, 47, 204; language, 55.

INDEX.

Customs duties, 94, 107; territories, 94.
Czechs, 4, 44, 45, 143, 144, 207; language and literature, 53.
Czernowitz T., 160, 161.
Czaslau, battle of, 198.

DACHSTEIN Mt., 9, 118.
Dalmatia, kingdom of, 94 and *n.*, 162, 202; exports and imports, 164.
Danube, 18, 109, 118, 136, 168; traffic on, 92.
Daun, General, 199.
Deaf mutes, number of, 37; schools for, 68.
Deaths, average number of, 39.
Debreczin T., 176.
Debt, National, see National Debt.
Delegations, the, 101.
Denmark, war with (1864), 205.
Deputies, House of, 102.
Diet, National, of Hungary, 101, 103, 203.
Diets, Provincial, 103.
Dinara Mt., 10, 162.
Dinaric Alps, 10, 162, 188.
Diocletian's palace, 165.
Dniester R., 18, 23, 155, 160.
Drave R., 21, 123, 126, 136, 168, 183.
Dreiherrenspitze, 9, 120.
Dresden, battle of, 202; peace of, 198.
Drina R., 188.
Dunajec R., 24, 155.
Dürnstein Mt., 110.

EARTHENWARE and porcelain, 88.
Education, progress of since 1848, 62; see Schools.
Eger R., 25, 140, 168; T., 147.
Egypt, trade with, 96.
Eipel R., 168.
Eisack R., 26, 136.
Eisthaler Thurm Mt., 13.
Elbe R., 18, 25; traffic on, 93.
Elbgebirge, 16.
England and Austria, 198, 199, 201, 203; see United Kingdom.
Enns R., 21, 110, 118, 121, 124.

Erlaf R., 110.
Erzgebirge, 10, 16, 140; Transylvanian, 178.
Ersatz-reserve, 105.
Essek T., 185, 186.
Esterhazy Gallery, the, 173.
Eugene, Prince, 197.
Exhibition of 1873, 117.
Exports, value of, and principal articles, 95, 96, 164.

FAIRS in Hungary, 171.
Fatragebirge, 13.
Fauna, 31.
Ferdinand I. of Germany, 144, 194; II., 195; III., 196; I. of Austria, 203, 204.
Finance 106; revenue and expenditure of monarchy, 107; of Austria, *ib.*; of Hungary, 108; national debt, *ib.*
Fiume T., 93, 94, 96, 183, 185, 186.
Flax and hemp, 71, 62; manufacture, 83, 142, 156.
Flora, 30.
Flour, value of, exported, 95, 96.
Forests, 30, 70, 71, 73, 188.
France, trade with, 96; wars with, 196, 197, 198, 200, 201, 202, 205.
Francis I., 198, 199; II., 200, 203.
Francis Joseph I., 204—207.
Franzensbad T., 11, 27, 141.
Franzens Canal, 23.
Frederic II., 192; III., 193; Elector Palatine, 195; the Great of Prussia, 198, 199.
Friulians, 50; language of, 56.
Fruits, 30, 71, 73, 136, 163, 169, 184.
Fünfkirchen, 167, 170.
Füred T., 27, 168.
Furniture, articles of, made, 89.

GABLONZ T., 143.
Galicia, kingdom of, 154, 199, 200.
Game, 31, 77.
Gardens and meadows, 70.
Gastein, 27, 121.
Gerlsdorfer Spitze, 13.
German Confederation, the, 202, 206; language 51; literature, 52.
Germans, 41, 42.

Germany, South, trade with, 94, 95.
Gesenke Mts., 148, 153.
Gipsies, 50, 171, 180.
Glass, manufacture of, 86, 143; value of exported, 95.
Gleichenberg T., 27, 124.
Gloves, manufacture of, 87.
Goats, 75, 163.
Gold, 78, 161, 170, 179; gold and silver articles, 86.
Golden Bull, *see* Aurea Bulla.
Göller Mt., 110; R., *ib.*
Görgei, General, 204.
Görz T., 134.
Görz and Gradisca, county of, 130.
Government, 100; emperor and king, *ib.*; executive and legislative power, *ib.*; duality of, 101; delegations, *ib.*; Reichsrath, 102; provincial diets, 103; Hungarian Reichstag or national diet, *ib.*
Grain crops, principal, 31; value of, 72; imported and exported, 95.
Gran R., 22, 168; T., 27.
Gratz T., 125.
Gravosa T., 96.
Great Rad Mt., 11.
Greece, trade with, 96.
Greek Catholic Church, 58, 59, 60.
Greek Oriental Church, 58, 59, 61.
Grintouc Mt., 128.
Grossglockner Mt., 8, 9, 126.
Gross Venediger Mt., 9, 120.
Grosswardein T., 168, 177.
Gurk R., 22, 126, 128; plain, *ib.*
Gustavus Adolphus, 195, 196.
Gymnasia, 64; real, *ib.*; under, *ib.*; subjects taught in, *ib.*

HABSBURG or Hapsburg dynasty, 193.
Habsburg-Lothringen or Hapsburg-Lorraine, house of, 100, 197.
Haydn, the composer, 122.
Haida T., 143.
Hall T., 27.
Hallein T., 121,
Halstädter L., 26, 118.
Hanna, district of, 149, 152.
Hapsburg, *see* Habsburg.
Hargitta Mts., 14.

Haynau, General, 204.
Hemp, 71, 72.
Henry I., Margrave, 192.
Hercynian Mts., 4, 10.
Hermannstadt T., 178, 181.
Hernad R., 23, 168.
Herzegovina, *see* Bosnia.
History, 191.
Hochkirch, battle of, 199.
Hops, 72, 141.
Horses, 73, 179.
Hubertsburg, peace of, 199.
Hungarian nobles, 203 *n.*
Hungary, kingdom of, 33, 34, 36, 37, 38, 39, 166, 193, 194, 195, 196, 197, 198, 200, 203, 204, 206, *et passim.*
Hunyady, John, 172, 177.
Huss, John, 53, 144.

IDRIA R., 131.
Iglau T., 151.
Ill R., 25, 136.
Imports, value of, 95, 96; principal articles, *ib.*
Industrial and trade schools, 64.
Inn R., 20, 118, 135, 136.
Innsbruck T., 136, 138.
Insane, number of, 37.
Insurrection of 1848, 203.
Ips, *see* Ybbs.
Ipsfeld, 110.
Iron, 79, 124, 127, 129, 142, 149, 153, 170; manufactures, 85, 124, 127, 143.
Iron Gate, the, 19, 20.
Ischl T., 27.
Isar R., 136.
Iser R., 140.
Isonzo R., 26, 131.
Isper R., 110; plain, *ib.*
Istria, 94 and *n.*, 130.
Italian language, 56; war of 1859, 205.
Italians, 41, 49.
Italy, trade with, 95, 96.

JABLUNKA PASS, 12, 153.
Jasomirgott, Henry, 192.
Javornik Mt., 12.
Jellachich, ban of Croatia, 203.

INDEX.

Jerome of Prague, 144.
Jewish religion, 58, 59, 62.
Jews, 50, 157.
Joint-stock companies, 98.
Joseph I., 197; II., 199.
Julian Alps, 9.
Jungholz, 94.

KAHLENGEBIRGE, 110.
Kamp R., 110; valley, *ib.*
Kapella, Great and Little, Mts., 182.
Kara, Mustapha, 197.
Karawank Mts., 126, 128.
Karlsbad T., 11, 27, 141.
Karst, the, 9, 128, 131, 183.
Kerka R., 162.
Kindergarten schools, 64.
Klagenfurt T., 127.
Klausenburg, T., 180.
Knighthood, orders of, 100.
Kokel, R., 178, 179.
Königgrätz, battle of, 205.
Körös R., 23, 168.
Kossuth, 204.
Kremnitz T., 170.
Krems R., 110; basin, *ib.*
Krimmler Ache R., 120, 121.
Kronstadt T., 180.
Kulpa R., 22, 183.
Kunersdorf, battle of, 199.

LADINS, 50; language, 56.
Ladislaus, Emperor, 144, 193.
Lago di Garda, 26, 136.
Lahatschowitz T., 27.
Laibach R., 22, 128, 129; T., 129, 130; plain, 128.
Lainsitz R., 110.
Landsturm, 105, 106.
Landwehr, 105, 106.
Languages and literatures, 51; German, *ib.*; Magyar, 52; Czech, 53; Polish, 54; Ruthenian, 55; Serbian, Croatian, and Slavonian, *ib.*; Italian, 56; Rhæto-Romanic, *ib.*; Roumanic, 57.
Lavant R., 126.
Luxenburg, 117.
Lead, 79, 127, 142.
Leather manufacture, 86, 157.

Lech R., 136; battle of, 195.
Leeches, 184, 186.
Leipsic, battle of, 202.
Leitha R., 21, 33, 168.
Leithagebirge, 110, 167.
Lemberg T., 99, 157, 158.
Leopold I. of Babenberg, margrave, 192; V. duke, *ib.*; duke, 193; I. emperor, 196; II., 200.
Leuthen, battle of, 199.
Lewis I. king of Hungary, 172; II., 144, 173.
Libraries, &c., 69.
Liegnitz, battle of, 199.
Lieser R., 126.
Linz T., 119; plain, 19, 118.
Lissa-hora Mt., 13.
Literatures, *see* Languages.
Lloyd's Company, Austrian, *see* Austrian Lloyd's Company.
Lobau Island, 19.
Lodomeria, 154, 199.
Lombardo-Venetia, 33, 200, 202, 203, 205, 206.
Lomnitza R., 155.
Lomnitzer Spitze, 13.
Lords, House of, 102.
Lorraine or Lothringen, duke of, 197.
Lubeck, peace of, 195.
Lueg Pass, 120.
Luneville, peace of, 201.
Lussin-piccolo T., 96.
Lutheran Church, 58, 59, 60.
Lutzen, battle of, 196.

Magdalena grotto, 128.
Magenta, battle of, 205.
Magnates, house of, 104.
Magyars, 41, 42, 172, 192; language and literature, 52.
Maize, 71, 131; estimated annual produce, 72; quantity exported, 96.
Males, 33, 34; proportion of to females, 35.
Mannhartsberg, 110.
Mantua T., 197.
Manufactures, 81; persons engaged in, 82; value of, *ib.*; cotton, *ib.*; flax and hemp, 83; woollen, 84;

silk, *ib.*; iron and steel, 85; copper, *ib.*; gold and silver articles, 86; scientific instruments, *ib.*; musical instruments, *ib.*; glass, *ib.*; leather, *ib.*; paper, 87; sugar, *ib.*; tobacco, *ib.*; beer, *ib.*; brandy, 88; porcelain and earthenware, *ib.*; chemicals, *ib.*; candles and soap, 89; wooden wares, 89.
Maraschino, 163, 165.
Marburg T., 126.
March R., 22, 110, 148, 168; feld, 110, 111.
Marcomanni, 144, 191.
Maria Theresa, 197, 198, 199.
Marienbad, 27, 141.
Marines, 105.
Maritime district, the, 130.
Maros R., 23, 168, 178, 179.
Marriages, average number of, 38.
Matthias, Emperor, 195.
Matzelgebirge, 123.
Maximilian I., 194; tomb of, 138; II., 194.
Mazurian Hills, 155.
Mehadia springs, 14, 27, 168.
Metternich, Prince, 202, 203.
Milan, 197.
Military, 33; schools, 68; *see* Army.
Military Frontier, the, 182, 184.
Mills, corn, &c., 89.
Millstädter L., 26, 126.
Mincio R., 136.
Mining, persons engaged in, 77; gold, 78; silver, *ib.*; iron, 79; copper, *ib.*; lead, *ib.*; quicksilver, *ib.*; tin, *ib.*; zinc, *ib.*; other metals, 80; coal, *ib.*; salt, *ib.*; other minerals, 81.
Mohacs, battle of, 173.
Moldau R., 25, 140.
Moldava or Moldawa R., 23, 160.
Möll R., 126.
Mond L., 26, 118.
Monetary crisis of 1873, 77 *n.*
Moravia, Margraviate of, 148.
Moravians, 44, 45.
Morlaks, 164.
Mozart, the composer, 122.
Mühl R., 118.

Mules, 74.
Mur R., 21, 121, 123.
Music schools, &c., 68.
Musical instruments, 86.

NAGY-BANHA Mountains, 178.
Nagy-Banya T., 170.
Namiest T., 150.
Naples, 197.
Napoleon Bonaparte, 200, 201.
Narenta R., 162, 188.
National Debt, 108.
National Diet, *see* Diet.
Navigation, river and canal, 93
Navy, 106, 107.
Nepomuk, St. John of, 145.
Netherlands, 197, 200.
Neusiedler L., 26, 167, 168.
Neutra R., 22.
Newspapers, number of, 57.
Nikolsburg, treaty of, 205.
Noric Alps, 8, 120, 167.
Norici, Noricum, 191.
Normal schools, 68.
Novara, battle of, 204.
Novi-Bazar T., 190.

OATS, 71; estimated produce of, 72.
Occupations of people, 38.
Oder R., 18, 24, 153.
Odergebirge, 148.
Oetscher Mt., 110.
Oetzthaler Ferner, 7.
Ofen, *see* Buda.
Olives, 71, 131, 163; oil of, 96.
Olmütz T., 152.
Olsa R., 153.
Oppa R., 24, 153.
Oravicza T., 170.
Orien Mt., 162.
Orphan Asylums, 64.
Ortler Alps, 7; Spitze, *ib.*, 135.
Ossiaker L., 26, 126.
Otto I., 192.
Ottokar, 192.

PANNONIA, 191.
Panslavic movement, 44.
Paper-making, 87.
Papuk Mt., 183.

INDEX.

Purad T., 168.
Parenzo T., 96.
Passanovicz, peace of, 197.
Pasterze glacier, 8, 126.
Pasture-land, 70, 71.
Peasant war in Hungary, 173.
Pesth, 174 ; *see* also Buda-Pesth.
Pellico, Silvio, 150.
Pianofortes, 86.
Piatra Mt., 14.
Pietrosa Mt., 13.
Piftjan T., 27.
Pilsen T., 147.
Pinzgauer swamps, 120.
Pirano, 96, 131, 134.
Plain, Croatia-Slavonian, 15 ; Galician, 15, 17, 155 ; of Hungary Great, 14, 19, 167 ; Little, 15, 19, 167.
Planina grotto, 128.
Platten L., *see* Balaton.
Podhorce R., 24, 155.
Podiebrad, George of, 144.
Podolian Highland, 155.
Pola T., 93, 96, 134.
Poland, partitions of, 199, 200.
Poles, 41, 44, 46, 157 ; language and literature of, 54.
Poprad R., 24, 155.
Population, 33, 34, density of, *ib.* ; proportion of males to females, 35 ; condition, 36 ; ages, *ib.* ; natives and foreigners, 37 ; occupations, 38 ; births, *ib.* ; marriages, *ib.* ; deaths, 39.
Portore T., 194.
Post-office statistics, 98.
Potatoes, 71, 72, 141.
Poultry, 76.
Pragmatic Sanction, 100, 197.
Prague, 99, 141, 144, 203 ; battle of, 199 ; treaty of, 206.
Prater island, 19 ; park, 117.
Pressburg T., 176 ; peace of, 201.
Priel Great Mt., 118.
Printing and lithographic establishments, 89.
Prossnitz T., 152.
Protestant religion, 58, 59, 60.
Provident Institutions, 98.
Provincial Diets, *see* Diets.

Prussia, trade with, 94, 95 ; war with, 205.
Pruth R., 23, 155, 160.
Püllna, 27, 141.
Pusterthal, 135.

QUADI, 191.
Quarnerian Islands, 130.
Quicksilver, 79, 129, 179.

RAAB R., 21, 124, 168.
Races, 40 ; German, 41, 42 ; Magyar, 41, 42 ; Slav, 41, 44, 45, 46 ; Czech, 45 ; Ruthenian, 46 ; Sloven or Wend, *ib.* ; Croat and Serb, *ib.*, 47 ; Roumanian or Wallachian, 48 ; Italian, 49 ; Ladin, 50 ; Friulian, Jewish, and other races, *ib.*
Radautz, 161.
Ragusa, 166.
Railways, 91 ; traffic on, 92 ; receipts, expenses, capital, &c., *ib.*
Rainfall, 29.
Rape-seed, 73.
Read and write, number able to, 63.
Real schools and gymnasia, 64 ; subjects taught in, 65.
Reichenberg T., 142, 147.
Reichsrath, 101, 102, 205, 206, 207.
Reichstag, *see* Diet, National.
Religion, 58 ; Roman Catholic, 59 ; Greek Catholic, 60 ; Protestant, *ib.* ; Oriental Greek, 61 ; Unitarian, *ib.* ; Jewish, 62.
Representatives, House of, 104.
Reschen L., 26.
Revenue and Expenditure, *see* Finance.
Rhætia, 191.
Rhætian Alps, 7.
Rhæto-Romanic or Romanic language, 56.
Rhine R., 18, 25, 136.
Riesengebirge, 11, 140.
Riesenkoppe, *see* Schneekoppe.
Roads, length of, &c., 91.
Rohitsch T., 27, 124.

INDEX.

Roman Catholic religion, 58, 59.
Rossbach, battle of, 199.
Roumania, trade with, 95.
Roumanians or Wallachians, 44, 48, 180; language of, 57.
Rovigno T. 93, 96.
Rudolf II., duke, 193; II. emperor, 195.
Rumburg T., 142.
Russia, trade with, 95.
Ruthenians, 41, 44, 46, 157; language and literature of, 55.
Rye, 71; estimated produce, 72.

SAALA R., 120.
Saddlery, 87.
Sadowa, battle of, 205.
Saidschitz springs, 141.
Salt, 80, 124, 137, 156, 163, 170, 179; monopoly, 107.
Salzach R., 20, 120.
Salzburg, Duchy of, 120; T., 121; Alps, 9.
Salzkammergut, 81.
San R., 24, 155.
San Servolo grotto, 131.
Sardinia, 197; king of, 203, 204.
Save R., 21, 124, 128, 183, 188.
Savings banks, statistics of, 97.
Saxon Switzerland, 11, 25.
Saxony, trade with, 94, 95.
Schemnitz T., 170.
Schmieda R., 110.
Schmöllnitz T., 170.
Schneeberg Mt., 9 (Lower Austria), 110.
Schneekoppe Mt., 11, 140.
Schönbrunn palace, 117.
School age, 62; attendance, 63.
Schools, elementary, kindergarten, &c., 63; middle—gymnasia and real, 64; high—universities and technical, 65; special—theological, law, commercial, navigation, mining, manufactures, agriculture, art, military, normal, &c., 66.
Schöpfel Mt., 110.
Schütt, Great and Little islands, 19, 167.
Schwechat R., 110.

Scientific instruments, 86.
Sdobba R., 131.
Seaports, principal, 93.
Sebenico T., 96, 165.
Sedlitz, 27, 141.
Semmering Pass, 9.
Serbs, Serbians, or Servians, 41, 44, 46, 47, 48; language of, 55.
Sered R., 155.
Sereth R., 23, 160, 161.
Seven Years' War, 199.
Sheep, 75, 149.
Shipping, 93, 95.
Sicily, 197.
Sigismund, emperor, 144, 193.
Silesia, Duchy of, 152, 198, 199.
Silkworm, 76, 163, 170.
Silk manufactures, 84; imported and exported, 95.
Silver, 78, 142, 170, 179.
Slavs, 41, 44, 45, 46.
Slovaks, 44, 45.
Slovens or Wends, 41, 44, 46; language of, 55.
Sobieski, John, 197.
Solferino, battle of, 205.
Soliman, or Solyman Sultan, 194.
Spalato T., 93, 96, 165.
Spanish Succession, war of, 197.
Spica, 207.
Spieglitzer Schneeberg, 11.
Steiner Alps, 128.
Steinschönau, 143.
Stelvio Pass, 8.
Steyer, Steyr, or Steier T., 85, 120.
Strehl R., 178.
Stry R., 24, 155.
Styria, Duchy of, 122; Alps, 9.
Suczawa R., 23, 160, 161.
Sudetes Mts., 11, 16, 148.
Sugar manufacture, 87, 157; exported, 96.
Sulzbach Alps, 123, 126, 128.
Swine, 75; imported and exported, 95.
Switzerland, trade with, 95.
Szamos R., 23, 168, 178, 179.
Szarviz R., 168.
Szegedin T., 176.
Szeklers, 180.

INDEX.

TÄNNENGEBIRGE, 120.
Tatra Mts., 13, 155.
Tauern, Greater and Lesser, Mts., 8.
Taurisci, 191.
Technical high schools, 66.
Telegraph statistics, 98.
Temes R., 23, 168.
Temesvar T., 177.
Teplitz (Bohemia), 11, 27, 141 (Carniola), 129 (Hungary), 168.
Terglou Mt., 9, 128.
Thaya R., 22, 110, 148.
Theiss R., 22, 168.
Theological seminaries, 66.
Thirty Years' War, 53, 195.
Tilly, General, 195.
Tin, 29.
Tobacco, 72, 136, 169; export and import of, 96; revenue from monopoly, 107.
Torgau, battle of, 199.
Toys, manufacture of, 89.
Trade and commerce, 93; persons engaged in, 94; internal, external, overland, by sea, *ib.*; principal countries with which carried on, *ib.*; value of imports and exports, and principal articles of, 95; trading vessels entering and leaving the different ports, *ib.*; value of imports and exports at different ports, 96; transit trade, *ib.*
Trade and manufacture, chambers of, 99; schools of, 67.
Traissen R., 110.
Transit trade, 96.
Trans-Leithania, 33, 34.
Transylvania, Grand Duchy of, 177, 197.
Transylvanian Alps, 14; Erzgebirge, *ib.*; Highlands, 13.
Traun L., 21, 26, 118; R., 12, 118, 124.
Trenck, Baron, 150, 151.
Trent T., 139.
Trientiner Alps, 7.
Trieste, 93, 94, 95, 96, 99, 130, 131, 132.
Troppau T., 154.

Tulner Basin, 15, 19, 110.
Turkey, trade with, 95, 96.
Turks, wars with the, 192, 194, 196, 200.
Turnips, 71.
Tyrol and Vorarlberg, county of, 135, 201.
Tyrolese, character of, 138.

UNITARIAN Church, 58, 59, 61.
United Kingdom, trade with, 95, 96; *see* England.
Universities, 65, 115.
Unna R., 22, 183, 188.
Untersberg, 121.
Utrecht, peace of, 197.
Uskoken Mountains, 128.

VALUE of grain crops, 72; of other products of soil, 73; manufactures, 82; exports and imports, 95.
Veldes L., 129.
Velebich Mts., 182.
Venice, 200, 201, 206.
Verbas R., 188.
Vertesgebirge, 167.
Vienna, 28, 85, 86, 99, 111-117, 194, 197, 201, 203, 204; Congress, 202; Exhibition of 1873, 117, 206; peace of, 201; plain or basin, 15, 17, 19, 30, 110.
Viennese, character of, 117.
Vindobona, 191.
Vine, vineyards, 30, 70, 71, 73, 110, 124.
Vistula R., 18, 24, 153, 155, 157; traffic on, 93.
Vorarlberg, *see* Tyrol and Vorarlberg.
Vöröspatak, 179.
Vrana L., 162.

WAAG R., 22, 168.
Wagram, battle of, 201.
Waidhofen on the Ybbs T., 85.
Wallachians, *see* Roumanians.
Wallenstein, General, 148, 196.
Waller L., 26.
Warasdiner Mts., 182.

Q

Wechsel Mt., 110, 123.
Welser Heath, 118.
Wends, *see* Slovens.
Wenzel IV., 144, 145.
Westphalia, peace of, 196.
Wheat, 71; estimated produce, 72.
White Hill, battle of, 195.
Wieliczka, 80, 156.
Wien R., 110, 112, 113.
Wiener-Neustadt T., 117; canal, 93, 117.
Wienerwald, 110.
Wiesbach-horn Mt., 9, 120.
Wild animals, 31, 77.
Wines, 73, 111, 131, 163, 169, 179, 184.
Wippach R., 131.
Wochiner L., 129.
Wolfgang, St., L., 26, 118.
Wood, value of, exported, 95.
Wool, 76, 149, 153, 170; imported and exported, 95.

Woollen manufactures, 84, 142, 150, 151, 153; imported and exported, 95.
Wörther L., 26, 126
Wurzner L., 129.

YBBS or Ips R., 110.

ZALANTHA, 179.
Zapolya, John, 173, 194.
Zara T., 93, 96, 163, 164.
Zator, *see* Auschwitz and Zator.
Zaya R., 110.
Zeller L., 121.
Zengg T., 94.
Zermagna R., 162.
Zeyer R., 128.
Zinc, 79, 127, 142.
Zirknitzer L. 129.
Zorndorf, battle of, 199.
Zurich, peace of, 205.
Zwittau T., 105.

THE END.

LONDON :
GILBERT AND RIVINGTON, PRINTERS,
ST. JOHN'S SQUARE.

A Catalogue of American and Foreign Books Published or Imported by MESSRS. SAMPSON LOW & CO. *can be had on application.*

Crown Buildings, 188, Fleet Street, London,
April, 1880.

A Selection from the List of Books

PUBLISHED BY

SAMPSON LOW, MARSTON, SEARLE, & RIVINGTON.

ALPHABETICAL LIST.

A CLASSIFIED Educational Catalogue of Works published in Great Britain. Demy 8vo, cloth extra. Second Edition, revised and corrected to Christmas, 1879, 5s.

About (Edmond). See "The Story of an Honest Man."

About Some Fellows. By an ETON BOY, Author of "A Day of my Life." Cloth limp, square 16mo, 2s. 6d.

Adventures of Captain Mago. A Phœnician's Explorations 1000 years B.C. By LEON CAHUN. Numerous Illustrations. Crown 8vo, cloth extra, gilt edges, 7s. 6d.; plainer binding, 5s.

Adventures of a Young Naturalist. By LUCIEN BIART, with 117 beautiful Illustrations on Wood. Edited and adapted by PARKER GILLMORE. Post 8vo, cloth extra, gilt edges, New Edition, 7s. 6d.

Afghan Knife (The). A Novel. By ROBERT ARMITAGE STERNDALE, Author of "Seonee." Small post 8vo, cloth extra, 6s.

Afghanistan and the Afghans. Being a Brief Review of the History of the Country, and Account of its People. By H. W. BELLEW, C.S.I. Crown 8vo, cloth extra, 6s.

Alcott (Louisa M.) Jimmy's Cruise in the "Pinafore." With 9 Illustrations. Second Edition. Small post 8vo, cloth gilt, 3s. 6d.

—— *Aunt Jo's Scrap-Bag.* Square 16mo, 2s. 6d. (Rose Library, 1s.)

—— *Little Men: Life at Plumfield with Jo's Boys.* Small post 8vo, cloth, gilt edges, 3s. 6d. (Rose Library, Double vol. 2s.)

—— *Little Women.* 1 vol., cloth, gilt edges, 3s. 6d. (Rose Library, 2 vols., 1s. each.)

A

Alcott (Louisa M.) Old-Fashioned Girl. Best Edition, small post 8vo, cloth extra, gilt edges, 3*s.* 6*d.* (Rose Library, 2*s.*)

—— *Work and Beginning Again.* A Story of Experience. Experience. 1 vol., small post 8vo, cloth extra, 6*s.* Several Illustrations. (Rose Library, 2 vols., 1*s.* each.)

—— *Shawl Straps.* Small post 8vo, cloth extra, gilt, 3*s.* 6*d.*

—— *Eight Cousins; or, the Aunt Hill.* Small post 8vo, with Illustrations, 3*s.* 6*d.*

—— *The Rose in Bloom.* Small post 8vo, cloth extra, 3*s.* 6*d.*

—— *Silver Pitchers.* Small post 8vo, cloth extra, 3*s.* 6*d.*

—— *Under the Lilacs.* Small post 8vo, cloth extra, 5*s.*

—— *Jack and Jill.* Small post 8vo, cloth extra, 5*s.*

"Miss Alcott's stories are thoroughly healthy, full of racy fun and humour . . . exceedingly entertaining . . . . We can recommend the 'Eight Cousins.'"—*Athenæum.*

Alpine Ascents and Adventures; or, Rock and Snow Sketches. By H. SCHÜTZ WILSON, of the Alpine Club. With Illustrations by WHYMPER and MARCUS STONE. Crown 8vo, 10*s.* 6*d.* 2nd Edition.

Andersen (Hans Christian) Fairy Tales. With Illustrations in Colours by E. V. B. Royal 4to, cloth, 25*s.*

Animals Painted by Themselves. Adapted from the French of Balzac, Georges Sands, &c., with 200 Illustrations by GRANDVILLE. 8vo, cloth extra, gilt, 10*s.* 6*d.*

Art Education. See "Illustrated Text Books."

Art in the Mountains: The Story of the Passion Play. By HENRY BLACKBURN, Author of "Artists and Arabs," "Breton Folk," &c. With numerous Illustrations, and an Appendix for Travellers, giving the Expenses of the Journey, Cost of Living, Routes from England, &c., Map, and Programme for 1880. 4to, cloth, 10*s.* 6*d.*

"Of the many previous accounts of the play, none, we are disposed to think, recalls that edifying and impressive spectacle with the same clearness and vividness as Mr. Blackburn's volume."—*Guardian.*

"He writes in excellent taste, and is interesting from the first page to the last."—*Saturday Review.*

Art of Reading Aloud (The) in Pulpit, Lecture Room, or Private Reunions. By G. VANDENHOFF, M.A. Crown 8vo, cloth extra, 6*s.*

Art Treasures in the South Kensington Museum. Published, with the sanction of the Science and Art Department, in Monthly Parts, each containing 8 Plates, price 1*s.* In this series are included representations of Decorative Art of all countries and all times from objects in the South Kensington Museum, under the following classes:—

    Sculpture : Works in Marble, Ivory, and Terra-Cotta.
    Bronzes : Statuettes, Medallions, Plaques, Coins.
    Decorative Painting and Mosaic.

Decorative Furniture and Carved Wood-Work.
Ecclesiastical Metal-Work.
Gold and Silversmiths' Work and Jewellery.
Limoges and Oriental Enamels.
Pottery of all Countries.
Glass: Oriental, Venetian, and German.
Ornamental Iron-Work : Cutlery.
Textile Fabrics : Embroidery and Lace.
Decorative Bookbinding.
Original Designs for Works of Decorative Art.
Views of the Courts and Galleries of the Museum.
Architectural Decorations of the Museum.

The Plates are carefully printed in atlas 8vo (13 in. by 9 in.), on thick ivory-tinted paper; and are included in a stout wrapper, ornamented with a drawing from "The Genoa Doorway" recently acquired by the Museum.

Asiatic Turkey: being a Narrative of a Journey from Bombay to the Bosphorus. By GRATTAN GEARY, Editor of the *Times of India*. 2 vols., crown 8vo, cloth extra, with many Illustrations, and a Route Map, 28s.

Australian Abroad (The). Branches from the Main Routes Round the World. Comprising the Author's Route through Japan, China, Cochin-China, Malasia, Sunda, Java, Torres Straits, Northern Australia, New South Wales, South Australia, and New Zealand. By JAMES HINGSTON ("J. H." of the *Melbourne Argus*). With Maps and numerous Illustrations from Photographs. 2 vols., 8vo, 14s. each.

Autobiography of Sir G. Gilbert Scott, R.A., F.S.A., &c. Edited by his Son, G. GILBERT SCOTT. With an Introduction by the DEAN OF CHICHESTER, and a Funeral Sermon, preached in Westminster Abbey, by the DEAN OF WESTMINSTER. Also, Portrait on steel from the portrait of the Author by G. RICHMOND, R.A. 1 vol., demy 8vo, cloth extra, 18s.

BAKER (Lieut.-Gen. Valentine, Pasha). See "War in Bulgaria."

THE BAYARD SERIES,
Edited by the late J. HAIN FRISWELL.

Comprising Pleasure Books of Literature produced in the Choicest Style as Companionable Volumes at Home and Abroad.

"We can hardly imagine better books for boys to read or for men to ponder over."—*Times*.

Price 2s. 6d. each Volume, complete in itself, flexible cloth extra, gilt edges, with silk Headbands and Registers.

The Story of the Chevalier Bayard. By M. DE BERVILLE.
De Joinville's St. Louis, King of France.

The Bayard Series (continued) :—

The Essays of Abraham Cowley, including all his Prose Works.

Abdallah ; or the Four Leaves. By EDOUARD LABOULLAYE.

Table-Talk and Opinions of Napoleon Buonaparte.

Vathek : An Oriental Romance. By WILLIAM BECKFORD.

The King and the Commons. A Selection of Cavalier and Puritan Songs. Edited by Prof. MORLEY.

Words of Wellington: Maxims and Opinions of the Great Duke.

Dr. Johnson's Rasselas, Prince of Abyssinia. With Notes.

Hazlitt's Round Table. With Biographical Introduction.

The Religio Medici, Hydriotaphia, and the Letter to a Friend. By Sir THOMAS BROWNE, Knt.

Ballad Poetry of the Affections. By ROBERT BUCHANAN.

Coleridge's Christabel, and other Imaginative Poems. With Preface by ALGERNON C. SWINBURNE.

Lord Chesterfield's Letters, Sentences, and Maxims. With Introduction by the Editor, and Essay on Chesterfield by M. DE STE.-BEUVE, of the French Academy.

Essays in Mosaic. By THOS. BALLANTYNE.

My Uncle Toby; his Story and his Friends. Edited by P. FITZGERALD.

Reflections; or, Moral Sentences and Maxims of the Duke de la Rochefoucauld.

Socrates : Memoirs for English Readers from Xenophon's Memorabilia. By EDW. LEVIEN.

Prince Albert's Golden Precepts.

<small>A Case containing 12 Volumes, price 31s. 6d.; or the Case separately, price 3s. 6.</small>

Beauty and the Beast. An Old Tale retold, with Pictures by E. V. B. 4to, cloth extra. 10 Illustrations in Colours. 12s. 6d.

Beumers' German Copybooks. In six gradations at 4d. each.

Biart (Lucien). See "Adventures of a Young Naturalist," "My Rambles in the New World," "The Two Friends," "Involuntary Voyage."

Bickersteth's Hymnal Companion to Book of Common Prayer
may be had in various styles and bindings from 1*d.* to 21*s*. Price List and Prospectus will be forwarded on application.

Bickersteth (Rev. E. H., M.A.) The Reef and other Parables.
1 vol., square 8vo, with numerous very beautiful Engravings, 2*s*. 6*d*.

—— *The Clergyman in his Home.* Small post 8vo, 1*s*.

—— *The Master's Home-Call; or, Brief Memorials of*
Alice Frances Bickersteth. 20th Thousand. 32mo, cloth gilt, 1*s*.

—— *The Master's Will.* A Funeral Sermon preached on the Death of Mrs. S. Gurney Buxton. Sewn, 6*d*. ; cloth gilt, 1*s*.

—— *The Shadow of the Rock.* A Selection of Religious Poetry. 18mo, cloth extra, 2*s*. 6*d*.

—— *The Shadowed Home and the Light Beyond.* 7th Edition, crown 8vo, cloth extra, 5*s*.

Bida. The Authorized Version of the Four Gospels, with the whole of the magnificent Etchings on Steel, after drawings by M. BIDA, in 4 vols., appropriately bound in cloth extra, price 3*l*. 3*s*. each. Also the four volumes in two, bound in the best morocco, by Suttaby, extra gilt edges, 18*l*. 18*s*., half-morocco, 12*l*. 12*s*.

"Bida's Illustrations of the Gospels of St. Matthew and St. John have already received here and elsewhere a full recognition of their great merits."—*Times*.

Biographies of the Great Artists, Illustrated. This Series is issued in the form of Handbooks. Each is a Monograph of a Great Artist, and contains Portraits of the Masters, and as many examples of their art as can be readily procured. They are Illustrated with from 16 to 20 Full-page Engravings. Cloth, large crown 8vo, 3*s*. 6*d*. per Volume.

Titian.	Rubens.	Tintoret and Veronese.
Rembrandt.	Leonardo.	Hogarth.
Raphael.	Turner.	Michelangelo.
Van Dyck and Hals.	The Little Masters.	Reynolds.
Holbein.	Delaroche & Vernet.	Gainsborough.
	Figure Painters of Holland.	

"A deserving Series, based upon recent German publications."—*Edinburgh Review.*
"Most thoroughly and tastefully edited."—*Spectator.*

Black (Wm.) Three Feathers. Small post 8vo, cloth extra, 6*s*.

—— *Lady Silverdale's Sweetheart, and other Stories.* 1 vol., small post 8vo, 6*s*.

—— *Kilmeny: a Novel.* Small post 8vo, cloth, 6*s*.

—— *In Silk Attire.* 3rd Edition, small post 8vo, 6*s*.

—— *A Daughter of Heth.* 11th Edition, small post 8vo, 6*s*.

—— *Sunrise.* 15 Monthly Parts, 1*s*. each.

Blackmore (R. D.) Lorna Doone. 10th Edition, cr. 8vo, 6s.
———— *Alice Lorraine.* 1 vol., small post 8vo, 6th Edition, 6s.
———— *Clara Vaughan.* Revised Edition, 6s.
———— *Cradock Nowell.* New Edition, 6s.
———— *Cripps the Carrier.* 3rd Edition, small post 8vo, 6s.
———— *Mary Anerley.* 3 vols., 31s. 6d.
———— *Erema; or, My Father's Sin.* With 12 Illustrations, small post 8vo, 6s.
Blossoms from the King's Garden : Sermons for Children. By the Rev. C. BOSANQUET. 2nd Edition, small post 8vo, cloth extra, 6s.
Blue Banner (The); or, The Adventures of a Mussulman, a Christian, and a Pagan, in the time of the Crusades and Mongol Conquest. Translated from the French of LEON CAHUN. With Seventy-six Wood Engravings. Imperial 16mo, cloth, gilt edges, 7s. 6d.; plainer binding, 5s.
Boy's Froissart (The). 7s. 6d. See "Froissart."
Brave Janet: A Story for Girls. By ALICE LEE. With Frontispiece by M. ELLEN EDWARDS. Square 8vo, cloth extra, 3s. 6d.
Brave Men in Action. By S. J. MACKENNA. Crown 8vo, 480 pp., cloth, 10s. 6d.
Brazil : the Amazons, and the Coast. By HERBERT H. SMITH. With 115 Full-page and other Illustrations. Demy 8vo, 650 pp., 21s.
Brazil and the Brazilians. By J. C. FLETCHER and D. P. KIDDER. 9th Edition, Illustrated, 8vo, 21s.
Breton Folk: An Artistic Tour in Brittany. By HENRY BLACKBURN, Author of "Artists and Arabs," "Normandy Picturesque," &c. With 171 Illustrations by RANDOLPH CALDECOTT. Imperial 8vo, cloth extra, gilt edges, 21s.
British Goblins : Welsh Folk-Lore, Fairy Mythology, Legends, and Traditions. By WIRT SYKES, United States Consul for Wales. With Illustrations by J. H. THOMAS. This account of the Fairy Mythology and Folk-Lore of his Principality is, by permission, dedicated to H.R.H. the Prince of Wales. Second Edition. 8vo, 18s.
British Philosophers.
Buckle (Henry Thomas) The Life and Writings of. By ALFRED HENRY HUTH. With Portrait. 2 vols., demy 8vo.
Burnaby (Capt.) See "On Horseback."
Burnham Beeches (Heath, F. G.). With numerous Illustrations and a Map. Crown 8vo, cloth, gilt edges, 3s. 6d. Second Edition.
"Writing with even more than his usual brilliancy, Mr. HEATH here gives the public an interesting monograph of the splendid old trees. . . . This charming little work."—*Globe.*

Butler (W. F.) The Great Lone Land; an Account of the Red
River Expedition, 1869-70. With Illustrations and Map. Fifth and Cheaper Edition, crown 8vo, cloth extra, 7s. 6d.

────── *The Wild North Land; the Story of a Winter Journey* with Dogs across Northern North America. Demy 8vo, cloth, with numerous Woodcuts and a Map, 4th Edition, 18s. Cr. 8vo, 7s. 6d.

────── *Akim-foo: the History of a Failure.* Demy 8vo, cloth, 2nd Edition, 16s. Also, in crown 8vo, 7s. 6d.

CADOGAN (Lady A.) Illustrated Games of Patience. Twenty-four Diagrams in Colours, with Descriptive Text. Foolscap 4to, cloth extra, gilt edges, 3rd Edition, 12s. 6d.

Caldecott (R.). See "Breton Folk."

Carbon Process (A Manual of). See LIESEGANG.

Ceramic Art. See JACQUEMART.

Changed Cross (The), and other Religious Poems. 16mo, 2s. 6d.

Chant Book Companion to the Book of Common Prayer. Consisting of upwards of 550 Chants for the Daily Psalms and for the Canticles; also Kyrie Eleisons, and Music for the Hymns in Holy Communion, &c. Compiled and Arranged under the Musical Editorship of C. J. VINCENT, Mus. Bac. Crown 8vo, 2s. 6d.; Organist's Edition, fcap. 4to, 5s.

Of various Editions of HYMNAL COMPANION, *Lists will be forwarded on application.*

Child of the Cavern (The); or, Strange Doings Underground. By JULES VERNE. Translated by W. H. G. KINGSTON. Numerous Illustrations. Sq. cr. 8vo, gilt edges, 7s. 6d.; cl., plain edges, 5s.

Child's Play, with 16 Coloured Drawings by E. V. B. Printed on thick paper, with tints, 7s. 6d.

────── *New.* By E. V. B. Similar to the above. *See* New.

Children's Lives and How to Preserve Them; or, The Nursery Handbook. By W. LOMAS, M.D. Crown 8vo, cloth, 5s.

Children's Magazine. Illustrated. See St. Nicholas.

Choice Editions of Choice Books. 2s. 6d. each, Illustrated by C. W. COPE, R.A., T. CRESWICK, R.A., E. DUNCAN, BIRKET FOSTER, J. C. HORSLEY, A.R.A., G. HICKS, R. REDGRAVE, R.A., C. STONEHOUSE, F. TAYLER, G. THOMAS, H. J. TOWNSHEND, E. H. WEHNERT, HARRISON WEIR, &c.

Bloomfield's Farmer's Boy.	Milton's L'Allegro.
Campbell's Pleasures of Hope.	Poetry of Nature. Harrison Weir.
Coleridge's Ancient Mariner.	Rogers' (Sam.) Pleasures of Memory.
Goldsmith's Deserted Village.	Shakespeare's Songs and Sonnets.
Goldsmith's Vicar of Wakefield.	Tennyson's May Queen.
Gray's Elegy in a Churchyard.	Elizabethan Poets.
Keat's Eve of St. Agnes.	Wordsworth's Pastoral Poems.

"Such works are a glorious beatification for a poet."—*Athenæum.*

Christ in Song. By Dr. PHILIP SCHAFF. A New Edition, Revised, cloth, gilt edges, 6s.

Cobbett (William). A Biography. By EDWARD SMITH. 2 vols., crown 8vo, 25s.

Comedy (The) of Europe, 1860—1890. A retrospective and prospective Sketch. Crown 8vo, 6s.

Conflict of Christianity with Heathenism. By Dr. GERHARD UHLHORN. Edited and Translated from the Third German Edition by G. C. SMYTH and C. J. H. ROPES. 8vo, cloth extra, 10s. 6d.

Continental Tour of Eight Days for Forty-four Shillings. By a JOURNEY-MAN. 12mo, 1s.
"The book is simply delightful."—*Spectator.*

Corea (The). See "Forbidden Land."

Covert Side Sketches: Thoughts on Hunting, with Different Packs in Different Countries. By J. NEVITT FITT (H.H. of the *Sporting Gazette*, late of the *Field*). 2nd Edition. Crown 8vo, cloth, 10s. 6d.

Crade-Land of Arts and Creeds; or, Nothing New under the Sun. By CHARLES J. STONE, Barrister-at-law, and late Advocate, High Courts, Bombay. 8vo, pp. 420, cloth, 14s.

Cripps the Carrier. 3rd Edition, 6s. See BLACKMORE.

Cruise of H.M.S. "Challenger" (The). By W. J. J. SPRY, R.N. With Route Map and many Illustrations. 6th Edition, demy 8vo, cloth, 18s. Cheap Edition, crown 8vo, some of the Illustrations, 7s. 6d.

Curious Adventures of a Field Cricket. By Dr. ERNEST CANDÈZE. Translated by N. D'ANVERS. With numerous fine Illustrations. Crown 8vo, cloth extra, gilt edges, 7s. 6d.

DANA (R. H.) Two Years before the Mast and Twenty-Four years After. Revised Edition with Notes, 12mo, 6s.

Daughter (A) of Heth. By W. BLACK. Crown 8vo, 6s.

Day of My Life (A); or, Every Day Experiences at Eton. By an ETON BOY, Author of "About Some Fellows." 16mo, cloth extra, 2s. 6d. 6th Thousand.

Day out of the Life of a Little Maiden (A): Six Studies from Life. By SHERER and ENGLER. Large 4to, in portfolio, 5s.

Diane. By Mrs. MACQUOID. Crown 8vo, 6s.

Dick Cheveley: his Fortunes and Misfortunes. By W. H. G. KINGSTON. 350 pp., square 16mo, and 22 full-page Illustrations. Cloth, gilt edges, 7s. 6d.

Dick Sands, the Boy Captain. By JULES VERNE. With nearly 100 Illustrations, cloth extra, gilt edges, 10s. 6d.

Dodge (Mrs. M.) Hans Brinker; or, the Silver Skates. An entirely New Edition, with 59 Full-page and other Woodcuts. Square crown 8vo, cloth extra, 5s.; Text only, paper, 1s.

Dogs of Assize. A Legal Sketch-Book in Black and White. Containing 6 Drawings by WALTER J. ALLEN. Folio, in wrapper, 6s. 8d.

EIGHT Cousins. See ALCOTT.

Eldmuir: An Art-Story of Scottish Home-Life, Scenery, and Incident. By JACOB THOMPSON, Jun. Illustrated with Engravings after Paintings of JACOB THOMPSON. With an Introductory Notice by LLEWELLYNN JEWITT, F.S.A., &c. Demy 8vo, cloth extra, 14s.

Elinor Dryden. By Mrs. MACQUOID. Crown 8vo, 6s.

Embroidery (Handbook of). By L. HIGGIN. Edited by LADY MARIAN ALFORD, and published by authority of the Royal School of Art Needlework. With 16 page Illustrations, Designs for Borders, &c. Crown 8vo, 5s.

English Catalogue of Books (The). Published during 1863 to 1871 inclusive, comprising also important American Publications. 30s.
  ⁎ Of the previous Volume, 1835 to 1862, very few remain on sale; as also of the Index Volume, 1837 to 1857.

—— *Supplements,* 1863, 1864, 1865, 3s. 6d. each; 1866 to 1880, 5s. each.

English Writers, Chapters for Self-Improvement in English Literature. By the Author of "The Gentle Life," 6s.; smaller edition, 2s. 6d.

English Philosophers. A Series of Volumes containing short biographies of the most celebrated English Philosophers, designed to direct the reader to the sources of more detailed and extensive criticism than the size and nature of the books in this Series would permit. Though not issued in chronological order, the series will, when complete, constitute a comprehensive history of English Philosophy. Two Volumes will be issued simultaneously at brief intervals, in square 16mo, price 2s. 6d.

The following are already arranged:—

Bacon. Professor FOWLER, Professor of Logic in Oxford.
Berkeley. Professor T. H. GREEN, Professor of Moral Philosophy, Oxford.
Hamilton. Professor MONK, Professor of Moral Philosophy, Dublin.
J. S. Mill. Miss HELEN TAYLOR, Editor of "The Works of Buckle," &c.
Mansel. Rev. J. H. HUCKIN, D.D., Head Master of Repton.
Adam Smith. Mr. J. A. FARRER, M.A., Author of "Primitive Manners and Customs."

English Philosophers, continued :—
> **Hobbes.** Mr. A. H. GOSSET, B.A., Fellow of New College, Oxford.
> **Bentham.** Mr. G. E. BUCKLE, M.A., Fellow of All Souls', Oxford.
> **Austin.** Mr. HARRY JOHNSON, B.A., late Scholar of Queen's College, Oxford.
> **Hartley.** } Mr. E. S. BOWEN, B.A., late Scholar of New College,
> **James Mill.** } Oxford.
> **Shaftesbury.** }
> **Hutcheson.** } Professor FOWLER.

Erchomenon ; or, The Republic of Materialism. Small post 8vo, cloth, 5s.

Erema ; or, My Father's Sin. See BLACKMORE.

Eton. See "Day of my Life," "Out of School," "About Some Fellows."

Evans (C.) Over the Hills and Far Away. By C. EVANS. One Volume, crown 8vo, cloth extra, 10s. 6d.

———— *A Strange Friendship.* Crown 8vo, cloth, 5s.

*F*AMILY *Prayers for Working Men.* By the Author of "Steps to the Throne of Grace." With an Introduction by the Rev. E. H. BICKERSTETH, M.A. Cloth, 1s. ; sewed, 6d.

Fern Paradise (The): A Plea for the Culture of Ferns. By F. G. HEATH. New Edition, entirely Rewritten, Illustrated with Eighteen full-page, numerous other Woodcuts, including 8 Plates of Ferns and Four Photographs, large post 8vo, cloth, gilt edges, 12s. 6d. Sixth Edition. In 12 Parts, sewn, 1s. each.
> "This charming Volume will not only enchant the Fern-lover, but will also please and instruct the general reader."—*Spectator.*

Fern World (The). By F. G. HEATH. Illustrated by Twelve Coloured Plates, giving complete Figures (Sixty-four in all) of every Species of British Fern, printed from Nature ; by several full-page Engravings. Cloth, gilt, 6th Edition, 12s. 6d. In 12 parts, 1s. each.
> "Mr. HEATH has really given us good, well-written descriptions of our native Ferns, with indications of their habitats, the conditions under which they grow naturally, and under which they may be cultivated."—*Athenæum.*

Few (A) Hints on Proving Wills. Enlarged Edition, 1s.

First Steps in Conversational French Grammar. By F. JULIEN. Being an Introduction to "Petites Leçons de Conversation et de Grammaire," by the same Author. Fcap. 8vo, 128 pp., 1s.

Five Years in Minnesota. By MAURICE FARRAR, M.A. Crown 8vo, cloth extra, 6s.

Flooding of the Sahara (The). See MACKENZIE.

Food for the People ; or, Lentils and other Vegetable Cookery. By E. E. ORLEBAR. Third Thousand. Small post 8vo, boards, 1s.

A Fool's Errand. By ONE OF THE FOOLS. Crown 8vo, cloth extra, 5s.

Footsteps of the Master. See STOWE (Mrs. BEECHER).

Forbidden Land (A): Voyages to the Corea. By G. OPPERT. Numerous Illustrations and Maps. Demy 8vo, cloth extra, 21s.

Four Lectures on Electric Induction. Delivered at the Royal Institution, 1878-9. By J. E. H. GORDON, B.A. Cantab. With numerous Illustrations. Cloth limp, square 16mo, 3s.

Foreign Countries and the British Colonies. Edited by F. S. PULLING, M.A., Lecturer at Queen's College, Oxford, and formerly Professor at the Yorkshire College, Leeds. A Series of small Volumes descriptive of the principal Countries of the World by well-known Authors, each Country being treated of by a Writer who from Personal Knowledge is qualified to speak with authority on the Subject. The Volumes will average 180 crown 8vo pages, will contain Maps, and, in some cases, a few typical Illustrations.

The following Volumes are in preparation:—

Denmark and Iceland.	Russia.	Canada.
Greece.	Persia.	Sweden and Norway.
Switzerland.	Japan.	The West Indies.
Austria.	Peru.	New Zealand.

Franc (Maude Jeane). The following form one Series, small post 8vo, in uniform cloth bindings:—

———— *Emily's Choice.* 5s.

———— *Hall's Vineyard.* 4s.

———— *John's Wife: a Story of Life in South Australia.* 4s.

———— *Marian; or, the Light of Some One's Home.* 5s.

———— *Silken Cords and Iron Fetters.* 4s.

———— *Vermont Vale.* 5s.

———— *Minnie's Mission.* 4s.

———— *Little Mercy.* 5s.

———— *Beatrice Melton.* 4s.

Friends and Foes in the Transkei: An Englishwoman's Experiences during the Cape Frontier War of 1877-8. By HELEN M. PRICHARD. Crown 8vo, cloth, 10s. 6d.

Froissart (The Boy's). Selected from the Chronicles of England, France, Spain, &c. By SIDNEY LANIER. The Volume will be fully Illustrated. Crown 8vo, cloth, 7s. 6d.

Funny Foreigners and Eccentric Englishmen. 16 coloured comic Illustrations for Children. Fcap. folio, coloured wrapper, 4s.

Games of Patience. See CADOGAN.

Gentle Life (Queen Edition). 2 vols. in 1, small 4to, 10s. 6d.

THE GENTLE LIFE SERIES.

Price 6s. each; or in calf extra, price 10s. 6d.; Smaller Edition, cloth extra, 2s. 6d.

A Reprint (with the exception of "Familiar Words" and "Other People's Windows") has been issued in very neat limp cloth bindings at 2s. 6d. each.

The Gentle Life. Essays in aid of the Formation of Character of Gentlemen and Gentlewomen. 21st Edition.

"Deserves to be printed in letters of gold, and circulated in every house."—*Chambers' Journal.*

About in the World. Essays by Author of "The Gentle Life."

"It is not easy to open it at any page without finding some handy idea."—*Morning Post.*

Like unto Christ. A New Translation of Thomas à Kempis' "De Imitatione Christi." 2nd Edition.

"Could not be presented in a more exquisite form, for a more sightly volume was never seen."—*Illustrated London News.*

Familiar Words. An Index Verborum, or Quotation Handbook. Affording an immediate Reference to Phrases and Sentences that have become embedded in the English language. 3rd and enlarged Edition. 6s.

"The most extensive dictionary of quotation we have met with."—*Notes and Queries.*

Essays by Montaigne. Edited and Annotated by the Author of "The Gentle Life." With Portrait. 2nd Edition.

"We should be glad if any words of ours could help to bespeak a large circulation for this handsome attractive book."—*Illustrated Times.*

The Countess of Pembroke's Arcadia. Written by Sir PHILIP SIDNEY. Edited with Notes by Author of "The Gentle Life." 7s. 6d.

"All the best things are retained intact in Mr. Friswell's edition."—*Examiner.*

The Gentle Life. 2nd Series, 8th Edition.

"There is not a single thought in the volume that does not contribute in some measure to the formation of a true gentleman."—*Daily News.*

The Silent Hour: Essays, Original and Selected. By the Author of "The Gentle Life." 3rd Edition.

"All who possess 'The Gentle Life' should own this volume."—*Standard.*

Half-Length Portraits. Short Studies of Notable Persons. By J. HAIN FRISWELL. Small post 8vo, cloth extra, 6s.

Essays on English Writers, for the Self-improvement of Students in English Literature.

"To all who have neglected to read and study their native literature we would certainly suggest the volume before us as a fitting introduction."—*Examiner.*

The Gentle Life Series (continued):—

Other People's Windows. By J. HAIN FRISWELL. 3rd Edition.
"The chapters are so lively in themselves, so mingled with shrewd views of human nature, so full of illustrative anecdotes, that the reader cannot fail to be amused."—*Morning Post.*

A Man's Thoughts. By J. HAIN FRISWELL.

German Primer. Being an Introduction to First Steps in German. By M. T. PREU. 2s. 6d.

Getting On in the World; or, Hints on Success in Life. By W. MATHEWS, LL.D. Small post 8vo, cloth, 2s. 6d.; gilt edges, 3s. 6d.

Gilpin's Forest Scenery. Edited by F. G. HEATH. Large post 8vo, with numerous Illustrations. Uniform with "The Fern World" and "Our Woodland Trees." 12s. 6d.
"Those who know Mr. HEATH's Volumes on Ferns, as well as his 'Woodland Trees,' and his little work on 'Burnham Beeches,' will understand the enthusiasm with which he has executed his task. . . . The Volume deserves to be a favourite in the boudoir as well as in the library."—*Saturday Review.*

Gordon (J. E. H.). See "Four Lectures on Electric Induction," "Physical Treatise on Electricity," &c.

Gouffé. The Royal Cookery Book. By JULES GOUFFÉ; translated and adapted for English use by ALPHONSE GOUFFÉ, Head Pastrycook to her Majesty the Queen. Illustrated with large plates printed in colours. 161 Woodcuts, 8vo, cloth extra, gilt edges, 2l. 2s.

—— Domestic Edition, half-bound, 10s. 6d.
"By far the ablest and most complete work on cookery that has eve been submitted to the gastronomical world."—*Pall Mall Gazette.*

Gouraud (Mdlle.) Four Gold Pieces. Numerous Illustrations. Small post 8vo, cloth, 2s. 6d. *See also* Rose Library.

Government of M. Thiers. By JULES SIMON. Translated from the French. 2 vols., demy 8vo, cloth extra, 32s.

Great Artists. See Biographies.

Greek Grammar. See WALLER.

Guizot's History of France. Translated by ROBERT BLACK. Super-royal 8vo, very numerous Full-page and other Illustrations. In 5 vols., cloth extra, gilt, each 24s.
"It supplies a want which has long been felt, and ought to be in the hands of all students of history."—*Times.*

—————————— *Masson's School Edition.* The History of France from the Earliest Times to the Outbreak of the Revolution; abridged from the Translation by Robert Black, M.A., with Chronological Index, Historical and Genealogical Tables, &c. By Professor GUSTAVE MASSON, B.A., Assistant Master at Harrow School. With 24 full-page Portraits, and many other Illustrations. 1 vol., demy 8vo, 600 pp., cloth extra, 10s. 6d.

Guizot's History of England. In 3 vols. of about 500 pp. each, containing 60 to 70 Full-page and other Illustrations, cloth extra, gilt, 24s. each.
> "For luxury of typography, plainness of print, and beauty of illustration, these volumes, of which but one has as yet appeared in English, will hold their own against any production of an age so luxurious as our own in everything, typography not excepted."—*Times.*

Guyon (Mde.) Life. By UPHAM. 6th Edition, crown 8vo, 6s.

HANDBOOK to the Charities of London. See Low's.

—— *of Embroidery;* which see.
—— *to the Principal Schools of England.* See Practical.

Half-Hours of Blind Man's Holiday; or, Summer and Winter Sketches in Black & White. By W. W. FENN. 2 vols., cr. 8vo, 24s.

Half-Length Portraits. Short Studies of Notable Persons. By J. HAIN FRISWELL. Small post 8vo, 6s.; Smaller Edition, 2s. 6d.

Hall (W. W.) How to Live Long; or, 1408 *Health Maxims,* Physical, Mental, and Moral. By W. W. HALL, A.M., M.D. Small post 8vo, cloth, 2s. Second Edition.

Hans Brinker; or, the Silver Skates. See DODGE.

Have I a Vote? A Handy Book for the Use of the People, on the Qualifications conferring the Right of Voting at County and Borough Parliamentary Elections. With Forms and Notes. By T. H. LEWIS, B.A., LL.B. Paper, 6d.

Heart of Africa. Three Years' Travels and Adventures in the Unexplored Regions of Central Africa, from 1868 to 1871. By Dr. GEORG SCHWEINFURTH. Numerous Illustrations, and large Map. 2 vols., crown 8vo, cloth, 15s.

Heath (Francis George). See "Fern World," "Fern Paradise," "Our Woodland Trees," "Trees and Ferns;" "Gilpin's Forest Scenery," "Burnham Beeches," "Sylvan Spring," &c.

Heber's (Bishop) Illustrated Edition of Hymns. With upwards of 100 beautiful Engravings. Small 4to, handsomely bound, 7s. 6d. Morocco, 18s. 6d. and 21s. An entirely New Edition.

Hector Servadac. See VERNE. 10s. 6d. and 5s.

Heir of Kilfinnan (The). New Story by W. H. G. KINGSTON, Author of "Snoe Shoes and Canoes," "With Axe and Rifle," &c. With Illustrations. Cloth, gilt edges, 7s. 6d.

History and Handbook of Photography. Translated from the French of GASTON TISSANDIER. Edited by J. THOMSON. Imperial 16mo, over 300 pages, 70 Woodcuts, and Specimens of Prints by the best Permanent Processes. Second Edition, with an Appendix by the late Mr. HENRY FOX TALBOT. Cloth extra, 6s.

History of a Crime (The) ; Deposition of an Eye-witness. By
VICTOR HUGO. 4 vols., crown 8vo, 42*s*. Cheap Edition, 1 vol., 6*s*.

────── *England. See* GUIZOT.

────── *France. See* GUIZOT.

────── *of Russia.* ee RAMBAUD.

────── *Merchant Shipping. See* LINDSAY.

────── *United States. See* BRYANT.

────── *Ireland.* STANDISH O'GRADY. Vols. I. and II., 7*s*. 6*d*. each.

────── *American Literature.* By M. C. TYLER. Vols. I. and II., 2 vols, 8vo, 24*s*.

History and Principles of Weaving by Hand and by Power. With several hundred Illustrations. By ALFRED BARLOW. Royal 8vo, cloth extra, 1*l*. 5*s*. Second Edition.

Hitherto. By the Author of " The Gayworthys." New Edition, cloth extra, 3*s*. 6*d*. Also, in Rose Library, 2 vols., 2*s*.

Home of the Eddas. By C. G. LOCK. Demy 8vo, cloth, 16*s*.

How to Live Long. See HALL.

How to get Strong and how to Stay so. By WILLIAM BLAIKIE. A Manual of Rational, Physical, Gymnastic, and other Exercises. With Illustrations, small post 8vo, 5*s*.

"Worthy of every one's attention, whether old or young."—*Graphic.*

Hugo (Victor) "*Ninety-Three.*" Illustrated. Crown 8vo, 6*s*.

────── *Toilers of the Sea.* Crown 8vo. Illustrated, 6*s*.; fancy boards, 2*s*.; cloth, 2*s*. 6*d*.; On large paper with all the original Illustrations, 10*s*. 6*d*.

──────. *See* " History of a Crime."

Hundred Greatest Men (The). 8 vols., containing 15 to 20 Portraits each, 21*s*. each. See below.

"Messrs. SAMPSON LOW & Co. are about to issue an important 'International' work, entitled, 'THE HUNDRED GREATEST MEN;' being the Lives and Portraits of the 100 Greatest Men of History, divided into Eight Classes, each Class to form a Monthly Quarto Volume. The Introductions to the volumes are to be written by recognized authorities on the different subjects, the English contributors being DEAN STANLEY, Mr. MATTHEW ARNOLD, Mr. FROUDE, and Professor MAX MÜLLER: in Germany, Professor HELMHOLTZ; in France, MM. TAINE and RENAN; and in America, Mr. EMERSON. The Portraits are to be Reproductions from fine and rare Steel Engravings."—*Academy.*

Hygiene and Public Health (A Treatise on). Edited by A. H. BUCK, M.D. Illustrated by numerous Wood Engravings. In 2 royal 8vo vols., cloth, one guinea each.

Hymnal Companion to Book of Common Prayer. See BICKERSTETH.

ILLUSTRATED Text-Books of Art-Education. A Series of Monthly Volumes preparing for publication. Edited by EDWARD J. POYNTER, R.A., Director for Art, Science and Art Department.

The first Volumes, large crown 8vo, cloth, 3s. 6d. each, will be issued in the following divisions:—

PAINTING.

Classic and Italian. | French and Spanish.
German, Flemish, and Dutch. | English and American.

ARCHITECTURE.

Classic and Early Christian. | Gothic, Renaissance, & Modern.

SCULPTURE.

Classic and Oriental. | Renaissance and Modern.

ORNAMENT.

Decoration in Colour. | Architectural Ornament.

Illustrations of China and its People. By J. THOMPSON F.R.G.S. Four Volumes, imperial 4to, each 3*l*. 3*s*.

In my Indian Garden. By PHIL ROBINSON. With a Preface by EDWIN ARNOLD, M.A., C.S.I., &c. Crown 8vo, limp cloth, 3*s*. 6*d*.

Involuntary Voyage (An). Showing how a Frenchman who abhorred the Sea was most unwillingly and by a series of accidents driven round the World. Numerous Illustrations. Square crown 8vo, cloth extra, 7*s*. 6*d*.

Irish Bar. Comprising Anecdotes, Bon-Mots, and Biographical Sketches of the Bench and Bar of Ireland. By J. RODERICK O'FLANAGAN, Barrister-at-Law. Crown 8vo, 12*s*. Second Edition.

JACK and Jill. By Miss ALCOTT. Small post 8vo, cloth, gilt edges, 5*s*.

Jacquemart (A.) History of the Ceramic Art. By ALBERT JACQUEMART. With 200 Woodcuts, 12 Steel-plate Engravings, and 1000 Marks and Monograms. Translated by Mrs. BURY PALLISER. Super-royal 8vo, cloth extra, gilt edges, 28*s*.

Jimmy's Cruise in the Pinafore. See ALCOTT.

KAFIRLAND: A Ten Months' Campaign. By FRANK N. STREATFIELD, Resident Magistrate in Kaffraria, and Commandant of Native Levies during the Kaffir War of 1878. Crown 8vo, cloth extra, 7*s*. 6*d*.

Keble Autograph Birthday Book (The). Containing on each left-hand page the date and a selected verse from Keble's hymns. Imperial 8vo, with 12 Floral Chromos, ornamental binding, gilt edges, 15*s*.

Khedive's Egypt (The); or, The old House of Bondage under
New Masters. By EDWIN DE LEON. Illustrated. Demy 8vo, 8s. 6d.

King's Rifle (The): From the Atlantic to the Indian Ocean;
Across Unknown Countries; Discovery of the Great Zambesi Affluents,
&c. By Major SERPA PINTO. With 24 full-page and about 100
smaller Illustrations, 13 small Maps, and 1 large one. Demy 8vo.

Kingston (W. H. G.). See "Snow-Shoes."
—— *Child of the Cavern.*
—— *Two Supercargoes.*
—— *With Axe and Rifle.*
—— *Begum's Fortune.*
—— *Heir of Kilfinnan.*
—— *Dick Cheveley.*

LADY Silverdale's Sweetheart. 6s. *See* BLACK.

Lenten Meditations. In Two Series, each complete in itself.
By the Rev. CLAUDE BOSANQUET, Author of "Blossoms from the
King's Garden." 16mo, cloth, First Series, 1s. 6d.; Second Series, 2s.

Lentils. See "Food for the People."

Liesegang (Dr. Paul E.) A Manual of the Carbon Process of
Photography. Demy 8vo, half-bound, with Illustrations, 4s.

Life and Letters of the Honourable Charles Sumner (The).
2 vols., royal 8vo, cloth. Second Edition, 36s.

Lindsay (W. S.) History of Merchant Shipping and Ancient
Commerce. Over 150 Illustrations, Maps and Charts. In 4 vols.,
demy 8vo, cloth extra. Vols. 1 and 2, 21s.; vols. 3 and 4, 24s. each.

Lion Jack: a Story of Perilous Adventures amongst Wild Men
and Beasts. Showing how Menageries are made. By P. T. BARNUM.
With Illustrations. Crown 8vo, cloth extra, price 6s.

Little King; or, the Taming of a Young Russian Count. By
S. BLANDY. 64 Illustrations. Crown 8vo, gilt edges, 7s. 6d.; plainer
binding, 5s.

Little Mercy; or, For Better for Worse. By MAUDE JEANNE
FRANC, Author of "Marian," "Vermont Vale," &c., &c. Small
post 8vo, cloth extra, 4s. Second Edition.

Long (Col. C. Chaillé) Central Africa. Naked Truths of
Naked People: an Account of Expeditions to Lake Victoria Nyanza
and the Mabraka Niam-Niam. Demy 8vo, numerous Illustrations, 18s.

Lost Sir Massingberd. New Edition, crown 8vo, boards, coloured
wrapper, 2s.

Low's German Series—

1. **The Illustrated German Primer.** Being the easiest introduction to the study of German for all beginners. 1s.
2. **The Children's own German Book.** A Selection of Amusing and Instructive Stories in Prose. Edited by Dr. A. L. MEISSNER. Small post 8vo, cloth, 1s. 6d.
3. **The First German Reader, for Children from Ten to Fourteen.** Edited by Dr. A. L. MEISSNER. Small post 8vo, cloth, 1s. 6d.
4. **The Second German Reader.** Edited by Dr. A. L. MEISSNER. Small post 8vo, cloth, 1s. 6d.

   Buchheim's Deutsche Prosa. Two Volumes, sold separately:—
5. **Schiller's Prosa.** Containing Selections from the Prose Works of Schiller, with Notes for English Students. By Dr. BUCHHEIM, Small post 8vo, 2s. 6d.
6. **Goethe's Prosa.** Selections from the Prose Works of Goethe, with Notes for English Students. By Dr. BUCHHEIM. Small post 8vo, 3s. 6d.

Low's International Series of Toy Books. 6d. each; or Mounted on Linen, 1s.

1. **Little Fred and his Fiddle,** from Asbjörnsen's "Norwegian Fairy Tales."
2. **The Lad and the North Wind,** ditto.
3. **The Pancake,** ditto.

Low's Standard Library of Travel and Adventure. Crown 8vo, bound uniformly in cloth extra, price 7s. 6d.

1. **The Great Lone Land.** By Major W. F. BUTLER, C.B.
2. **The Wild North Land.** By Major W. F. BUTLER, C.B.
3. **How I found Livingstone.** By H. M. STANLEY.
4. **The Threshold of the Unknown Region.** By C. R. MARKHAM. (4th Edition, with Additional Chapters, 10s. 6d.)
5. **A Whaling Cruise to Baffin's Bay and the Gulf of Boothia.** By A. H. MARKHAM.
6. **Campaigning on the Oxus.** By J. A. MACGAHAN.
7. **Akim-foo: the History of a Failure.** By MAJOR W. F. BUTLER, C.B.
8. **Ocean to Ocean.** By the Rev. GEORGE M. GRANT. With Illustrations.
9. **Cruise of the Challenger.** By W. J. J. SPRY, R.N.
10. **Schweinfurth's Heart of Africa.** 2 vols., 15s.
11. **Through the Dark Continent.** By H. M. STANLEY. 1 vol., 12s. 6d.

Low's Standard Novels. Crown 8vo, 6s. each, cloth extra.

My Lady Greensleeves. By HELEN MATHERS, Authoress of "Comin' through the Rye," "Cherry Ripe," &c.
Three Feathers. By WILLIAM BLACK.
A Daughter of Heth. 13th Edition. By W. BLACK. With Frontispiece by F. WALKER, A.R.A.
Kilmeny. A Novel. By W. BLACK.
In Silk Attire. By W. BLACK.
Lady Silverdale's Sweetheart. By W. BLACK.
History of a Crime: The Story of the Coup d'État. By VICTOR HUGO.
Alice Lorraine. By R. D. BLACKMORE.
Lorna Doone. By R. D. BLACKMORE. 8th Edition.
Cradock Nowell. By R. D. BLACKMORE.
Clara Vaughan. By R. D. BLACKMORE.
Cripps the Carrier. By R. D. BLACKMORE.
Erema; or My Father's Sin. By R. D. BLACKMORE.
Innocent. By Mrs. OLIPHANT. Eight Illustrations.
Work. A Story of Experience. By LOUISA M. ALCOTT. Illustrations. *See also* Rose Library.
The Afghan Knife. By R. A. STERNDALE, Author of "Sconee."
A French Heiress in her own Chateau. By the author of "One Only," "Constantia," &c. Six Illustrations.
Ninety-Three. By VICTOR HUGO. Numerous Illustrations.
My Wife and I. By Mrs. BEECHER STOWE.
Wreck of the Grosvenor. By W. CLARK RUSSELL.
Elinor Dryden. By Mrs. MACQUOID.
Diane. By Mrs. MACQUOID.
Poganuc People, Their Loves and Lives. By Mrs. BEECHER STOWE.
A Golden Sorrow. By Mrs. CASHEL HOEY.

Low's Handbook to the Charities of London. Edited and revised to date by C. MACKESON, F.S.S., Editor of "A Guide to the Churches of London and its Suburbs," &c. 1s.

MACGAHAN (J. A.) Campaigning on the Oxus, and the Fall of Khiva. With Map and numerous Illustrations, 4th Edition, small post 8vo, cloth extra, 7s. 6d.

Macgregor (John) "Rob Roy" on the Baltic. 3rd Edition, small post 8vo, 2s. 6d.

—— *A Thousand Miles in the "Rob Roy" Canoe.* 11th Edition, small post 8vo, 2s. 6d.

Macgregor (John) Description of the "*Rob Roy*" *Canoe*, with Plans, &c., 1*s*.

—— *The Voyage Alone in the Yawl* "*Rob Roy*." New Edition, thoroughly revised, with additions, small post 8vo, 5*s*.; boards, 2*s*. 6*d*.

Mackenzie (D). The Flooding of the Sahara. By DONALD MACKENZIE. 8vo, cloth extra, with Illustrations, 10*s*. 6*d*.

Macquoid (Mrs.) Elinor Dryden. Crown 8vo, cloth, 6*s*.

—— *Diane.* Crown 8vo, 6*s*.

Magazine (Illustrated) for Young People. See "St. Nicholas."

Markham (C. R.) The Threshold of the Unknown Region. Crown 8vo, with Four Maps, 4th Edition. Cloth extra, 10*s*. 6*d*.

Maury (Commander) Physical Geography of the Sea, and its Meteorology. Being a Reconstruction and Enlargement of his former Work, with Charts and Diagrams. New Edition, crown 8vo, 6*s*.

Memoirs of Madame de Rémusat, 1802—1808. By her Grandson, M. PAUL DE RÉMUSAT, Senator. Translated by Mrs. CASHEL HOEY and and Mr. JOHN LILLIE. 4th Edition, cloth extra. This work was written by Madame de Rémusat during the time she was living on the most intimate terms with the Empress Josephine, and is full of revelations respecting the private life of Bonaparte, and of men and politics of the first years of the century. Revelations which have already created a great sensation in Paris. 8vo, 2 vols. 32*s*.

Men of Mark: a Gallery of Contemporary Portraits of the most Eminent Men of the Day taken from Life, especially for this publication, price 1*s*. 6*d*. monthly. Vols. I., II., III., and IV., handsomely bound, cloth, gilt edges, 25*s*. each.

Michael Strogoff. 10*s*. 6*d*. and 5*s*. *See* VERNE.

Mitford (Miss). See "Our Village."

Montaigne's Essays. See "Gentle Life Series."

My Brother Jack; or, The Story of Whatd'yecallem. Written by Himself. From the French of ALPHONSE DAUDET. Illustrated by P. PHILIPPOTEAUX. Imperial 16mo, cloth extra, gilt edges, 7*s*. 6*d*.; plainer binding, 5*s*.

My Lady Greensleeves. By HELEN MATHERS, Authoress of "Comin' through the Rye," "Cherry Ripe," &c. 1 vol. edition, crown 8vo, cloth, 6*s*.

My Rambles in the New World. By LUCIEN BIART, Author of "The Adventures of a Young Naturalist." Numerous full-page Illustrations. Crown 8vo, cloth extra, gilt edges, 7s. 6d.; plainer binding, 5s.

Mysterious Island. By JULES VERNE. 3 vols., imperial 16mo. 150 Illustrations, cloth gilt, 3s. 6d. each; elaborately bound, gilt edges, 7s. 6d. each. Cheap Edition, with some of the Illustrations, cloth, gilt, 2s.; paper, 1s. each.

NARES (Sir G. S., K.C.B.) Narrative of a Voyage to the Polar Sea during 1875-76, in H.M.'s Ships "Alert" and "Discovery." By Captain Sir G. S. NARES, R.N., K.C.B., F.R.S. Published by permission of the Lords Commissioners of the Admiralty. With Notes on the Natural History, edited by H. W. FEILDEN, F.G.S., C.M.Z.S., F.R.G.S., Naturalist to the Expedition. Two Volumes, demy 8vo, with numerous Woodcut Illustrations, Photographs, &c. 4th Edition, 2l. 2s.

National Music of the World. By the late HENRY F. CHORLEY. Edited by H. G. HEWLETT. Crown 8vo, cloth, 8s. 6d.

"What I have to offer are not a few impressions, scrambled together in the haste of the moment, but are the result of many years of comparison and experience."—*From the Author's "Prelude."*

New Child's Play (A). Sixteen Drawings by E. V. B. Beautifully printed in colours, 4to, cloth extra, 12s. 6d.

New Guinea (A Few Months in). By OCTAVIUS C. STONE, F.R.G.S. With numerous Illustrations from the Author's own Drawings. Crown 8vo, cloth, 12s.

New Ireland. By A. M. SULLIVAN, M.P. for Louth. 2 vols., demy 8vo, 30s. Cheaper Edition, 1 vol., crown 8vo, 8s. 6d.

New Novels. Crown 8vo, cloth, 10s. 6d. per vol. :—

Mary Anerley. By R. D. BLACKMORE, Author of "Lorna Doone," &c. 3 vols.
The Sisters. By G. EBERS, Author of "An Egyptian Princess." 2 vols., 16mo, 2s. each.
Countess Daphne. By RITA, Authoress of ",Vivienne" and "Like Dian's Kiss." 3 vols.
Sunrise. By W. BLACK. In 15 Monthly Parts, 1s. each.
Wait a Year. By HARRIET BOWRA, Authoress of "A Young Wife's Story." 3 vols.
Sarah de Beranger. By JEAN INGELOW. 3 vols.
The Braes of Yarrow. By C. GIBBON. 3 vols.
Elaine's Story. By MAUD SHERIDAN. 2 vols.
Prince Fortune and His Friends. 3 vols.

Noble Words and Noble Deeds. Translated from the French of E. MULLER, by DORA LEIGH. Containing many Full-page Illustrations by PHILIPPOTEAUX. Square imperial 16mo, cloth extra, 7s. 6d.

North American Review (The). Monthly, price 2s. 6d.

Notes on Fish and Fishing. By the Rev. J. J. MANLEY, M.A. With Illustrations, crown 8vo, cloth extra, leatherette binding, 10s. 6d.

Nursery Playmates (Prince of). 217 Coloured pictures for Children by eminent Artists. Folio, in coloured boards, 6s.

OBERAMMERGAU Passion Play. See "Art in the Mountains."

Ocean to Ocean: Sandford Fleming's Expedition through Canada in 1872. By the Rev. GEORGE M. GRANT. With Illustrations. Revised and enlarged Edition, crown 8vo, cloth, 7s. 6d.

Old-Fashioned Girl. See ALCOTT.

Oliphant (Mrs.) Innocent. A Tale of Modern Life. By Mrs. OLIPHANT, Author of "The Chronicles of Carlingford," &c., &c. With Eight Full-page Illustrations, small post 8vo, cloth extra, 6s.

On Horseback through Asia Minor. By Capt. FRED BURNABY, Royal Horse Guards, Author of "A Ride to Khiva." 2 vols., 8vo, with three Maps and Portrait of Author, 6th Edition, 38s.; Cheaper Edition, crown 8vo, 10s. 6d.

Our Little Ones in Heaven. Edited by the Rev. H. ROBBINS. With Frontispiece after Sir JOSHUA REYNOLDS. Fcap., cloth extra, New Edition—the 3rd, with Illustrations, 5s.

Our Village. By MARY RUSSELL MITFORD. Illustrated with Frontispiece Steel Engraving, and 12 full-page and 157 smaller Cuts of Figure Subjects and Scenes. Crown 4to, cloth, gilt edges, 21s.

Our Woodland Trees. By F. G. HEATH. Large post 8vo, cloth, gilt edges, uniform with "Fern World" and "Fern Paradise," by the same Author. 8 Coloured Plates (showing leaves of every British Tree) and 20 Woodcuts, cloth, gilt edges, 12s. 6d. Third Edition.

"The book, as a whole, meets a distinct need; its engravings are excellent, its coloured leaves and leaflets singularly accurate, and both author and engraver appear to have been animated by a kindred love of their subject."—*Saturday Review.*

PAINTERS of All Schools. By Louis Viardot, and other Writers. 500 pp., super-royal 8vo, 20 Full-page and 70 smaller Engravings, cloth extra, 25s. A New Edition is issued in Half-crown parts, with fifty additional portraits, cloth, gilt edges, 31s. 6d.

Palliser (Mrs.) A History of Lace, from the Earliest Period. A New and Revised Edition, with additional cuts and text, upwards of 100 Illustrations and coloured Designs. 1 vol. 8vo, 1l. 1s.
"One of the most readable books of the season; permanently valuable, always interesting, often amusing, and not inferior in all the essentials of a gift book."—*Times.*

—— *Historic Devices, Badges, and War Cries.* 8vo, 1l. 1s.

—— *The China Collector's Pocket Companion.* With upwards of 1000 Illustrations of Marks and Monograms. 2nd Edition, with Additions. Small post 8vo, limp cloth, 5s.

Petites Leçons de Conversation et de Grammaire: Oral and Conversational Method; being Lessons introducing the most Useful Topics of Conversation, upon an entirely new principle, &c. By F. Julien, French Master at King Edward the Sixth's School, Birmingham. Author of "The Student's French Examiner," "First Steps in Conversational French Grammar," which see.

Phillips (L.) Dictionary of Biographical Reference. 8vo, 1l. 11s. 6d.

Photography (History and Handbook of). See Tissandier.

Physical Treatise on Electricity and Magnetism. By J. E. H. Gordon, B.A. With about 200 coloured, full-page, and other Illustrations. Among the newer portions of the work may be enumerated: All the more recent investigations on Striæ by Spottiswoode, De la Rue, Moulton, &c. An account of Mr. Crooke's recent researches. Full descriptions and pictures of all the modern Magnetic Survey Instruments now used at Kew Observatory. Full accounts of all the modern work on Specific Inductive Capacity, and of the more recent determination of the ratio of Electric units (v). It is believed that in respect to the number and beauty of the Illustrations, the work will be quite unique. 2 vols., 8vo, 36s.

Picture Gallery of British Art (The). 38 Permanent Photographs after the most celebrated English Painters. With Descriptive Letterpress. Vols. 1 to 5, cloth extra, 18s. each. Vols. 6, 7, and 8, commencing New Series, demy folio, 31s. 6d.

Pinto (Major Serpa). See "King's Rifle."

Placita Anglo-Normannica. The Procedure and Constitution of the Anglo-Norman Courts (William I.—Richard I.), as shown by Contemporaneous Records. With Explanatory Notes, &c. By M. M. Bigelow. Demy 8vo, cloth, 21s.

Plutarch's Lives. An Entirely New and Library Edition. Edited by A. H. CLOUGH, Esq. 5 vols., 8vo, 2*l.* 10*s.*; half-morocco, gilt top, 3*l.* Also in 1 vol., royal 8vo, 800 pp., cloth extra, 18*s.*; half-bound, 21*s.*

—— *Morals.* Uniform with Clough's Edition of "Lives of Plutarch." Edited by Professor GOODWIN. 5 vols., 8vo, 3*l.* 3*s.*

Poems of the Inner Life. A New Edition, Revised, with many additional Poems. Small post 8vo, cloth, 5*s.*

Poganuc People: their Loves and Lives. By Mrs. BEECHER STOWE. Crown 8vo, cloth, 6*s.*

Polar Expeditions. See KOLDEWEY, MARKHAM, MACGAHAN, and NARES.

Practical (A) Handbook to the Principal Schools of England. By C. E. PASCOE. New Edition, crown 8vo, cloth extra, 3*s.* 6*d.*

Prejevalsky (N. M.) From Kulja, across the Tian Shan to Lobnor. Translated by E. DELMAR MORGAN, F.R.G.S. Demy 8vo, with a Map. 16*s.*

Prince Ritto; or, The Four-leaved Shamrock. By FANNY W. CURREY. With 10 Full-page Fac-simile Reproductions of Original Drawings by HELEN O'HARA. Demy 4to, cloth extra, gilt, 10*s.* 6*d.*

Publishers' Circular (The), and General Record of British and Foreign Literature. Published on the 1st and 15th of every Month, 3*d.*

*R*AMBAUD *(Alfred). History of Russia, from its Origin to the Year 1877.* With Six Maps. Translated by Mrs. L. B. LANG. 2 vols., demy 8vo, cloth extra, 38*s.*

Recollections of Writers. By CHARLES and MARY COWDEN CLARKE. Authors of "The Concordance to Shakespeare," &c.; with Letters of CHARLES LAMB, LEIGH HUNT, DOUGLAS JERROLD, and CHARLES DICKENS; and a Preface by MARY COWDEN CLARKE. Crown 8vo, cloth, 10*s.* 6*d.*

Reminiscences of the War in New Zealand. By THOMAS W. GUDGEON, Lieutenant and Quartermaster, Colonial Forces, N.Z. With Twelve Portraits. Crown 8vo, cloth extra, 10*s.* 6*d.*

Rémusat (Madame de). See "Memoirs of."

Robinson (Phil). See "In my Indian Garden."

Rochefoucauld's Reflections. Bayard Series, 2*s.* 6*d.*

Rogers (S.) Pleasures of Memory. See "Choice Editions of Choice Books." 2*s.* 6*d.*

Rose in Bloom. See ALCOTT.

Rose Library (The). Popular Literature of all countries. Each volume, 1*s.*; cloth, 2*s.* 6*d.* Many of the Volumes are Illustrated—

1. **Sea-Gull Rock.** By JULES SANDEAU. Illustrated.
2. **Little Women.** By LOUISA M. ALCOTT.
3. **Little Women Wedded.** Forming a Sequel to "Little Women."
4. **The House on Wheels.** By MADAME DE STOLZ. Illustrated.
5. **Little Men.** By LOUISA M. ALCOTT. Dble. vol., 2*s.*; cloth, 3*s.* 6*d.*
6. **The Old-Fashioned Girl.** By LOUISA M. ALCOTT. Double vol., 2*s.*; cloth, 3*s.* 6*d.*
7. **The Mistress of the Manse.** By J. G. HOLLAND.
8. **Timothy Titcomb's Letters to Young People, Single and Married.**
9. **Undine, and the Two Captains.** By Baron DE LA MOTTE FOUQUÉ. A New Translation by F. E. BUNNETT. Illustrated.
10. **Draxy Miller's Dowry, and the Elder's Wife.** By SAXE HOLM.
11. **The Four Gold Pieces.** By Madame GOURAUD. Numerous Illustrations.
12. **Work.** A Story of Experience. First Portion. By LOUISA M. ALCOTT.
13. **Beginning Again.** Being a Continuation of "Work." By LOUISA M. ALCOTT.
14. **Picciola; or, the Prison Flower.** By X. B. SAINTINE. Numerous Graphic Illustrations.
15. **Robert's Holidays.** Illustrated.
16. **The Two Children of St. Domingo.** Numerous Illustrations.
17. **Aunt Jo's Scrap Bag.**
18. **Stowe (Mrs. H. B.) The Pearl of Orr's Island.**
19. ——— **The Minister's Wooing.**
20. ——— **Betty's Bright Idea.**
21. ——— **The Ghost in the Mill.**
22. ——— **Captain Kidd's Money.**
23. ——— **We and our Neighbours.** Double vol., 2*s.*
24. ——— **My Wife and I.** Double vol., 2*s.*; cloth, gilt, 3*s.* 6*d.*
25. **Hans Brinker; or, the Silver Skates.**
26. **Lowell's My Study Window.**
27. **Holmes (O. W.) The Guardian Angel.**
28. **Warner (C. D.) My Summer in a Garden.**

The Rose Library, continued :—

    29. **Hitherto.** By the Author of "The Gayworthys." 2 vols., 1s. each.
    30. **Helen's Babies.** By their Latest Victim.
    31. **The Barton Experiment.** By the Author of "Helen's Babies."
    32. **Dred.** By Mrs. BEECHER STOWE. Double vol., 2s. Cloth, gilt, 3s. 6d.
    33. **Warner (C. D.) In the Wilderness.**
    34. **Six to One.** A Seaside Story.

Russell (W. H., LL.D.) The Tour of the Prince of Wales in India. By W. H. RUSSELL, LL.D. Fully Illustrated by SYDNEY P. HALL, M.A. Super-royal 8vo, cloth extra, gilt edges, 52s. 6d.; Large Paper Edition, 84s.

SANCTA Christina: a Story of the First Century. By ELEANOR E. ORLEBAR. With a Preface by the Bishop of Winchester. Small post 8vo, cloth extra, 5s.

Scientific Memoirs: being Experimental Contributions to a Knowledge of Radiant Energy. By JOHN WILLIAM DRAPER, M.D., LL.D., Author of "A Treatise on Human Physiology," &c. With Steel Portrait of the Author. Demy 8vo, cloth, 473 pages, 14s.

Scott (Sir G. Gilbert.) See " Autobiography."

Sea-Gull Rock. By JULES SANDEAU, of the French Academy. Royal 16mo, with 79 Illustrations, cloth extra, gilt edges, 7s. 6d. Cheaper Edition, cloth gilt, 2s. 6d. *See also* Rose Library.

Seonee: Sporting in the Satpura Range of Central India, and in the Valley of the Nerbudda. By R. A. STERNDALE, F.R.G.S. 8vo, with numerous Illustrations, 21s.

The Serpent Charmer: a Tale of the Indian Mutiny. By LOUIS ROUSSELET, Author of "India and its Native Princes." Numerous Illustrations. Crown 8vo, cloth extra, gilt edges, 7s. 6d. ; plainer binding, 5s.

Shakespeare (The Boudoir). Edited by HENRY CUNDELL. Carefully bracketted for reading aloud; freed from all objectionable matter, and altogether free from notes. Price 2s. 6d. each volume, cloth extra, gilt edges. Contents :—Vol I., Cymbeline—Merchant of Venice. Each play separately, paper cover, 1s. Vol. II., As You Like It—King Lear—Much Ado about Nothing. Vol. III., Romeo and Juliet—Twelfth Night—King John. The latter six plays separately, paper cover, 9d.

Shakespeare Key (The). Forming a Companion to "The Complete Concordance to Shakespeare." By CHARLES and MARY COWDEN CLARKE. Demy 8vo, 800 pp., 21*s*.

Shooting: its Appliances, Practice, and Purpose. By JAMES DALZIEL DOUGALL, F.S.A., F.Z.A. Author of "Scottish Field Sports," &c. Crown 8vo, cloth extra, 10*s*. 6*d*.
"The book is admirable in every way. . . . . We wish it every success."—*Globe*.
"A very complete treatise. . . . . Likely to take high rank as an authority on shooting."—*Daily News*.

Silent Hour (The). See "Gentle Life Series."

Silver Pitchers. See ALCOTT.

Simon (Jules). See "Government of M. Thiers."

Six to One. A Seaside Story. 16mo, boards, 1*s*.

Smith (G.) Assyrian Explorations and Discoveries. By the late GEORGE SMITH. Illustrated by Photographs and Woodcuts. Demy 8vo, 6th Edition, 18*s*.

—————— *The Chaldean Account of Genesis*. By the late G. SMITH, of the Department of Oriental Antiquities, British Museum. With many Illustrations. Demy 8vo, cloth extra, 6th Edition, 16*s*.

Snow-Shoes and Canoes; or, the Adventures of a Fur-Hunter in the Hudson's Bay Territory. By W. H. G. KINGSTON. 2nd Edition. With numerous Illustrations. Square crown 8vo, cloth extra, gilt edges, 7*s*. 6*d*.; plainer binding, 5*s*.

Songs and Etchings in Shade and Sunshine. By J. E. G. Illustrated with 44 Etchings. Small 4to, cloth, gilt tops, 25*s*.

South Kensington Museum. Monthly 1*s*. See "Art Treasures."

Stanley (H. M.) How I Found Livingstone. Crown 8vo, cloth extra, 7*s*. 6*d*.; large Paper Edition, 10*s*. 6*d*.

—————— *"My Kalulu," Prince, King, and Slave.* A Story from Central Africa. Crown 8vo, about 430 pp., with numerous graphic Illustrations, after Original Designs by the Author. Cloth, 7*s*. 6*d*.

—————— *Coomassie and Magdala.* A Story of Two British Campaigns in Africa. Demy 8vo, with Maps and Illustrations, 16*s*.

—————— *Through the Dark Continent*, which see.

St. Nicholas Magazine. 4to, in handsome cover. 1*s*. monthly. Annual Volumes, handsomely bound, 15*s*. Its special features are, the great variety and interest of its literary contents, and the beauty and profuseness of its Illustrations, which surpass anything yet attempted in any publication for young people, and the stories are by the best living authors of juvenile literature. Each Part contains, on an average, 50 Illustrations.

Story without an End. From the German of Carové, by the late Mrs. SARAH T. AUSTIN. Crown 4to, with 15 Exquisite Drawings by E. V. B., printed in Colours in Fac-simile of the original Water Colours; and numerous other Illustrations. New Edition, 7s. 6d.

—— square 4to, with Illustrations by HARVEY. 2s. 6d.

Stowe (Mrs. Beecher) Dred. Cheap Edition, boards, 2s. Cloth, gilt edges, 3s. 6d.

—— *Footsteps of the Master.* With Illustrations and red borders. Small post 8vo, cloth extra, 6s.

—— *Geography,* with 60 Illustrations. Square cloth, 4s. 6d.

—— *Little Foxes.* Cheap Edition, 1s.; Library Edition, 4s. 6d.

—— *Betty's Bright Idea.* 1s.

—— *My Wife and I; or, Harry Henderson's History.* Small post 8vo, cloth extra, 6s.*

—— *Minister's Wooing.* 5s.; Copyright Series, 1s. 6d.; cl., 2s.*

—— *Old Town Folk.* 6s.; Cheap Edition, 2s. 6d.

—— *Old Town Fireside Stories.* Cloth extra, 3s. 6d.

—— *Our Folks at Poganuc.* 10s. 6d.

—— *We and our Neighbours.* 1 vol., small post 8vo, 6s. Sequel to "My Wife and I."*

—— *Pink and White Tyranny.* Small post 8vo, 3s. 6d.; Cheap Edition, 1s. 6d. and 2s.

—— *Queer Little People.* 1s.; cloth, 2s.

—— *Chimney Corner.* 1s.; cloth, 1s. 6d.

—— *The Pearl of Orr's Island.* Crown 8vo, 5s.*

—— *Little Pussey Willow.* Fcap., 2s.

* *See also* Rose Library.

Stowe (Mrs. Beecher) Woman in Sacred History. Illustrated with 15 Chromo-lithographs and about 200 pages of Letterpress. Demy 4to, cloth extra, gilt edges, 25*s.*

Student's French Examiner. By F. JULIEN, Author of "Petites Leçons de Conversation et de Grammaire." Square crown 8vo, cloth, 2*s.*

Studies in German Literature. By BAYARD TAYLOR. Edited by MARIE TAYLOR. With an Introduction by the Hon. GEORGE H. BOKER. 8vo, cloth extra, 10*s.* 6*d.*

Studies in the Theory of Descent. By Dr. AUG. WEISMANN, Professor in the University of Freiburg. Translated and edited by RAPHAEL MELDOLA, F.C.S., Secretary of the Entomological Society of London. Part I.—"On the Seasonal Dimorphism of Butterflies," containing Original Communications by Mr. W. H. EDWARDS, of Coalburgh. With two Coloured Plates. Price of Part. I. (to Subscribers for the whole work only) 8*s*; Part II. (6 coloured plates), 16*s.*; Part III., 6*s.*

Sugar Beet (The). Including a History of the Beet Sugar Industry in Europe, Varieties of the Sugar Beet, Examination, Soils, Tillage, Seeds and Sowing, Yield and Cost of Cultivation, Harvesting, Transportation, Conservation, Feeding Qualities of the Beet and of the Pulp, &c. By L. S. WARE. Illustrated. 8vo, cloth extra, 21*s.*

Sullivan (A. M., M.P.). See "New Ireland."

Sulphuric Acid (A Practical Treatise on the Manufacture of). By A. G. and C. G. LOCK, Consulting Chemical Engineers. With 77 Construction Plates, and other Illustrations.

Sumner (Hon. Charles). See Life and Letters.

Sunrise: A Story of These Times. By WILLIAM BLACK, Author of "A Daughter of Heth," &c. To be published in 15 Monthly Parts, commencing April 1st, 1*s.* each.

Surgeon's Handbook on the Treatment of Wounded in War. By Dr. FRIEDRICH ESMARCH, Professor of Surgery in the University of Kiel, and Surgeon-General to the Prussian Army. Translated by H. H. CLUTTON, B.A. Cantab, F.R.C.S. Numerous Coloured Plates and Illustrations, 8vo, strongly bound in flexible leather, 1*l.* 8*s.*

Sylvan Spring. By FRANCIS GEORGE HEATH. Illustrated by 12 Coloured Plates, drawn by F. E. HULME, F.L.S., Artist and Author of "Familiar Wild Flowers;" by 16 full-page, and more than 100 other Wood Engravings. Large post 8vo, cloth, gilt edges, 12*s.* 6*d.*

Tauchnitz's English Editions of German Authors.
Each volume, cloth flexible, 2*s.* ; or sewed, 1*s.* 6*d.* (Catalogues post free on application.)

—— (*B.*) *German and English Dictionary.* Cloth, 1*s.* 6*d.*; roan, 2*s.*

—— *French and English.* Paper, 1*s.* 6*d.*; cloth, 2*s.*; roan, 2*s.* 6*d.*

—— *Italian and English.* Paper, 1*s.* 6*d.*; cloth, 2*s.*; roan, 2*s.* 6*d.*

—— *Spanish and English.* Paper, 1*s.* 6*d.*; cloth, 2*s.*; roan, 2*s.* 6*d.*

—— *New Testament.* Cloth, 2*s.*; gilt, 2*s.* 6*d.*

Taylor (Bayard). See "Studies in German Literature."

Textbook (A) of Harmony. For the Use of Schools and Students. By the late CHARLES EDWARD HORSLEY. Revised for the Press by WESTLEY RICHARDS and W. H. CALCOTT. Small post 8vo, cloth extra, 3*s.* 6*d.*

Through the Dark Continent: The Sources of the Nile; Around the Great Lakes, and down the Congo. By HENRY M. STANLEY. 2 vols., demy 8vo, containing 150 Full-page and other Illustrations, 2 Portraits of the Author, and 10 Maps, 42*s.* Seventh Thousand. Cheaper Edition, crown 8vo, with some of the Illustrations and Maps. 1 vol., 12*s.* 6*d.*

Tour of the Prince of Wales in India. See RUSSELL.

Trees and Ferns. By F. G. HEATH. Crown 8vo, cloth, gilt edges, with numerous Illustrations, 3*s.* 6*d.*
"A charming little volume."—*Land and Water.*

Turkistan. Notes of a Journey in the Russian Provinces of Central Asia and the Khanates of Bokhara and Kokand. By EUGENE SCHUYLER, Late Secretary to the American Legation, St. Petersburg. Numerous Illustrations. 2 vols, 8vo, cloth extra, 5th Edition, 2*l.* 2*s.*

Two Friends. By LUCIEN BIART, Author of "Adventures of a Young Naturalist," "My Rambles in the New World," &c. Small post 8vo, numerous Illustrations, gilt edges, 7*s.* 6*d.*; plainer binding, 5*s.*

Two Supercargoes (The); or, Adventures in Savage Africa. By W. H. G. KINGSTON. Numerous Full-page Illustrations. Square imperial 16mo, cloth extra, gilt edges, 7*s.* 6*d.*; plainer binding, 5*s.*

Up and Down; or, Fifty Years' Experiences in Australia, California, New Zealand, India, China, and the South Pacific. Being the Life History of Capt. W. J. BARRY. Written by Himself. With several Illustrations. Crown 8vo, cloth extra, 8*s.* 6*d.*

"*Jules Verne, that Prince of Story-tellers.*"—Times.

BOOKS BY JULES VERNE.

WORKS. (LARGE CROWN 8VO)	Containing 350 to 600 pp. and from 50 to 100 full-page illustrations.		Containing the whole of the text with some illustrations.	
	In very handsome cloth binding, gilt edges.	In plainer binding, plain edges.	In cloth binding, gilt edges, smaller type.	Coloured Boards.
	s. d.	s. d.	s. d.	
Twenty Thousand Leagues under the Sea. Part I. Ditto. Part II.	10 6	5 0	3 6	2 vols., 1s. each.
Hector Servadac	10 6	5 0		
The Fur Country	10 6	5 0	3 6	2 vols., 1s. each.
From the Earth to the Moon and a Trip round it	10 6	5 0	2 vols., 2s. each.	2 vols., 1s. each.
Michael Strogoff, the Courier of the Czar	10 6	5 0		
Dick Sands, the Boy Captain	10 6			
				s. d.
Five Weeks in a Balloon	7 6	3 6	2 0	1 0
Adventures of Three Englishmen and Three Russians	7 6	3 6	2 0	1 0
Around the World in Eighty Days	7 6	3 6	2 0	1 0
A Floating City	7 6	3 6	2 0	1 0
The Blockade Runners			2 0	1 0
Dr. Ox's Experiment			2 0	
Master Zacharius	7 6	3 6	2 0	1 0
A Drama in the Air				
A Winter amid the Ice			2 0	1 0
The Survivors of the "Chancellor"	7 6	3 6	2 0	2 vols. 1s. each.
Martin Paz			2 0	1 0
THE MYSTERIOUS ISLAND, 3 vols.:—	22 6	10 6	6 0	3 0
Vol. I. Dropped from the Clouds	7 6	3 6	2 0	1 0
Vol. II. Abandoned	7 6	3 6	2 0	1 0
Vol. III. Secret of the Island	7 6	3 6	2 0	1 0
The Child of the Cavern	7 6	3 6		
The Begum's Fortune	7 6			
The Tribulations of a Chinaman	7 6			

CELEBRATED TRAVELS AND TRAVELLERS. 3 vols. Demy 8vo, 600 pp., upwards of 100 full-page illustrations, 12s. 6d.; gilt edges, 14s. each :—
(1) THE EXPLORATION OF THE WORLD.
(2) THE GREAT NAVIGATORS OF THE EIGHTEENTH CENTURY.

WALLER (*Rev. C. H.*) *The Names on the Gates of Pearl*, and other Studies. By the Rev. C. H. WALLER, M.A. Second edition. Crown 8vo, cloth extra, 6s.

——— *A Grammar and Analytical Vocabulary of the Words in* the Greek Testament. Compiled from Brüder's Concordance. For the use of Divinity Students and Greek Testament Classes. By the Rev. C. H. WALLER, M.A. Part I., The Grammar. Small post 8vo, cloth, 2s. 6d. Part II. The Vocabulary, 2s. 6d.

——— *Adoption and the Covenant.* Some Thoughts on Confirmation. Super-royal 16mo, cloth limp, 2s. 6d.

Wanderings in the Western Land. By A. PENDARVES VIVIAN, M.P. With many Illustrations from Drawings by Mr. BIERSTADT and the Author, and 3 Maps. 1 vol., demy 8vo, cloth extra, 18s.

War in Bulgaria: a Narrative of Personal Experiences. By LIEUTENANT-GENERAL VALENTINE BAKER PASHA. Maps and Plans of Battles. 2 vols., demy 8vo, cloth extra, 2l. 2s.

Warner (*C. D.*) *My Summer in a Garden.* Rose Library, 1s.

——— *Back-log Studies.* Boards, 1s. 6d.; cloth, 2s.

——— *In the Wilderness.* Rose Library, 1s.

——— *Mummies and Moslems.* 8vo, cloth, 12s.

Weaving. See "History and Principles."

Whitney (*Mrs. A. D. T.*) *Hitherto.* Small post 8vo, 3s. 6d. and 2s. 6d.

——— *Sights and Insights.* 3 vols., crown 8vo, 31s. 6d.

——— *Summer in Leslie Goldthwaite's Life.* Cloth, 3s. 6d.

Wills, A Few Hints on Proving, without Professional Assistance. By a PROBATE COURT OFFICIAL. 5th Edition, revised with Forms of Wills, Residuary Accounts, &c. Fcap. 8vo, cloth limp, 1s.

With Axe and Rifle on the Western Prairies. By W. H. G. KINGSTON. With numerous Illustrations, square crown 8vo, cloth extra, gilt edges, 7s. 6d.; plainer binding, 5s.

Witty and Humorous Side of the English Poets (*The*). With a variety of Specimens arranged in Periods. By ARTHUR H. ELLIOTT. 1 vol., crown 8vo, cloth, 10s. 6d.

Woolsey (*C. D., LL.D.*) *Introduction to the Study of International Law;* designed as an Aid in Teaching and in Historical Studies. 5th Edition, demy 8vo, 18s.

Words of Wellington: Maxims and Opinions, Sentences and Reflections of the Great Duke, gathered from his Despatches, Letters, and Speeches (Bayard Series). 2s. 6d.

Wreck of the Grosvenor. By W. CLARK RUSSELL. 6s. Third and Cheaper Edition.

London:
SAMPSON LOW, MARSTON, SEARLE, & RIVINGTON,
CROWN BUILDINGS 188, FLEET STREET.

www.ingramcontent.com/pod-product-compliance
Lightning Source LLC
Chambersburg PA
CBHW031929230426
43672CB00010B/1864